ble
St. Maarten/St. Martin,
Anguilla & St. Barts

4th Edition

by Alexis Lipsitz Flippin

WILEY

John Wiley & Sons, Inc.

Published by:

JOHN WILEY & SONS, INC.

111 River St.

Hoboken, NJ 07030-5774

ISBN 978-1-118-36899-2 (paper); ISBN 978-1-118-51813-7 (ebk);
ISBN 978-1-118-51814-4 (ebk)

Editors: Andrea Kahn, Fiona Quinn
Production Editors: Lindsay Beineke, Lindsay Conner
Cartographer: Guy Ruggiero
Photo Editor: Richard Fox
Production by Wiley Indianapolis Composition Services

Front cover photo: Boats in Island Harbour on Anguilla © James Schwabel / Alamy
Images

For information on our other products and services or to obtain technical support,
please contact our Customer Care Department within the U.S. at 877/762-2974,
outside the U.S. at 317/572-3993 or fax 317/572-4002.

Wiley also publishes its books in a variety of electronic formats. Some content that
appears in print may not be available in electronic formats.

Manufactured in the United States of America

5   4   3   2   1

CONTENTS

9 PLANNING YOUR TRIP TO ST. MAARTEN/ST. MARTIN, ANGUILLA & ST. BARTS 159

LIST OF MAPS

ABOUT THE AUTHOR

A former Frommer's Senior Editor, **Alexis Lipsitz Flippin** is the author of *Frommer's Turks & Caicos* and *Frommer's New York City with Kids* and a coauthor of *Frommer's Caribbean* and *Frommer's 500 Extraordinary Islands*. She has written and edited for numerous consumer magazines and websites, including *Self*, *American Health*, CNN.com, Weather.com, and *Rolling Stone*.

HOW TO CONTACT US

In researching this book, we discovered many wonderful places—hotels, restaurants, shops, and more. We're sure you'll find others. Please tell us about them, so we can share the information with your fellow travelers in upcoming editions. If you were disappointed with a recommendation, we'd love to know that, too. Please write to:

Frommer's Portable St. Maarten/St. Martin,
Anguilla & St. Barts, 4th Edition
John Wiley & Sons, Inc. • 111 River St. • Hoboken, NJ 07030-5774
frommersfeedback@wiley.com

ADVISORY & DISCLAIMER

Travel information can change quickly and unexpectedly, and we strongly advise you to confirm important details locally before traveling, including information on visas, health and safety, traffic and transport, accommodations, shopping, and eating out. We also encourage you to stay alert while traveling and to remain aware of your surroundings. Avoid civil disturbances, and keep a close eye on cameras, purses, wallets, and other valuables.

While we have endeavored to ensure that the information contained within this guide is accurate and up-to-date at the time of publication, we make no representations or warranties with respect to the accuracy or completeness of the contents of this work and specifically disclaim all warranties, including without limitation warranties of fitness for a particular purpose. We accept no responsibility or liability for any inaccuracy or errors or omissions, or for any inconvenience, loss, damage, costs, or expenses of any nature whatsoever incurred or suffered by anyone as a result of any advice or information contained in this guide.

The inclusion of a company, organization, or website in this guide as a service provider and/or potential source of further information does not mean that we endorse them or the information they provide. Be aware that information provided through some websites may be unreliable and can change without notice. Neither the publisher nor author shall be liable for any damages arising herefrom.

FROMMER'S STAR RATINGS, ICONS & ABBREVIATIONS

Every hotel, restaurant, and attraction listing in this guide has been ranked for quality, value, service, amenities, and special features using a **star-rating system.** In country, state, and regional guides, we also rate towns and regions to help you narrow down your choices and budget your time accordingly. Hotels and restaurants are rated on a scale of zero (recommended) to three stars (exceptional). Attractions, shopping, nightlife, towns, and regions are rated according to the following scale: zero stars (recommended), one star (highly recommended), two stars (very highly recommended), and three stars (must-see).

In addition to the star-rating system, we also use *seven feature icons* that point you to the great deals, in-the-know advice, and unique experiences that separate travelers from tourists. Throughout the book, look for:

🎁 **special finds**—those places only insiders know about

💬 **fun facts**—details that make travelers more informed and their trips more fun

😀 **kids**—best bets for kids and advice for the whole family

📷 **special moments**—those experiences that memories are made of

✋ **overrated**—places or experiences not worth your time or money

✎ **insider tips**—great ways to save time and money

🏷 **great values**—where to get the best deals

The following abbreviations are used for credit cards:

AE American Express	DISC Discover	V Visa
DC Diners Club	MC MasterCard	

TRAVEL RESOURCES AT FROMMERS.COM

Frommer's travel resources don't end with this guide. Frommer's web-site, **www.frommers.com**, has travel information on more than 4,000 destinations. We update features regularly, giving you access to the most current trip-planning information and the best airfare, lodging, and car-rental bargains. You can also listen to podcasts, connect with other Frommers.com members through our active-reader forums, share your travel photos, read blogs from guidebook editors and fellow travelers, and much more.

THE BEST OF ST. MAARTEN/ ST. MARTIN, ANGUILLA & ST. BARTS

S t. Maarten/St. Martin and its neighbors Anguilla and St. Barts offer something for everyone: bewitching beaches, duty-free shopping, exceptional watersports, and nightlife aplenty. You can stay in charming Creole cottages or world-class resorts. And you can dine very well indeed at casual beach barbecues or grand temples of gastronomy. Whatever your tastes and budget, this chapter will guide you to the best these beautiful islands have to offer.

THE most unforgettable EXPERIENCES

o **Day-Tripping to Offshore Islands:** Take a trip to a real-life desert island when you visit one of the little gems off the shores of St. Martin and Anguilla. Here you can snorkel in gin-clear waters, sip rum punches, and eat lobster fresh off the grill. There are few more relaxing diversions than wading in the gentle lagoon at **Îlet Pinel (Isle of Pinel)** near St. Martin's Anse Marcel, or taking off-island forays to Anguilla's **Sandy Island, Prickly Pear,** or **Dog Island.** See p. 24 and 97.

o **Becoming a High-Flying Yachtsman, St. Maarten:** If you've ever dreamed of racing in an America's Cup yachting competition, here's your chance. St. Maarten's 12-Metre Challenge lets you race real America's Cup boats in one of four regattas a day. See p. 27.

o **People-Watching at a Sidewalk Cafe:** Take a seat on the Great Bay Boardwalk in **Philipsburg,**

St. Maarten/St. Martin, Anguilla & St. Barts

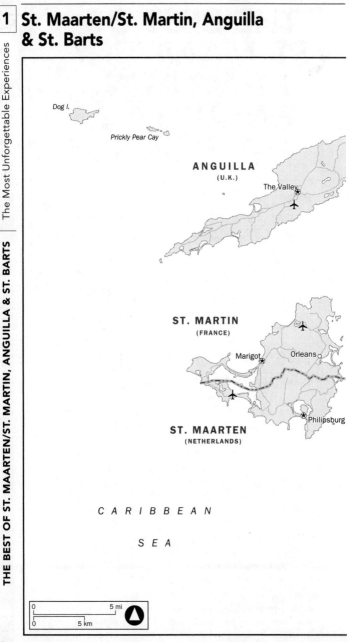

Scrub I.

I. Tintamarre

ATLANTIC

OCEAN

I. Fourchue

I. Frégate   I. Toc Vers

I. Chevreau

La Tortue

ST. BARTHÉLEMY
(FRANCE)   Gustavia

where leviathan cruise ships make fishing dinghies look like toy boats. Stroll the U-shaped port of St. Barts's fairy-tale harbor town, **Gustavia**. See chapter 3, and p. 160.

o **Chilling in an Anguilla Beach Bar:** No place nails the beach-bar culture as perfectly as Anguilla, where barbecue is smoking on the grill, the music is infectious, and the setting is sublime. See p. 108.

o **Swimming and Snorkeling the Anguilla Beaches:** The beach is the thing here, and the pleasure of simply immersing yourself in the clear, warm, turquoise seas of Anguilla cannot be underestimated—from the powdery sands of Shoal Bay to the gentle swells of Meads Bay. See p. 94.

o **Beach-Hopping in St. Barts:** Everyone does it, and here's how you do it: Pack a beach umbrella (your hotel can provide one for you)—shade is hard to find on St. Barts's beaches—towels, a beach book, a snorkel and mask, picnic fare, and Ligne St. Barth sunscreen, and prepare for a day of luxuriating on some of the world's finest stretches of sand. See p. 132.

o **Kitesurfing the Grand Cul-de-Sac on St. Barts:** This windswept, protected lagoon is made for kitesurfing; here billowing kites seem to skim the clouds. It's a thrill to watch and a thrill to do, as you practically skate across the glassy seas. See p. 135.

o **Shopping in St. Barts:** When it comes to shopping, it's hard to top St. Barts, where you'll find stylish, high-quality goods in even the most basic shops. The famously exquisite French skin-care lines and toiletries are a pleasure to browse in local pharmacies, and even the grocery stores are a marvel, with imported French cheeses, pâtés, wine, and—ooh-la-la!—the French version of canned ravioli. See p. 136.

THE best BEACH EXPERIENCES

o **Watching the Sun Rise at Dawn Beach, St. Maarten:** Swim or snorkel with views of St. Barts. Sunrise is spectacular, but it's an enchanting spot at any time of day. See p. 23.

o **Snorkeling the Rocks along Mullet Bay, St. Maarten:** This beautiful beach has a sprinkling of umbrellas and chairs and a couple of beach shacks serving food and drinks, but nowhere near the activity it once enjoyed as the silky strand fronting the Mullet Bay Resort, the island's first resort that's now in a state of (seemingly) perpetual ruin after Hurricane Luis took it out of commission in 1995. The blue pearlescent waters are calm, and the snorkeling isn't bad along the rocks. See p. 22.

o **Ducking the Passing Planes at Maho Bay, St. Maarten:** Okay, so some reckless fools get a little too close for comfort, but you can't deny the thrill of being buzzed by a massive 747 on its landing into Princess Juliana International Airport, just feet from the white sands of Maho Bay beach. See p. 22.

o **Admiring the Passing Parade at Orient Bay, St. Martin:** This happening strand may be clothing optional, but it also happens to be one gorgeous beach. If you're looking for watersports action and a simmering beach-bar scene, this is the place to find it. See p. 25.

o **Spending the Day on Isle of Pinel, St. Martin:** This tiny offshore cay with a perfect lagoon in which to paddle makes for a wonderful day trip. See p. 24.

o **Hanging out on Shoal Bay East, Anguilla:** Not to be confused with Shoal Bay West, this beach offers some of Anguilla's most popular beach bars plus seclusion, with fine snorkeling on its less-trafficked eastern flank. See p. 96.

o **Strolling the Serene Sands of Rendezvous Bay, Anguilla:** This powdery, picture-perfect beach curls and stretches for nearly 3 miles—with plenty of space to find a secluded strand of white sand. See p. 94.

o **Swimming and Sunbathing on Meads Bay, Anguilla:** Here, swooping pelicans shadow big, languorous rolls and sparkling turquoise seas. Snorkel the rocks beneath the old Malliouhana resort. See p. 95.

o **Having a Castaway Adventure on Anguilla's Offshore Cays:** Head out for such delicious spits of sand as Dog Island, Prickly Pear, Sandy Island, and even Scilly Cay, just offshore—the latter three also have charmingly dilapidated beach bars where lobster is grilled to perfection. See p. 97.

o **Circling the Rock at St-Jean Beach, St. Barts:** This beach is split into two beaches by "the rock," upon which sits Eden Rock hotel. Both beaches are lovely and just steps away from shopping and dining. See p. 122.

o **Hiking to Colombier Beach, St. Barts:** Known as "Rockefeller's Beach," Colombier can be reached only by a hiking trail—a 25-minute walk along a rocky goat path—or by boat. The calm waters make it a dream for swimming and snorkeling. See p. 134.

o **Body-Surfing the Waves at Flamands Beach, St. Barts:** The island's biggest beach, Flamands, is mighty fetching, a sweep of fine sand and decent body-surfing waves. See p. 134.

o **Picnicking the Powdery Sands at Grande Saline Beach, St. Barts:** From the parking lot, it's a 10- or 15-minute walk over pebbly terrain to this protected cove with body-surfable waves. It's one of two clothing-optional beaches on St. Barts (the other is Gouverneur), so don't be shocked to see folks dining on fresh picnic fare in the buff. See p. 133.

THE best FAMILY EXPERIENCES

o **Watching Children Dip Their Toes in the Calm, Clear Waters at Le Galion Beach, St. Martin:** It's not called the "children's beach" for nothing. Gentle waves lap a white-sand beach, and the shallow waters seem to go on forever. It's the perfect place for kids to learn the delights of swimming in the sea. But the steady breezes lure windsurfers, too. It's a great place to glide, and a great place to learn how. See p. 26.

o **Chasing Blue Morpho Butterflies at the Butterfly Farm, St. Martin:** It's small and sweetly modest, but the butterflies are anything but. Kids love enticing these beautiful creatures to alight on their hands. See p. 18.

o **Visiting Loterie Farm, St. Martin:** Head over to this nature reserve to ride the ziplines (or the Ti-Tarzan adventure for the little ones) or hike through virgin rainforest, followed by a meal in the treetops at the Hidden Forest Café. See p. 20.

o **Sailing the Blue Seas of Anguilla:** Sailing is the island's national sport, and local kids learn the ropes from a young age. The **Anguilla Sailing Association** (www.sailanguilla.com; © **264/584-7245**) is the force behind the Anguilla Regatta in early May and offers sailing lessons for kids and adults at its Optimist Sailing School on Sandy Ground. See p. 99.

o **Playing in the Grand Cul-de-Sac, St. Barts:** From kitesurfing to sailing to kayaking to pedal-boating, this wide, shallow lagoon is a kids' dreamy playground.

THE best FOOD & DRINK EXPERIENCES

o **Sampling the International Cuisine in St. Maarten:** From Italian to French to Indian, the cuisine of St. Maarten reflects the island's global influences. It's culinarily cosmopolitan too, with fine-dining restaurants like **Temptation,** Cupecoy, St.

Maarten, offering some of the island's most creative fare. See p. 36.

- **Dining on Restaurant Row in Grand Case, St. Martin:** This fishing village has an appealingly ramshackle vibe. But don't let its languorous style fool you: The beachfront strip of the "Gourmet Capital of the Caribbean" has an amazing concentration of top-notch eateries. See p. 42.

- **Savoring Lip-Smacking Barbecue at the Lolos in St. Maarten/St. Martin:** The island's modest outdoor barbecue joints, known as lolos, dish out heaping helpings of home-cooked Creole fare at bargain prices. Look for state-of-the-art lolos like **Talk of the Town** in Grand Case and **Enoch's Place** on the Marigot waterfront. See p. 45.

- **Breakfasting at La Samanna, St. Martin:** The views alone will have you swooning: high above Baie Longue, the white-sand beach caressing the curve of the bay. The food isn't bad either: a grand buffet of breakfast favorites plus fresh island fruits and juices. See p. 77.

- **Enjoying the Caribbean's Top Restaurants in Anguilla:** From **Blanchards** and **Jacala** on Meads Bay to **da'Vida,** Crocus Bay, and **Veya,** Sandy Ground, the island has arguably the best dining—led by a cadre of top-caliber chefs—in the region. See chapter 7.

- **Kicking Back in Anguilla's Beach Shacks:** Rollicking music, smokin' barbecue, and an irresistible barefoot vibe make Anguilla's beach-shack scene unparalleled. You can't go wrong with old-timers like **Johnno's Beach Stop,** Sandy Ground, or **Dune Preserve,** Rendezvous Bay, the latter a multitiered beachfront bar crafted out of old boats and beach salvage. But equally fun are **Blanchards' Beach Shack,** next door to the Blanchards restaurant, and da'Vida's casual sibling next door, **Bayside Grill,** home to the best johnnycakes in Anguilla. See p. 108.

- **Making the Pilgrimage to Palm Grove, Anguilla:** Down a long, winding potholed road that cuts through scrub brush is this idyllic strand, home to the rough-hewn culinary domain of Nat Richardson and a nice little spot to snorkel. Nat's place is little more than a beach shack, but his barbecued specialties (lobster, crawfish, ribs, chicken, fresh fish) are well worth the trip. The johnnycakes are first-rate. See p. 108.

- **Thrilling to Finely Tuned French Cuisine on St. Barts:** It doesn't get any better than **Le Gaïac,** Anse de Toiny, in the Le

Toiny hotel, where the ambience is swooningly romantic and the food sublime. See p. 146.

o **Dining Beachside on St. Barts:** You can do it high (**Santa Fe,** overlooking **Gouverneur Beach**) or you can do it low (**Dõ Brazil,** on the sands of Shell Beach), but dining on St. Barts's beaches is divine. Try it casual (**O'Corrail,** Grand Cul-de-Sac) or fancy (Eden Rock's **On the Rocks,** overlooking Baie St-Jean). See chapter 8.

THE best HOTELS & RESORTS

o **Hôtel L'Esplanade,** Grand Case, St. Martin: High up on a bluff overlooking Grand Case and Grand Case Beach, this 24-room hotel is decked out in colorful tiles and pillowed in a profusion of tropical blooms. The rooms manage to be utterly private, beautifully outfitted, and comfortably homey all at once. You're just 5 minutes away from bustling Grand Case below, but this tranquil spot feels like a world apart. See p. 80.

o **La Samanna,** Baie Longue, St. Martin: This is a rarity among resorts in its class, offering posh pampering with little pretension. The main restaurant sits high up over Baie Longue—a breathtakingly beautiful setting. See p. 77.

o **Cap Juluca,** Maundays Bay, Anguilla: Always at or near the top of everyone's "Best Of" lists—and a refashioning of the lobby and public spaces has made the place feel fresh and vigorous again. It's a favorite of celebrities and captains of industry, but regular folks get the royal treatment, too. See p. 112.

o **The Villas at CuisinArt Resort & Spa,** Anguilla: Discreet and private, each of the six sun-dappled, white, adobe villas at the east end of the resort has its own gated entry courtyard, shaded by palms and trailing bougainvillea. Choose one with a private pool and solarium for the utmost in secluded romance. See p. 113.

o **Eden Rock,** Baie de St-Jean, St. Barts: Its lodgings are staggered on either side of the titular bluff that cleaves the bay. This remains one of the Caribbean's most elegant enclaves. See p. 148.

o **Hôtel Guanahani and Spa,** Grand Cul-de-Sac, St. Barts: A purring machine of meticulous hospitality and seamless efficiency; just relax and let the pros pamper you. The vibrantly colored rooms are crammed with state-of-the-art amenities, the beach looks out on the beauteous Cul-de-Sac lagoon, and the food is terrific. The capper? All this luxury is yours without pomp or attitude. See p. 149.

o **Hôtel St. Barth Isle de France,** Baie des Flamands, St. Barts: Better than anywhere else, this warm, wonderful boutique hotel (37 rooms) exemplifies the island's easy luxury. It opens right onto Flamands Beach, and the extravagantly sized, beautifully designed rooms and suites are dreamy. See p. 150.

o **Le Toiny,** St. Barts: Ensconced in your impeccably furnished villa, you don't have to see or be seen by anyone. From your tiled terrace—complete with private plunge pool—the views are simply ravishing. See p. 152.

o **The Villas at Le Sereno,** Grand Cul-de-Sac, St. Barts: Simply spectacular, with panoramic views of Grand Cul-de-Sac and big plunge pools. Oh, and leave your pots and pans at home: Le Sereno stocks its ultra-designer kitchens with brands like Le Creuset. See p. 151.

THE best SHOPPING EXPERIENCES

o **Front Street, Philipsburg, St. Maarten:** A mind-boggling display of rampant consumerism. And it's all duty-free, from luxury watches to diamonds to Delft china. See chapter 6.

o **Marigot, French St. Martin:** Skip the icy air-conditioned and marbled West Indies Mall and explore the streets of this charming village for atmospheric wine stores, French pharmacies, and shops selling *prêt-à-porter*. The cobbled warrens and back alleys around the marina reveal little boutiques. See chapter 6.

o **Artists' ateliers, French St. Martin:** These are particularly notable, showcasing Gallic expats working in a variety of media and traditions. Many open their studios to visitors. See chapter 6.

o **Gustavia, St. Barts**: This island capital is lined with stores selling couture and *prêt-à-porter*. Many of the luxury brands are here: Bulgari, Cartier, Giorgio Armani, Louis Vuitton, and Hermès. See chapter 8.

o **St-Jean, St. Barts:** This town has several small shopping plazas along the main road leading toward Lorient: Les Galeries du Commerce, La Villa Creole, La Sodexa, and L'Espace Neptune, each filled with boutiques selling the stylishly casual St. Barts clothing we covet. See chapter 8.

- **La Ligne St. Barth,** Lorient, St. Barts: This brand produces scents and skin-care and cosmetic products made with extracts from Caribbean flowers and seeds. The company's main laboratory/shop, on Route de Salines in Lorient, often offers very slightly damaged products at good discounts. See p. 137.

EXPLORING ST. MAARTEN/ ST. MARTIN

St. Maarten/St. Martin is a fizzy cocktail of French cuisine, Dutch tolerance, and Caribbean relaxation set on a 96-square-kilometer (37-square-mile) island in a sparkling sea of aquamarine. Here you can also snorkel in gin-clear waters, sip rum punches, and soak up the sun on your choice of 39 beaches.

THINGS TO DO   Stroll the seaside boardwalk of Dutch Philipsburg. Take in views of the quaint French town of Marigot, its harbor, and the island of Anguilla from the hillside ruins of Fort Louis. The island's pristine beaches invite barefoot strolls, snorkeling in reefs just offshore, or sunbathing to the strains of reggae from a nearby beach bar. At Orient Bay, the adventurous can partake in parasailing or windsurfing. Inland, discover your inner Tarzan in the jungle canopy of Loterie Farm's Fly Zone, with rope bridges and tree-to-tree zipline flights.

SHOPPING   Browse duty-free shops in Philipsburg for cameras, watches, and island-made Guavaberry rum. Front Street is a mind-boggling display of high-end shops, from Tiffany to Tommy Hilfiger. Day-trippers head to Marigot to browse French Riviera–style boutiques, with their striped awnings and wrought-iron balconies. Harborside, a lively morning market buzzes with vendors selling spices, fruit, and handicrafts. Wander the marble staircases and browse designer brands in Le West Indies Mall.

NIGHTLIFE & ENTERTAINMENT   Bars come in all shapes and sizes, from rickety rum shops to neon-streaked nightclubs. You can gamble and dance around the clock in Simpson Bay. In downtown Philipsburg, salsa dancers spill out of clubs and bars, and free entertainment and zouk party music abounds. Many restaurants (notably in Simpson Bay) and beach bars (especially on Orient Bay) host beachside barbecues with live calypso or soca rhythms. Afterward hit the slots or the big-game tables at the seaside casinos.

RESTAURANTS & DINING   The "Gourmet Capital of the Caribbean" has a strong concentration of top-notch restaurants. Ignite your palate with Creole specialties such as *crabe farci* (stuffed crab) or fresh local seafood. Wash it down with local rum mixed with fresh juices: mango, guava, papaya, or tangy tamarind. Mix with the locals at a lolo—an outdoor barbecue joint and a St. Martin institution—for hearty and delicious helpings of barbecued ribs, lobster, chicken, or fish grilled on split metal drums.

ISLAND LAYOUT

St. Maarten/St. Martin is a hilly island, with splendid panoramas of the coast, and offshore islets from numerous lookouts. One main road essentially circumnavigates the island; a detour from Marigot to Cole Bay on the Dutch side hugs the eastern shore of the Simpson Bay lagoon and bypasses traffic around the airport and bustling Maho area during rush hours.

The island is shaped—very roughly—like a boot. The toe at the western point encompasses the French **Lowlands (Terres Basses),** a tony residential area with several stunning beaches. Following the main road east takes you through **Sandy Ground,** a strip of land crammed with tour-group-style hotels, restaurants, shops, and beach bars. It's bordered on the north by **Baie Nettlé** and on the south by **Simpson Bay,** the Caribbean's largest enclosed body of water. **Marigot,** the French side's capital, is just over 2km (1¼ miles) to the northeast. Ferries depart its harbor for **Anguilla.** The main route ambles north, with turnoffs west on rutted roads to fine beaches, as well as east to **Pic du Paradis** (the island's highest peak at 424m/1,391 ft.) before reaching **Grand Case,** site of the tiny interisland L'Espérance Airport and beloved by foodies for its superlative eateries. The highway runs east, with a fork at Mont Vernon. The north turnoff accesses **French Cul-de-Sac** (embarkation point for ferries to the offshore cays) and a side road to Anse Marcel, home of a marina and the Radisson resort. The other turnoff accesses the beautiful **Orient Bay** beach and continues south through the residential **Orléans** quarter, straddling the Dutch border at **Oyster Pond** and its marina.

Dawn Beach, site of increased development (and the Westin resort), is the first major strand on the Dutch side. The main highway turns slightly inland and passes the Great Salt Pond on its way to the Dutch capital, **Philipsburg,** which unfurls along **Great Bay.** The major cruise ships dock here; there are also several marinas offering boat rentals and excursions. **Pointe Blanche** forms the very flat heel. From Philipsburg, the highway parallels the south coast, rising and dipping over Cay and Cole Bay Hills. Traffic here in both directions is often dreadful, especially on weekends: the "Caribbean's longest parking lot," as locals joke. Party central begins at **Simpson Bay,** where the highway officially becomes Airport Road. Marinas, bars, restaurants, timeshare units, casinos, and strip malls line both sides, continuing almost unabated past Princess Juliana International Airport to **Maho Beach,** another nightlife nirvana. The road passes Mullet Bay and the lively **Cupecoy** area in the Dutch Lowlands before hitting the French border.

THE MAIN SIGHTS
Dutch St. Maarten

Philipsburg ★, capital of the Dutch side, is named, perhaps surprisingly, for an 18th-century Scottish governor. The town has always enjoyed a lovely setting at the headlands of Great Bay, on a spit of land separating the Caribbean from the Great Salt Pond. Its superb, deep natural harbor can accommodate such enormous cruise ships as the *Queen Mary II*. With at least one large ship in port most days, cruise-ship passengers have become a reliable presence in the town's everyday landscape. They come to shop at the duty-free stores lining the pedestrianized main drag, **Front Street** (see chapter 4), ride Segways along the boardwalk, sample island dishes at beachside cafes, and stroll past handsome colonial buildings, including the ornate white 1792 **Wathey Courthouse** (still in use), complete with a cupola, at **Wathey Square,** which roughly bisects Front Street.

Buffeted by hurricanes and for a long time somewhat dilapidated, Philipsburg is looking pretty spiffy these days. Shaded by royal palms and lined with cast-iron street lamps, the wide, red-brick boardwalk (Great Bay Beach Promenade) makes Philipsburg's beachfront a delightful place to stroll, stare at cruise ships and megayachts, or sunbathe in the white sand.

The continuing makeover includes a revamped tourist office, an expanded ferry and cruise dock, and the rejuvenation of Back Street. Eventually, the beautification will extend to the Great Salt Pond (where locals still fish for mullet), with boardwalk paving and planting on tap all the way north to the French border.

Fort Amsterdam ★   Built in 1631 on the peninsula between Great and Little Bays as the Caribbean's first Dutch bastion, Fort Amsterdam was promptly captured by the Spaniards, who made it their most important garrison outside El Morro in San Juan before

St. Maarten/St. Martin

ST. MARTIN
EXPLORING ●
Butterfly Farm **14**
Loterie Farm **11**

HOTELS ■
Alamanda Resort **12**
Club Orient Naturist Resort **13**
Esmeralda Resort **9**
La Samanna **1**
Hotel La Plantation **10**
Le Domaine de Lonvilliers **6**
Mercure St. Martin and Marina **2**
Radisson Blu Resort Marina
 & Spa, St. Martin **7**

RESTAURANTS ◆
C Le Restaurant **7**
La Cigale **3**
Le Santal **4**
Mario's Bistro **5**
Sol é Luna **8**
Chez Yvette's **15**

Airport ✈
Beach ⌁
Mountain ▲

Pointe
Arago

Pointe
du Bluff

see Marigot
map p.19

Baie de
Marigot
Marigot

Pointe
du Plum

**Baie
Rouge**

Baie Nettlé

**Baie aux
Prunes** ⌁

**Baie
Nettlé
Beach** ⌁

2 **3** ⌁ **4** **5**

**Marigot
Fort**

Baie Longue ⌁ **1**

Simpson Bay Lagoon

**Cupecoy
Beach** ⌁ **32**

*Border
Monument*

Mullet Bay Beach ⌁

*Princess Juliana
Int'l Airport*

CARIBBEAN SEA

31 **30** ⌁ **29** **28**

Maho Beach ⌁ ✈

**Simpson
Bay Beach**

26 **27** ⌁ **25**
24

Koolbaai

Kimsha Beach ⌁

23

*Cole
Bay*

ST. MAARTEN
EXPLORING ●
St. Maarten Zoological Park **20**

HOTELS ■
Divi Little Bay Beach Resort **21**
Horny Toad Guesthouse **28**
La Vista Hotel/La Vista Beach
 Resort **23**
Mary's Boon Beach Resort **30**
Oyster Bay Beach Resort **16**
Princess Heights **19**
Sonesta Maho Beach Hotel & Casino **31**
Turquoise Shell Inn **24**
Westin St. Maarten Dawn Beach
 Resort & Spa **18**

RESTAURANTS ◆
La Gondola **32**
Mr. Busby's Beach Bar/Daniel's
 by the Sea **17**
Rare **32**
Saratoga **25**
SkipJack's Seafood Grill, Bar &
 Fish Market **27**
Temptation **32**
The Tides **29**
Topper's **26**

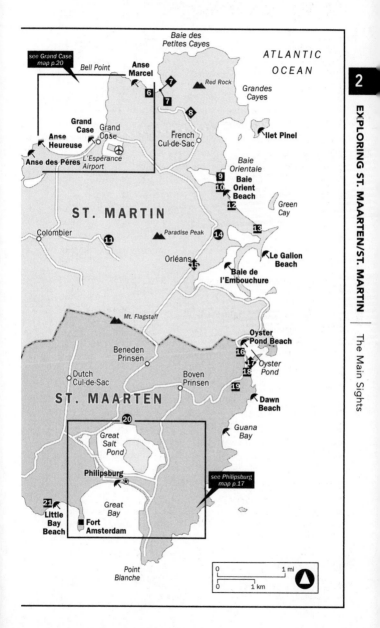

*Baie des
Petites Cayes*

ATLANTIC
OCEAN

Bell Point

see *Grand Case*
map p.20

**Anse
Marcel**

7

Red Rock

*Grandes
Cayes*

6

7

8

**Grand
Case**

**Anse
Heureuse**

Grand
Case

French
Cul-de-Sac

Ilet Pinel

Anse des Péres

*L'Espérance
Airport*

*Baie
Orientale*

ST. MARTIN

9

10

**Baie
Orient
Beach**

12

*Green
Cay*

Colombier

11

▲ *Paradise Peak*

14

13

Orléans

15

**Le Galion
Beach**

**Baie de
l'Embouchure**

▲ *Mt. Flagstaff*

**Oyster
Pond Beach**

16

Beneden
Prinsen

Boven
Prinsen

17

18

*Oyster
Pond*

Dutch
Cul-de-Sac

19

ST. MAARTEN

**Dawn
Beach**

20

*Great
Salt
Pond*

*Guana
Bay*

Philipsburg

⊛

see *Philipsburg*
map p.17

21

**Little
Bay
Beach**

*Great
Bay*

■ **Fort
Amsterdam**

*Point
Blanche*

0   1 mi

0   1 km

abandoning it in 1648. Only one small intact storage building, a few walls, and rusted cannons remain, but it's most noteworthy for its smashing views of Philipsburg. Easiest access is via the Divi Little Bay Beach Resort (guards will let you pass if you tell them you're hiking to the fort).

On the peninsula between Great and Little bays. No phone.

St. Maarten National Heritage Museum ★ This deceptively modest-looking museum is packed with relics from the island's past. Documenting island history and culture, the museum starts with an impressive collection of indigenous Arawak tools, pottery shards, and *zemis* (spiritual totems) that date back over 2 millennia. The plantation and piracy era yields its own artifacts (including cargo salvaged from an 1801 wreck), period clothes (contrasted with slave beads), and weapons. The environment is represented by exhibits on typical flora, fauna, geology, and coral reefs. The final multimedia display recounts the catastrophic effects of Hurricane Luis in 1995. The museum also organizes guided hikes and sells terrific printed walking guides to historic Philipsburg.

7 Front St. http://museumsintmaarten.org. © **599/542-4917.** Admission $5. Weekdays 10am–4pm.

St. Maarten Zoological Park ★ ☺ Just east of Philipsburg, this is the largest park of its kind in the Caribbean. It's been battered by hurricanes and tropical storms but soldiers on with more than 500 animals comprising 80 different species from the Caribbean basin and Amazon rainforest—many of them endangered. There are no cages or bars of any kind; rather, environmentally conscious "naturalistic" boundaries carefully protect both animals and visitors while creating typical habitats. An example is Squirrel Monkey Island: The capuchins and vervets are separated by a moat (replicating the streams that draw them in the wild) stocked with water lilies, turtles, and freshwater fish. Nicely landscaped botanic gardens (with interpretive signs) alternate with various environments, from a caiman marsh to a tropical forest to a boulder-strewn savannah. Walk-through aviaries hold more than 200 birds: red ibis, macaws, toucans, and the Caribbean's largest display of exotic parrots. Other residents include capybaras, ocelots, peccaries, coatis, baboons, and the endangered cotton-top tamarin. The zoo even features the island's largest playground (slides and, of course, a jungle gym).

Arch Rd., Madame Estate. www.stmaartenzoo.com. © **599/543-2030.** Admission $10, $5 children 3–11. Daily 9am–5pm.

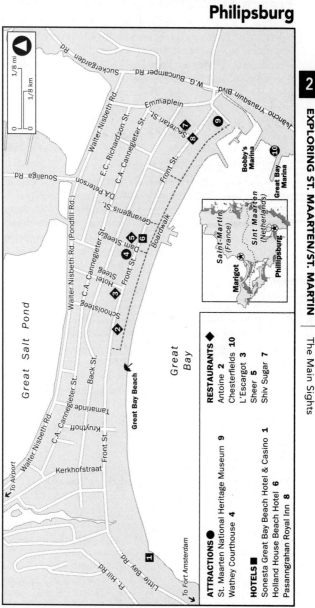

ATTRACTIONS ●
St. Maarten National Heritage Museum **9**
Wathey Courthouse **4**

HOTELS ■
Sonesta Great Bay Beach Hotel & Casino **1**
Holland House Beach Hotel **6**
Pasanngrahan Royal Inn **8**

RESTAURANTS ◆
Antoine **2**
Chesterfields **10**
L'Escargot **3**
Sheer **5**
Shiv Sugar **7**

17

French St. Martin

Marigot, the capital of French St. Martin, has lots of old-world charm, where gas lamps, breezy sidewalk *boîtes,* and vintage Creole gingerbread-trimmed wood houses ring the harbor, as well as a separate marina, **Marina Port La Royale.** The marina area is ringed by boutiques and shops (see chapter 4). The waterfront **Market** is a hub for vendors and farmers; it's busiest in the early morning, when islanders converge to buy fresh-caught fish, fruits, vegetables, and herbs. A crafts market is there on Wednesdays and Saturdays, but there is little that is original or locally made here; vendors tend to offer many of the same goods—colorful dolls, spices, drums, trinkets, and clothing.

Butterfly Farm ★ ☺ Some 40 species of butterflies from around the world (including such rarities as the Central American postman, Malaysian malachite, and Brazilian blue morpho) flit and flutter through this hot and humid miniature bamboo rainforest. The lengths that butterflies go to in order to preserve the species is nature at its canniest: Some lay eggs that look like bird poop; others have camouflaged wings. Most have an incredibly short life span; the spectacularly beautiful blue morpho lives just 2 weeks. The atmosphere here is hypnotically calming, between tinkling waterfalls, ponds stocked with splashing koi, passing chickens, and classical music. Wear bright colors or floral scents to entice butterflies to land on you. Multilingual docents conduct 25-minute hands-on tours following the typical life cycle from egg to caterpillar and on to adulthood. The ramshackle shop sells butterfly earrings, wind chimes, pewter figurines, fridge magnets, and framed mounted sets. The website tells you what to plant to attract butterflies at home.

Rte. Le Galion, Quartier d'Orléans. www.thebutterflyfarm.com. ✆ **590/87-31-21.** Admission $14, $7 children 3–12. Daily 9am–3:30pm (last tour starts at 3pm).

Fort Louis ★ It's a steep, steep climb up some 114 steps from the Marigot harbor side (near the splashy West Indies Mall) to Fort Louis. But the trek up is worth it: The fort sits on one of the island's highest hills, rewarding visitors with sensational 180-degree vistas of Marigot, Simpson Bay lagoon, and most of the French coast, with Anguilla shimmering in the background. The bastion was erected around 1789 to repel English incursions and was the site of a spirited battle in 1808, when 200 British soldiers from a marine frigate attacked the undermanned garrison to loot warehouses for coffee beans. You can climb your way up (stone steps start just to the right of L'Oizeau restaurant) or drive to a parking

Marigot

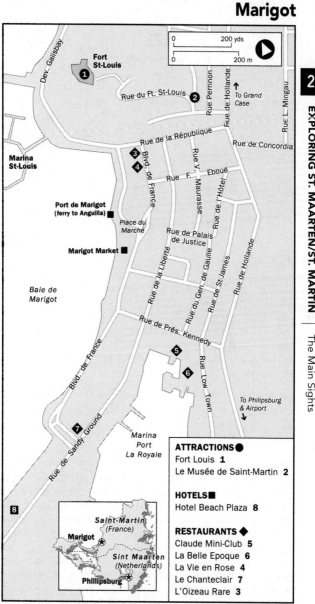

0   200 yds

0   200 m

↑ To Grand Case

Fort St-Louis

Rue du Ft. St-Louis

Rue Perrinon

Rue de Hollande

Rue L. Mingau

Rue de la République

Rue de Concordia

Marina St-Louis

Blvd. de France

Rue V. Maurasse

Rue F. Eboué

Rue de l''Hôtel

Port de Marigot
(ferry to Anguilla)

Place du Marché

Rue de Palais de Justice

Marigot Market

Rue de la Liberté

Rue du Gen. de Gaulle

Rue de St-James

Rue de Hollande

Baie de Marigot

Rue de Prés. Kennedy

Blvd. de France

Rue Low Town

To Philipsburg & Airport ↓

Rue de Sandy Ground

Marina Port La Royale

ATTRACTIONS ●
Fort Louis **1**
Le Musée de Saint-Martin **2**

HOTELS ■
Hotel Beach Plaza **8**

RESTAURANTS ◆
Claude Mini-Club **5**
La Belle Epoque **6**
La Vie en Rose **4**
Le Chanteclair **7**
L'Oizeau Rare **3**

Saint-Martin
(France)

Marigot

Sint Maarten
(Netherlands)

Phillipsburg

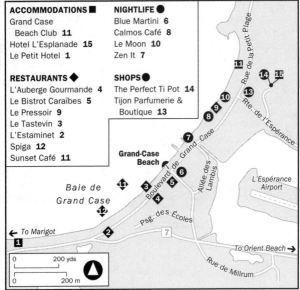

Grand Case

ACCOMMODATIONS ■
Grand Case
  Beach Club **11**
Hotel L'Esplanade **15**
Le Petit Hotel **1**

RESTAURANTS ◆
L'Auberge Gourmande **4**
Le Bistrot Caraïbes **5**
Le Pressoir **9**
Le Tastevin **3**
L'Estaminet **2**
Spiga **12**
Sunset Café **11**

NIGHTLIFE ●
Blue Martini **6**
Calmos Café **8**
Le Moon **10**
Zen It **7**

SHOPS ●
The Perfect Ti Pot **14**
Tijon Parfumerie &
  Boutique **13**

Baie de
Grand Case

Grand-Case
Beach

Boulevard de Grand-Case

Allée des Lambis

L'Espérance
Airport

Rte. de l'Espérance

Rue de la petit Plage

← To Marigot

Psg. des Écoles

7

Rue de Millrum

To Orient Beach →

0   200 yds
0   200 m

lot at the Sous Préfecture (at the foot of the fort)—where you'll still have plenty of steps to tackle if you want to reach the top.

Marigot waterfront. Free admission. Daily 24 hr.

Loterie Farm ★★ ☺   Located along the turnoff to Pic du Paradis halfway between Marigot and Grand Case, this splendid sanctuary—by far the greenest spot on island—merits a stop. It was a famed sugar plantation between 1721 and 1848 (the original slave walls still surround the property). In the farm's modern heyday a half-century ago, the Fleming family hosted Fortune 500 elite and celebrities. But after Hurricane Luis ravaged the property in 1995, it became derelict. Californian B. J. Welch purchased the land in 2003 with the goal of establishing a nature retreat, preserving the island's last remaining virgin rainforest. Literally thousands of plant species, including towering mahogany, mango, papaw, and guavaberry trees, have reclaimed a hillside of rock formations and running streams. Iguanas, parrots, hummingbirds, monkeys, and mongoose run wild. Well-maintained trails zig and zag from the foothills to the top of Pic Paradis, the island's highest point, where a viewing platform offers sweeping 360-degree panoramas. You can trek on your own or take one of the farm's guided tours, from a mild

DINNER IN THE treehouse

Set on a *carbet* (covered wood patio) at Loterie Farm's entrance, the **Hidden Forest Café** (www.loteriefarm.com) serves delicious lunches and dinners; it's open from noon to 3pm and 6:30 to 9:30pm Tuesday through Saturday and noon to 6pm Sunday. It sports a funky-chic treehouse look and is the domain of Canadian-born, self-taught chef Julia Purkis, who says her surroundings provide inspiration (and, of course, fresh ingredients from the organic gardens and forest). Her sophisticated culinary techniques and presentation (including often-edible floral garnishes) are all the more impressive given the basic kitchen and frequent power outages. You might start with spicy crab cakes, or brie in puff pastry with mango chutney. Standout main courses include a Caribbean gumbo (with plantains), a green curry coconut fish, and Julia's signature curried spinach-stuffed chicken.

sunset walk to a wild, strenuous eco-challenge. Along the way, enthusiastic guides discourse on local history, geology, wildlife, and bush medicine. The **Fly Zone** (35€) lets you fly over the forest canopy on ropes and cables suspended high in the air. The newest attraction, **Fly Zone Extreme** (55€), gives you even more adrenaline chills with a challenging hike uphill and a thrilling ride on a high-tech zipline down. Kids can fly on slightly lower suspended bridges and swinging rope on the park's **Ti-Tarzan** (20€) attraction. The **Hidden Forest Café** (see below) is a delightful place to dine. The **Tree Lounge** is a bar perched 7.5m (25 ft.) off the ground; it serves tapas and pizza (along with cocktails) and is open Tuesday to Sunday from noon to midnight.

Rte. de Pic Paradis, Rambaud. www.loteriefarm.com. ✆ **590/87-86-16.** Admission for self-guided hikes 5€. Tues–Sun 9am–4pm.

Le Musée de Saint-Martin   This museum details island history and culture going back 2,500 years through the colonial era. It holds a fine collection of ancient Arawak pottery unearthed at Hope Estate (near Grand Case) and a treasure trove of maps, prints, daguerreotypes, and newspapers spanning the 18th to early 20th centuries. Ask the clerks about guided tours of the island, including those that visit archaeological digs (even some that are closed to the general public).

7 rue Fichot. www.museesaintmartin.com. ✆ **690/56-78-92.** Admission $5. Mon–Fri 9am–5pm; Sat 9am–1pm.

BEACHES

Coves scissor the island, with 39 beautiful beaches of varying length and hue. All are public, though access is often via a rutted dirt road and/or through a fancy resort. Beaches on the western leeward half of the island are generally hotter and calmer; those on the eastern windward side are, predictably, breezier with rougher swells (when not reef protected). **Warning:** If a beach is too secluded, be careful. Robberies have been reported on some remote strips. Never carry valuables on a trip to the beach, and if you do, never leave them in the car.

Wherever you stay, you're never far from the water. You can sometimes use the changing facilities at bigger resorts for a small fee. Beach bars often rent chairs and umbrellas, but may waive the charge if you order lunch or drinks. Those who prefer topless sunbathing should head for the French side of the island; for clothing optional, go to Orient Bay or Cupecoy (on the French and Dutch sides, respectively).

Dutch St. Maarten

Cupecoy Beach ★   This popular beach is close to the Dutch–French border at the island's southwest tip. It's a string of three sand beaches set against a backdrop of caves, rock formations, and dramatically eroded limestone cliffs, which offer privacy to sunbathers at this clothing-optional beach. There are two parking lots, one near Cupecoy and Sapphire beach clubs, the other a short distance to the west; parking costs $2. You must descend stone-carved steps to reach the sands. Cupecoy is also the island's major gay beach. **Warning:** The steep drop-off and high swells make the beach hazardous for young children and weak swimmers; the beach can also become eroded from the prevailing weather. The Cupecoy area is seeing considerable new development, including the sprawling Porto Cupecoy complex.

Mullet Bay Beach ★★   The next strand down from Cupecoy (west of the airport) is a palm-shaded, white-sand strip framed in seagrapes. It was once the busiest beach on the island, but St. Maarten's largest resort, Mullet Bay, has been shuttered (save for a timeshare section) since Hurricane Luis in 1995, so it's rarely crowded, though locals flock here on weekends. Watersports equipment can be rented at a local kiosk, and a couple of beach shacks sell refreshments. Snorkeling is not bad along the rocks.

Maho Beach ★   Located at the west end of the airport runway and bordering the Sonesta Maho Beach Hotel and Casino, this a classic Caribbean crescent, bustling with sunbathers, vendors hawking colorful wares, and impromptu beach barbecues. But it's best known as the beach that is buzzed daily by incoming jumbo jets that nearly decapitate the palm trees. When you spot a 747 coming into view, hang on to your hats, towels, and partner.

Simpson Bay Beach ★   West of Philipsburg before the airport, the 2km-long (1¼-mile) soft ivory sands of crescent-shaped Simpson Bay beach ring the lagoon and are set against a backdrop of brightly hued fishing boats, yachts, and town homes. This beach is ideal for a stroll or a swim (beware the steep drop-off), with calm waters and surprisingly few crowds.

Great Bay Beach ★   This 2km-long (1¼-mile) beach along the boardwalk in Philipsburg is sandy and calm; despite bordering the busy capital, it's surprisingly clean and a pleasant place to kick back after shopping or admiring the cruise ships from one of many strategically placed bars along the boardwalk. On a clear day, you'll have a view of the island of Saba in the distance. Immediately to the west, at the foot of Fort Amsterdam, is picturesque **Little Bay Beach,** but it can be overrun with tourists disgorged by cruise ships.

Dawn Beach ★   On the island's east coast, Dawn Beach is noted for its underwater life and incredible sunrises, with some of the island's most beautiful reefs immediately offshore. Dawn has plenty of wave action, but it's suitable for swimming and snorkeling out by the reef. Dawn Beach is the site of the **Westin Resort** (p. 73). This, in addition to the expansion of **Oyster Bay Resort** (p. 74), has diminished its peaceful allure, but its remarkable reef, soft pearly sand, and views of St. Barts remain unchanged.

French St. Martin

Baie Longue (Long Bay) ★   On the island's western Caribbean flank, this beach is home to the chic, expensive **La Samanna** hotel (p. 77), but it's otherwise blissfully undeveloped and uncrowded. Its reef-protected waters are ideal for snorkeling, but beware the strong undertow and steep drop-off. Baie Longue is to the north of Cupecoy Beach, reached via the Lowlands Road. Don't leave valuables in your car, as break-ins have been reported along this stretch of road.

Baie aux Prunes (Plum Bay)   Plum Bay's ivory sand stretches luxuriantly around St. Martin's northwest point. This is a romantic sunset perch (bring your own champagne, as there are no facilities) that also offers good surfing and snorkeling near the rocks. Access it via the Lowlands Road past Baie Longue.

Baie Rouge (Red Beach) ★   Baie Rouge is a charmer, from its serene waters to its views of Anguilla. It's tucked between two

A GRAND DAY ON pinel ★★

Imagine a secluded tropical island where bathers dip in a glassy lagoon fringed by palm trees and a curtain of jade mountains. Gentle surf laps a beach dotted with *palapas* and parasols. The scent of barbecued meat and coconut oil waft in the salt air. Welcome to **Îlet Pinel (Isle of Pinel),** a tiny island a 5-minute boat ride from French Cul-de-Sac. A day trip to this uninhabited island is highly recommended. You'll find two beach bistros, each with its own section of beach chairs and umbrellas (20€ for the day), and food and drink. Among them, **Karibuni ★** (© **690/39-67-00**) is the country's longest-running beach bar and serves fresh grilled lobster, shrimp salad, and burgers. (If you want to save money, bring along a picnic lunch.) Small ferryboats ($6 per passenger) run from the French Cul-de-Sac on St. Martin's northeast coast to Pinel daily on the hour from 9am to 4pm (to 5pm Sun). Take care not to miss the last return trip, at 4:30pm.

craggy headlands where flocks of gulls and terns descend at dusk—its western end is dubbed Falaise des Oiseaux (Birds' Bluff). The other side is marked by the Trou du Diable (Devil's Hole), a collapsed cave with two natural arches where the sea churns. You'll find good snorkeling here, but beware the powerful undertow. Several stands hawk sarongs, shorts, and sunbonnets.

Baie Nettlé (Nettle Bay)   Baie Nettlé lies between the Caribbean and Simpson Bay, just west of Marigot. Access is right off the main highway running through Sandy Ground. The area has become increasingly developed, with hotels, apartment complexes, watersports franchises (waterskiing and kiteboarding are quite popular), and tiny beach bars alternating with fancier restaurants. The view on the Caribbean side frames Anguilla; Marigot's harbor, to the north; and the ruins of La Belle Creole, along the Pointe du Bluff, to the south.

Anse des Pères (Friar's Bay Beach) ★   This isolated beach lies at the end of a winding, bumpy country road; its clearly sign-posted entrance intersects with the main highway between Grand Case and Marigot. This is a pretty, less-visited beach with ample parking. Shelling, snorkeling, and sunset-watching are all favored. Two beloved beach bars organize themed bashes. Stop in at **Kali's Beach Bar** (© **690/49-06-81**), a thatched bamboo hut splashed in Rasta colors, where Kali himself serves some of the island's best

A TRIP TO tintamarre

Pinel is just one of several Robinson Crusoe cays off the island's east coast. You can go even farther afield to wild, 10-sq.-km (4-sq.-mile) **Tintamarre,** patois for "noisy sea" after the nesting birds (and bleating goats). The island features pristine snow-white beaches (including the aptly named Baie Blanche), striking ocher cliffs, and wrecks such as an upright tugboat encrusted in coral reef. You can clamber through the scrub and woodlands, discovering the ruins of a 19th-century stone farmhouse and an airport for regional carriers abandoned half a century ago. But nothing matches slathering yourself with mineral-rich mud from the flats, adding sea water, and baking, avocado-colored, in the sun—nature's exfoliant. Many tour operators run snorkeling trips to Tintamarre, including **Scuba Zen** (www.scubazensxm.com; ℂ **590/87-36-13**), which offers Friday morning snorkeling/picnic trips to Tintamarre.

barbecue. Kali's legendary "full-moon parties" feature reggae bands on the beach along with a bonfire and plenty of drink.

Anse Heureuse (Happy Bay) ★ A 10-minute walk north through underbrush over a hill from Friar's Bay (pause to drink in the views of Anguilla), Happy Bay richly deserves its name, thanks to the tranquillity offered by its seas, fine snorkeling, and white-sand beach.

Grand Case Beach This narrow, mile-long ribbon of sand right in the middle of Grand Case is a small, pleasant beach that can get crowded on weekends and during sunset salutations. The waters are very calm, so swimming is good—although it's become a popular parking spot for visiting boats. A large section of the water has been roped off to allow kids to swim in safety. You can find seaglass on the beach in front of the Grand Case lolos. Nicer still is **Petite Plage,** on the north side of the Grand Case Beach Club resort, where you can snorkel around the rocks.

Baie Orientale (Orient Bay) ★★ Nestled on the island's eastern shore, Orient Bay is where the action is. It's also a beauty of a beach and the French side's designated "clothing-optional" beach. Eating, drinking, and people-watching qualify as sports, and many beach bistro/bars offer not only grilled crayfish Creole, but also live music, boutiques (with fashion shows), massages, para-sailing, jet-ski rentals, kiteboard instruction, and more. The beach's southern end contains the naturist resort, **Club Orient.**

Baie de l'Embouchure ★ Embracing **Le Galion** and **Coconut Grove** beaches, just south of Orient, this is part of the St. Martin Réserve Sous-Marine Régionale, established to protect migrant waterfowl habitats and rebuild mangrove swamps. A coral reef encloses the bay. You can wade far out into the calm, shallow waters here, making it an ideal swimming spot for small children—its nickname is "Baby Beach." It's the only beach on the French side where topless sunbathing is discouraged. Up in the hills facing the bay is a handsome white house that was long the home of Romare Bearden, the celebrated American artist and collagist.

OUTDOOR ACTIVITIES

If it's aquatic, St. Maarten/St. Martin offers it: from sailing to scuba diving, big-game fishing to boogie boarding. It almost seems the island has more marinas per square mile than anywhere else on earth (one even changed its name to Dock Maarten, neatly combining two local economic mainstays—boating and shopping). Needless to say, the island offers everything from booze cruises to eco-kayaking on all manner of pleasure craft, including banana boats, catamarans, and dinghies. Land-based excursions are less popular, though hiking and mountain biking can be rewarding.

Cruisin': Boat Excursions & Charters

The best way to really experience the island is by boat. The following operators offer a range of ways to get out on the water, whether on **sightseeing trips, lagoon tours, sunset cruises, island-hopping excursions, dinner cruises, shopping trips,** or some combination thereof. Keep in mind that in addition to the following, many of the boat operators listed under "Outdoor Activities," below, also offer a range of scheduled cruises and private charters.

Tour operator **Scoobidoo** (www.scoobidoo.com; ✆ **590/52-02-53**) is led by longtime resident Stéphane Mazurier. The sleek 23m (75-ft.) catamaran **ScoobiToo** sails from the Anse Marcel marina and Grand Case to Tintamarre, Anguilla, Prickly Pear, and St. Barts on sunset cruises, dinner cruises, or some combination of the above; it also does private charters and minicruises. **Scoobifree** is an 18m (60-ft.) catamaran that specializes in luxury charters and mini cruises. **ScoobiCat,** launched in late 2008, is a 12m (36-ft.) catamaran that can zip passengers (18 max) to neighboring islands and coves for snorkeling trips or on shopping expeditions to Marigot or even Gustavia, St. Barts. Most regular excursions ($60–$155) include snorkeling equipment, lunch, and an open bar.

If you're looking for a guaranteed party cruise, **Eagle Tours** at Bobby's Marina in Philipsburg (www.sailingsxm.com; © **721/542-3323**) offers lagoon sightseeing tours aboard the flatboat *Explorer,* stopping in Marigot for shopping before heading home; mimosas and rum punches flow copiously to pulsing music. The custom-designed *Golden Eagle* catamaran (originally built for the prestigious Whitbread Around the World Race) cruises to various deserted strands and cays for snorkeling and soaking up both tropical ambience and drinks (the pampering service includes a floating bar).

Aqua Mania Adventures offers active trips out of Pelican Marina, Simpson Bay (www.stmaarten-activities.com; © **721/544-2640**). In addition to a parasail outfit, a PADI dive shop, high-speed-ferry service to Saba and St. Barts, and a boutique abounding in beach toys and resortwear, its three party-hearty boats patrol the waters several times daily for lagoon tours, snorkeling trips, dinner cruises, shopping trips, and more. The spacious 19m (63-ft.) catamaran *Lambada* cruises to Anguilla and Prickly Pear for snorkeling and beach barbecues ($85 adults, $40 children 4–12). *Sand Dollar* clings closer to St. Martin with a half-day snorkeling excursion to Creole Rock ($45 adults, $25 children 4–12). For Children's Lagoon Cruises, kids can take turns piloting the *Calypso* in Simpson Bay's serene lagoon waters ($25); prizes and bobbing blow-up animals keep things happy. Dinner cruises (some aboard, others stopping at restaurants in Marigot's Marina Royale) are genial affairs; the return voyage toward St. Maarten's blazing skyline is memorable indeed.

The 12m (40-ft.) catamaran **Celine** departs the dock at Skipjack's restaurant at Simpson Bay (www.sailstmaarten.com;

🅾 Come Sail Away

Ever dreamed of racing a state-of-the-art yacht? You can—and no previous sailing experience is necessary—when you sign on to crew aboard one of five famed America's Cup yachts in the **St. Maarten 12-Metre Challenge ★★** in Philipsburg at Bobby's Marina (www.12metre.com; © **721/542-0045**). Among the prestigious yachts are Dennis Conner's champion *Stars & Stripes, True North,* and *Canada II.* Each boat takes 9 to 18 sailors (12 and up) for a 3-hour race ($80–$100 per person). It's great fun and a thrilling sail: The captains and mates brief their swabs-for-a-day on the basics, from grinding a winch to tacking. Celebrate your win (or just finishing) with a complimentary rum punch.

© **721/526-1170**) for mellow sunset cruises ($35). But it's most famous for the thrice-weekly Lagoon Pub Crawl/Progressive Dinner around Simpson Bay, often led by *Celine* skipper Neil Roebert. The 3-hour bender costs a mere $75. *Celine* can also be charted for full-day trips to Pinel, Tintamarre, Baie Longue, Friar's Bay, and more.

Staying Active

DEEP-SEA FISHING   The island hosts several highly regarded competitions that lure an impressive international roster of entrants. The waters teem with tuna, wahoo, snapper, grouper, jack, pompano, yellowtail, marlin, and other big-game fish. The crew from **Lee's Roadside Grill,** on Welfare Road 84, Simpson Bay (www.leesfish.com; © **721/544-4233**) knows where to catch the big boys, since they supply their own popular seafood haunt. Charter one of their 9.3m (31-ft.) Bertrams for a half-, ¾-, or full-day excursion with a minimum of four people (maximum six). Drinks are included in the half-day trip ($150 per person), and lunch and drinks are included in the ¾- and full-day excursions ($200 and $250 per person, respectively). And yes, they'll cook your trophy up at the restaurant for no extra cost.

   Pelican Watersports, on the Dutch side, at the Pelican Resort Club, Simpson Bay (© **721/544-2640**), has boats available for deep-sea-fishing expeditions priced at $150 per person for a half-day (7:30–11:30am) or $300 per person for a full-day (7:30am–3pm) excursion. In high season, reservations must be made 1 week in advance.

GOLF   Constructed in 1970, the **Mullet Bay Golf Course** (© **721/545-2850**) is the island's only golf course. It's a battered 18-hole, Joe Lee–designed course whose fate has hung in the balance, based on ongoing court battles, for years. Surrounding the course are the ruins of the island's vaunted flagship resort—described in a vintage guidebook as a "golf and tennis Shangri-La"—severely damaged by Hurricane Luis in 1995. No one has ever gotten around to cleaning up the mess (more to the point: No one will take financial responsibility for the cleanup, not even its zillionaire developers). But golfers find their way here anyway and putter along on the lumpy, poorly kempt course. Greens fees are $50 for 9 holes or $80 for 18 holes; rental carts are $50.

HIKING & MOUNTAIN BIKING   Despite its small size, the island offers terrain ranging from limestone plateaus to a central volcanic ridge topped by 424m (1,391-ft.) Pic du Paradis, and ecosystems from semiarid to tropical rainforest. Birders will sight coots, black-necked stilts, and ospreys nesting amid the swamps and cliffs.

The **St. Martin Trails Hiking Club (SXM Trails)** has weekly hikes on St. Martin and neighboring islands; individual hikes are free and visitors are welcome (www.stmartintrails.com). Offering both biking and hiking tours is **TriSport,** 14B Airport Rd., Simpson Bay (www.trisportsxm.com; ✆ **721/545-4384**). Hikes include a Guana Bay tour ($29–$39) and a Cross the Border Hike ($49). Bike tours include the Philipsburg Historical tour ($49). Bikers can rent Trek mountain bikes and hybrids ($20 half-day, $25 full day, $110 per week)—TriSport will deliver the bikes to your hotel for a $20 fee.

HORSEBACK RIDING Lucky Stables (http://luckystables. shoreadventures.net; ✆ **721/544-5255**) offers a daily romantic Sunset Champagne ride ($100 per person) that includes a marshmallow roast or a beach and trail jaunt (from $65) into secluded, stony, unspoiled Cay Bay (aka Cape Bay), from which you can glimpse Saba, Statia, St. Kitts, and Nevis on the horizon.

KAYAKING TriSport (www.trisportsxm.com; ✆ **721/545-4384**) also ventures into the open water with snorkeling/kayaking tours around Anse Guichard's hulking Henry Moore–ish boulders and Caye Verte. The 2½-hour **Simpson Bay Lagoon tour** ($49) includes instruction and a stop at deserted Grand Îlet, whose mangrove system houses critters from sea cucumbers to upside-down jellies. You can rent kayaks for $15 per hour; a double kayak costs $19 per hour.

SAILING Hop aboard a 16.5m (54-ft.) traditional sailboat for fun-filled snorkel and swimming daysails around the island with **Random Wind** (www.randomwind.com; ✆ **721/587-5742**). Leaving from the dock at Skipjack's restaurant in Simpson Bay, the *Random Wind* takes small groups (18–20 passengers max) on excursions to such beaches as Baie Rouge, Baie Longue, and Mullet Bay, lunch included.

SCUBA DIVING Although the nearby island of **Saba** is considered to be the area's top dive sight, the scuba diving is quite good around **St. Martin,** with reef, wreck, night, cave, and drift diving; the depth of dives is 6 to 21m (20–69 ft.). Off the northeastern coast on the French side, dive sites include Îlet Pinel, for shallow diving; Green Key, a barrier reef; and Tintamarre, for sheltered coves and geologic faults. To the north, Anse Marcel and neighboring Anguilla are good choices. The waters around **St. Maarten** offer good dive wrecks, including the 1770 British man-of-war, **HMS *Proselyte,*** which came to a watery grave on a reef 2km (1¼ miles) off Philipsburg in 1801. Most of the big resorts have facilities for scuba diving and can provide information about underwater tours, photography, and night diving.

Operating out of a small office in little Grand Case, **Octopus Diving** (www.octopusdiving.com; ☎ **590/29-11-27**) offers some of the best scuba services on island. Its multinational staff provides PADI courses, night dives, and underwater photography at some 30 dive sites around the island—and boats take out no more than six people maximum. One-site dives go for $99, and two-site dives $149, all equipment included.

Another top dive operation is **Scuba Zen** (formerly Scuba Fun), whose dive center is at the Great Bay Marina, Dock Maarten, Philipsburg (www.scubazensxm.com; ☎ **590/87-36-13**). It offers morning and afternoon dives in deep and shallow water, wreck dives, and reef dives. A resort course for first-time divers with reasonable swimming skills costs 75€ and includes instruction in shallow water and a one-tank dive above a coral reef. A morning two-tank dive (certified divers only) costs 85€.

Ocean Explorers, at Kim Sha Beach (www.stmaartendiving. com; ☎ **721/544-5252**), is the island's oldest dive operation.

SEGWAY TOURS Explore the Philipsburg boardwalk while handling your own personal Segway on 90-minute tours with **Caribbean Segway Tours** (www.stmaartensegway.com).

SNORKELING ★★ The calm waters ringing the island's shallow reefs and tiny coves make it a snorkeler's heaven. The waters off the northeastern shores of French St. Martin have been classified as a regional underwater nature reserve, **Réserve Sous-Marine Régionale,** which protects the area around Tintamarre, Îlet Pinel, Green Key, Proselyte, and Petite Clef. Equipment can be rented at almost any hotel, and most beaches have watersports kiosks. All of the operators listed under "Cruisin': Boat Excursions & Charters," above, offer snorkeling excursions.

Both **Octopus Diving** and **Scuba Zen** (see "Scuba Diving," above) provide guided snorkeling trips to the island's teeming off-shore reefs. Favorite snorkeling spots include Creole Rock and Turtle Reef, both in Grand Case Bay; sightings have included dolphin, barracuda, eagle rays, and turtles. Snorkeling trips to two sites with Octopus Diving cost $40 (including all equipment). Snorkeling trips with Scuba Zen cost 35€ for a half-day, plus 7.50€ for equipment rental.

TENNIS You can try the courts at most of the large resorts, but you must call first for a reservation. Preference, of course, is given to hotel guests.

WINDSURFING Most windsurfers gravitate to the eastern part of the island, most notably Coconut Grove/Le Galion Beach, Orient Beach, and, to a lesser extent, Dawn Beach, all in French St. Martin. The top outfitter here, **Tropical Wave,** Le Galion Beach,

Baie de l'Embouchure (www.sxm-orientbeach.com/chezpat; © 590/87-37-25), capitalizes on the near-ideal combination of wind and calm waters. The outfitter rents Mistral windsurfboards and also offers instruction. They also rent snorkeling gear, pedal boats, and kayaks (tours can be arranged).

WHERE TO EAT ON ST. MAARTEN/ST. MARTIN

3

Without a doubt, St. Maarten/St. Martin has some of the best dining in the Caribbean. Both the French and Dutch sides offer epicurean experiences galore, with nearly 500 restaurants to choose from. The island has become a competitive training ground for a number of classically trained culinary wizards and Michelin-bound chefs. Although the Dutch side is much more Americanized (you'll spot KFC and Burger King, among fast-food chains), some of the island's most exciting international restaurants are here—this, after all, is the melting pot of the Caribbean.

Truth be told, the standards are so high on both sides of this tiny island that few restaurateurs can get away with mediocrity for long; even the hotel restaurants are better than most. You can eat well pretty much anywhere you go. You'll find French bistros in **Marigot,** in restaurants lining the waterfront and at Marina Port la Royale. **Philipsburg,** for all its slightly tawdry tendencies, has a number of truly fine eateries around Front Street. Numerous options have sprouted in St. Maarten's **Maho district,** while its neighbor **Simpson Bay** has dozens of casual watering holes overlooking the lagoon, where fresh seafood reflects the community's longtime fishing heritage. But if the island has a culinary mecca, it is the ramshackle fishing village of **Grand Case,** perched near the northern tip of St. Martin: No other Caribbean town offers so many wonderful restaurants per capita, sitting cheek-by-jowl along the narrow mile-long Boulevard de Grand Case.

DUTCH ST. MAARTEN

Rates are quoted in dollars on Dutch St. Maarten. Unlike in French St. Martin, restaurants do not include a service charge, and gratuities are appreciated.

LA BELLE créole

Befitting its turbulent colonial history, St. Maarten/St. Martin is a rich culinary melting pot. The local cuisine, symbol of the island's voyage on many levels, is primarily a savory blend of Arawak (indigenous), French, African, and even East Indian influences. The Arawaks contributed native tubers like yuca (aka cassava) and dasheen (whose leaves, similar to spinach, are also used), as well as cilantro, lemon grass, and achiote for flavoring. The slave ships introduced plantains, sweet potatoes, green pigeon peas, and assorted peppers. The various European influences bore fruit in fresh garden staples like onions (and breadfruit imported from Tahiti because it proved cheaper for feeding slaves). The East Indians brought curry—an essential ingredient of Colombo, a meat or chicken dish of Tamil origin—as well as exotic spices.

True Creole cuisine is fast vanishing: It requires patience and work, long hours marinating and pounding. But you can still find authentic dishes whose seasonings ignite the palate. Look for specialties such as *crabe farci* (stuffed crab), *féroce* (avocado with shredded, spicy codfish called *chiquetaille*), *accras* (cod fritters), *blaff* (seafood simmered in seasoned soup), *boudin* (spicy blood sausage), and *bébélé* and *matéte* (tripe dishes stewed with anything from breadfruit to bananas). Conch (*lambi*) and whelks are found in fritters and stews with fiery *sauce chien.* Wash them down with local juices: mango, guava, papaya, and less familiar flavors such as the tart, tangy tamarind; milky mouth-puckering soursop; pulpy passion fruit; bitter yet refreshing mauby (made from tree bark); and the milkshakelike, reputedly aphrodisiacal sea moss. And try a *ti' punch* aperitif: deceptively sweet, fruit-infused 100-proof rum.

—Jordan Simon

Philipsburg
EXPENSIVE

Antoine ★ FRENCH/CREOLE   In a scenic seaside setting, Antoine serves comforting bistro food with warmth and style. The handsome room is decked out with jungle-themed Haitian masterworks, Delft tile, hurricane lanterns, old phonographs, and towering floral arrangements. Start with the chef's savory kettle of fish soup, escargots de Bourgogne, or the almost translucent sea scallops Nantaise. You can't go wrong with the baked red snapper filet delicately flavored with shallots and a white-wine butter sauce, shrimp scampi flambéed with Pastis, or grilled local lobster. And desserts are satisfyingly sinful. Antoine is also open for lunch,

Restaurant Price Categories

All restaurants tend to be quite expensive, the most expensive being in St. Barts. The following is an approximate guideline to price categories.

Very Expensive	$35 and up
Expensive	$25–$35
Moderate	$15–$25
Inexpensive	$15 and under

serving pastas, burgers, sandwiches, and salads, and has a basic kids' menu. A grove of palm trees planted out front makes a fine spot to lounge.

119 Front St. www.antoinerestaurant.com. (C) **721/542-2964.** Reservations recommended. Main courses $20–$40 dinner; lobster thermidor $46. AE, DISC, MC, V. Daily 11am–10pm.

L'Escargot ★★ FRENCH/CREOLE   It's a temple to garlic and color and bonhomie—and a memorable evening out in Philipsburg. You can't miss the wildly painted shutters and tropical Toulouse-Lautrec–style murals on the butter-yellow exterior of this 160-year-old Creole cottage. The high spirits continue within, thanks to the colorful, candlelit decor and mellow staff, which does double duty performing the Friday-night cabaret drag show, "La Cage aux Folles." The chef is deft with fish, particularly classic preparations such as meunière, and hearty bistro classics. The *coeur de filet a la confiture d'oignons* (filet of beef in a sweet onion dressing perfumed with grenadine) will melt in your mouth. Apropos of the name, the menu always lists at least six preparations of snails (try the sampler plate), including *sur champignons* (in fresh mushroom caps), *en croustade au safran* (in a crust with chardonnay and saffron sauce), and in cherry tomatoes with garlic butter.

96 Front St. www.lescargotrestaurant.com. (C) **721/542-2483.** Reservations recommended. Main courses $19–$31. AE, DISC, MC, V. Mon–Fri 11am–3pm and 6–10pm; Sat–Sun 6–10pm.

Sheer ★ FRENCH/CARIBBEAN   This upscale spot adds a coolly elegant tenor to the city's dining scene. The owner, hotel professional Valentin Davis, has pulled out all the stops—and the series of mirrored rooms done in beige-and-cream monochromes shows he means business. Start with a crab salad with an avocado, apple, and red pepper coulis, or the coconut shrimp cakes topped with lemon-grass cream. For entrees, look for fresh fish or lobster

tail, or try the grilled pork tenderloin with a sweet potato pave and
sautéed greens.

44 Front St., Promenade Mall. www.sheerrestaurant.com. **721/542-9635.**
Reservations recommended. Main courses $28–$45. AE, MC, V. Daily 11am–
3pm and 6:30–11pm.

MODERATE

The harborfront **Pasanggrahan Restaurant** ★, 19 Front St.
(www.pasanroyalinn.com; **721/542-3588**), in the Pasanggrahan Inn, is a peaceful, shady oasis for lunch or a drink. The seafood
is fresh off the boat, and the views of Great Bay are simply
wonderful.

Chesterfields ★ CARIBBEAN/INTERNATIONAL The
"house" restaurant at the Great Bay Marina has a carefree, seafar-
ing feel. It's the ideal spot for an après-snorkeling or sailing outing.
Set right on the dock of the marina, with boats cruising in and salt
air wafting, Chesterfields has a classic nautical decor of rough-
hewn timbers, wooden tables, and walls tacked with mounted fish.
A friendly staff oversees the comings and goings of sunburned
sailors, grizzled captains, and day-trippers revitalized after a morning of exploring offshore islets. Look for pub fare such as burgers,
steaks, salads, and sandwiches, as well as island specialties like
garlic shrimp, stuffed mahimahi, and conch chowder. The food is
simple and tasty—testament to Chesterfields' nearly 30 years of
solid customer service.

Dock Maarten, Great Bay Marina. www.chesterfields-restaurant.com.
721/542-3484. Main courses $7.95–$16 lunch, $16–$23 dinner. DISC, MC,
V. Mon–Wed 7:30am–10pm; Thurs–Sun 9am–10pm.

Mr. Busby's Beach Bar/Daniel's by the Sea ★ CARIB-
BEAN Little more than a sprinkling of wooden *palapas* set in the
sand on Dawn Beach, Mr. Busby's is the place to relax and let your
hair down with a real cross section of St. Maarteners. Cooled by
shady palms and sea breezes, this is the quintessential beach bar,
but it's also a fine breakfast and lunch destination. It's a lively spot
(but nowhere near as rowdy as the beach bars around Maho, say),
and a supremely chill place to sip a Carib beer against a backdrop
of low-key reggae or calypso music. But Mr. Busby's is serious

Mapping It

For locations of dining establishments listed in this chapter,
please refer to the St. Maarten/St. Martin, Marigot, Philipsburg,
and Grand Case maps on p. 14, 19, 17, and 20, respectively.

about its food, and it shows. Everything is fresh and tasty—home-made johnnycakes, eggs to order, and bloody marys make this one of the top breakfast spots on island. Lunch is jumping, too, with a menu that includes grilled Saba lobster, shrimp kebab over rice, conch or lobster salad, and Busby's own barbecued ribs. Be sure to sample the potato salad; it's addictive. Following the 4 to 6pm happy hour (try the guavaberry colada), the space becomes **Daniel's by the Sea,** which offers Italian fare. The restaurant is located next door to the Oyster Bay Beach Resort.

Dawn Beach. http://dawnbeachsxm.com. *©* **721/543-6828.** Mr. Busby's main courses $5–$14; lobster $23; sandwiches/burgers $7–$9. Daniel's main courses $16–$32. DISC, MC, V. Mr. Busby's daily 7:30am–6pm. Daniel's daily 6–10pm.

Shiv Sagar INDIAN   The island's first Indian eatery remains its best, emphasizing Kashmiri and Mughlai specialties. The best tables in the large second-floor split-level space overlook Front Street. Black lacquer chairs, hand-carved chess tables, and tradi-tional Indian silkscreens depicting scenes from such great epics as the *Mahabharata* set the stage for tempting tandooris, Madras fish curry, and vegetarian dishes such as *saag panir* (spinach in garlicky curried yogurt), hearty enough to convert even the most dedicated carnivore.

20 Front St. www.shivsagarsxm.com. *©* **721/542-2299.** Main courses $11–$22. AE, DISC, MC, V. Mon–Sat noon–10pm; Sun noon–3pm.

Maho & Cupecoy Beach Areas
VERY EXPENSIVE

Rare ★★ STEAK   Dino Jagtiani, the whiz behind the adjacent Temptation (see below), opened this take on the classic chophouse in 2005. The futuristic-yet-retro space is wittily designed. The only steakhouse in St. Maarten to carry USDA Prime dry-aged certified Angus beef, Rare offers choices from a 12-ounce filet mignon to a 28-ounce porterhouse. Those seeking lighter fare can savor sashimi-grade tuna with wasabi mash, or Parmigiano-crusted salmon. Anyone could make a meal of the home-baked bread and dips (hummus, pesto, tapenade). Dino's creativity truly shines in his sauces (nine, including chipotle-ketchup and spicy peanut). Desserts include an inspired s'mores cobbler, with chocolate, gra-ham crackers, marshmallow crust, caramel, and vanilla ice cream.

Atlantis World Casino, 106 Rhine Rd., Cupecoy. www.rareandtemptation. com. *©* **721/545-5714.** Reservations required. Main courses $27–$45. AE, DISC, MC, V. Mon–Sat 6:30–10:30pm.

Temptation ★★★ NOUVEAU CARIBBEAN   The name may sound like a strip club, but this innovative gem is one of the finest restaurants on the island. Owner/chef Dino Jagtiani, who hails from a multigenerational East Indian family, is a native and a graduate of the prestigious Culinary Institute of America. His mother, Asha, graciously greets diners. Dino's Asian-inspired cuisine is exciting, often utilizing unorthodox pairings. Main courses include "Quack Quack Chow Mein," orange-ginger-glazed duck breast with Asian veggie stir-fried rice; chicken 'n' shrimp pad Thai; and veal *osso buco* braised in red wine. You'll find the perfect wine complement on one of the island's top wine lists.

Atlantis World Casino, 106 Rhine Rd., Cupecoy. www.rareandtemptation. com. (✆ **721/545-2254.** Main courses $36–$42. AE, MC, V. Tues–Sun 6:30–10:30pm.

EXPENSIVE

La Gondola ★ ITALIAN   In a warm, expansive room, with a swooning *Mamma Mia* ambience, guests dine on fresh pasta and well-prepared Italian classics. The overriding palette is bordello red, accented by winged cherubs and gilt. The food, too, hews to the tried-and-true. But the minestrone is pitch-perfect and the tomato sauce sparkles. For something richly decadent, try the lobster ravioli in a lobster sauce—it's not overkill, trust me—or the baked veal manicotti. The congenial staff makes this dining experience extra pleasurable.

Atlantis World Casino, 106 Rhine Rd., Cupecoy. (✆ **721/545-3938.** Reservations recommended. Main courses $18–$32. AE, MC, V. Daily 6–10pm.

Simpson Bay Area
EXPENSIVE

Saratoga ★ INTERNATIONAL/SEAFOOD   This restaurant, owned and run by Culinary Institute of America grad John Jackson, occupies a beautiful setting, resembling a Spanish colonial structure from the outside and lined with rich mahogany inside. Seating is either indoors or on a marina-side veranda. The food is beautifully presented. Although the menu changes frequently, it leans toward light and healthy: It generally offers some six different salads, a gazpacho with lobster, and lots of grilled local fish—like grouper plucked from the marine-rich waters around Saba. If you're looking for good and rich, opt for the linguine primavera, prepared here with both smoked ham and bacon. Jackson dips into Thai and classic Chinese preparations, including salt-and-pepper-fried whole black sea bass.

Simpson Bay Yacht Club, Airport Rd. www.sxmsaratoga.com. (✆ **721/544-2421.** Reservations recommended. Main courses $18–$38. AE, MC, V. Mon–Sat 6:30–10pm. Closed Aug to mid-Oct.

MODERATE

SkipJack's Seafood Grill, Bar & Fish Market ★ SEA-FOOD   Of the many shipshape seafood spots on Simpson Bay, this pleasant, breezy restaurant is one of the best. You can pick your fish on ice and both Maine and Caribbean lobster from a tank and pool, then enjoy the breezes on the handsome and expansive wooden deck, from which you can watch the big yachts muscle their way in and out of Simpson Bay. The entrees range from fresh grilled lobster to blackened grouper to shrimp potpie. The steamed shrimp, hot and piled on the plate, was some of the best we've ever had. Other excellent starters include tuna carpaccio, a hearty New England clam chowder, a seared ahi salad, and Chesapeake Bay–style crab cakes with caper mayo. SkipJack's does justice to its namesake, the old-time, single-mast fishing boats that plied the Chesapeake.

Airport Rd. www.skipjacks-sxm.com. ✆ **721/544-2313.** Main courses $20–$27. MC, V. Daily noon–10:30pm. Closed Sun lunch.

The Tides CARIBBEAN/INTERNATIONAL   This modest, old-fashioned dining room is tucked into the sea-facing side of **Mary's Boon Beach Resort** (p. 74). The head chef, Leona, has been cooking here for almost 40 years. The food is simple but good, and you're so close to Simpson Bay that the sea spray practically perfumes your meal. The dinner menu is sprinkled with international classics—Caesar salad, chicken cordon bleu, pasta Bolognese, shrimp Creole—but ask about the special Caribbean menu.

Mary's Boon Beach Resort. www.marysboon.com. ✆ **721/545-7000.** Reservations recommended. Main courses $18–$30. AE, MC, V. Mon–Sat 7:30am–3pm and 6:30–9:30pm.

Topper's ★ AMERICAN   I was first clued into this spot by other travelers, who raved about the fat, juicy steaks and well-poured drinks served up by a gentleman of a certain age in what was essentially a roadside Creole shack. Topper's is indeed a hoot, but someone in the kitchen has a real touch with beef—where else on St. Maarten will you find meltingly tender brisket, served with real homemade mashed potatoes and whiskey carrots? Other classics include Caesar salad, shrimp cocktail, and meatloaf. The steaks are big and juicy indeed, and the atmosphere is fun. Best of all, the prices are reasonable for pricey St. Maarten. A second location, **Topper's by the Sea,** is at the Flamingo Beach Resort in Pelican Key (✆ **721/544-6002**).

113 Welfare Rd. www.sxmtoppers.com. ✆ **721/544-3500.** Reservations recommended. Main courses $13–$24. AE, MC, V. Mon–Sat 11am–10pm.

INEXPENSIVE

Travelers in the know (and those who watch the Travel Channel's Anthony Bourdain as he chases his appetite around the globe) are already clued in to **Hilma's Windsor Castle,** located on airport road in Simpson Bay (next door to RBTT Bank). Even by shack standards, Hilma's is rudimentary, basically a small trailer with an awning and four stools. Hilma's specialty? Johnnycakes filled with all sorts of delicious things, like ham, eggs, or cheese. The star is a saltfish johnnycake, spiced with peppers and onions ($2). Hilma's is open Monday through Saturday 7:30am to 3pm.

FRENCH ST. MARTIN

In the French Quarter in Orleans, **Chez Yvette** ★ (✆ 590/87-32-03; closed Mon) serves up Creole cuisine in a vintage cottage trimmed in gingerbread. This is home cooking, St. Martin style, with dishes like fish, conch, and goat stew; ribs; and stewed chicken served with heaping platters of rice and peas and sides of freshly made johnnycakes. Yvette passed away several years ago, but her husband, Felix, is the master chef in charge. For those looking for an authentic island meal, this is it. A platter costs around $20.

Note: Rates are quoted in either euros or dollars, depending on how establishments quoted them at press time. Prices in St. Martin restaurants include taxes and a 15% service charge, but you may want to add a little extra gratuity if the service warrants it.

Marigot
EXPENSIVE

La Vie en Rose ★ FRENCH   The "Grande Dame" of St. Martin dining still resides in its balconied second-floor perch, enjoying the breezes sweeping in from Marigot harbor. It's French through and through, from its pink-tinged dining room with gold gilt mirrors and candle lamps to the time-honored classic French cuisine. Lunches are relatively simple affairs, with an emphasis on meal-size salads, simple grills like beefsteak with shallot sauce, brochettes of fresh fish, and pastas. Dinners are more elaborate (attracting a dressier crowd) and might begin with a lobster salad with passion-fruit dressing. Main courses might include filet of red snapper simmered in a champagne sauce with pumpkin risotto; breast of duck in a foie gras sauce; lobster paired with boneless rabbit in honey-vanilla sauce; and roasted rack of lamb in a mushroom and truffle sauce. The lobster bisque in puff pastry is a must.

Bd. de France at rue de la République. ✆ **590/87-54-42.** Reservations recommended. Main courses 10€–18€ lunch, 19€–33€ dinner. AE, DISC, MC, V. Mon–Sat noon–2:30pm and 6:30–10pm; Sun 6:30–10pm.

resources **FOR SELF-CATERING**

As a large provisioning hub for passing boats, St. Maarten has plenty of options for visitors with self-catering capabilities, whether a hotel kitchenette or a fully equipped kitchen. You can buy meats, fresh fruits and vegetables, snacks, drinks, and kitchen supplies at **Le Grand Marché,** a full-service grocery chain with four locations on the island: Simpson Bay, Cupecoy, Cole Bay, and Bush Road (www.legrandmarche.net; ℂ **721/542-4400**). The **U.S. Market Super Marché** (ℂ **590/52-87-14**), a supermarket chain on the French side, has three spacious stores (Sandy Ground, Concordia, and outside Grand Case in the Hope Estate district)—all stocked with grocery basics as well as a good selection of French wines, imported cheeses, and seafood. You can also find takeout foods at *traiteurs* (takeout/caterers), *pâtisseries* (pastry shops), and *boulangeries* (baked goods). For an excellent selection of wine and spirits, head to **Vinissimo,** at 1 rue de Low Town, Marigot (ℂ **590/877-078**) or **Le Goût du Vin,** rue de L'Anguille, Marigot (ℂ **590/87-25-03**). For fresh fish, head over to the **Simpson Bay Fish Market,** an open-air seafood market facing the lagoon (next to the dreawbridge), which sells Simpson Bay's fresh catches daily. **SkipJack's Seafood Grill,** in Simpson Bay (see above), also has a small fresh-seafood market (ℂ **721/544-2313**).

Le Chanteclair ★ FRENCH   This simple yet elegant eatery is perfectly positioned on the marina boardwalk. Both the decor (from turquoise deck to orange and yellow napery) and the cuisine are sun-drenched. Chef Stéphane Decluseau, formerly of L'Astrolabe, brings his award-winning cooking to Le Chanteclair. The "Chef's Discovery" and "Gastronomic Lobster" menus at 56€ are comparative bargains, with an aperitif and four courses. The foie gras is top-notch, as is the duck in puff pastry with foie gras sauce. Among the many desserts, the Innommable ("No Name") stands out—pastry bursting with semi-sweet chocolate paired with vanilla ice cream in its own pastry shell swimming in vanilla sauce.

Marina Port la Royale. www.lechanteclair.com. ℂ **590/87-94-60.** Reservations recommended. Main courses 25€–39€. AE, MC, V. Daily 6–10:30pm.

Le Réservé ★★ FRENCH/CARIBBEAN   La Samanna's signature restaurant offers a sublime fine-dining experience in a setting that's hard to beat: high above the glittering curve of Baie Longue. The menu features classic seafood and beef dishes but does much more than pay mere lip service to vegetarian needs. Mushroom ravioli arrives drizzled in a cheeky cashew-nut sauce, and a *"coeur de boeuf"* tomato is cooked *en papillote*—baked in a feathery parchment. No matter what you order, the resort's celebrated wine cellar provides the perfect complement to the meal. Children of highchair age are not permitted during the restaurant's two nightly seatings.

La Samanna Resort, Baie Longue. www.lasamanna.com. 𝄞 **590/87-64-00.** Reservations recommended. Main courses $22–$38. AE, MC, V. Daily 6:45– 9:45pm (2 seatings nightly).

Mario's Bistro ★★ FRENCH   The setting defines romance, with tables staggered along a balcony overlooking Sandy Ground Bridge and the silvery waters of the Marigot Channel. Chef Mario Tardif inspires passion with his architectural presentations and inventive "contemporary French" cooking spiced with Asian, Moroccan, and Southwestern accents. Start with hoisin-braised duck roll and cacao foie gras, or the sautéed lobster tails in puff pastry. For mains try the crab-crusted baked mahimahi or the bouillabaisse with green Thai curry and lemon grass.

Sandy Ground Bridge. www.mariosbistro.com. 𝄞 **590/87-06-36.** Reservations highly recommended. Main courses 24€–35€. DISC, MC, V. Mon–Sat 6:30–10:30pm. Closed Aug–Sept.

MODERATE

Claude Mini-Club ★ CREOLE/FRENCH   For more than 3 decades, this has been a favorite among locals and discerning visitors. The building was constructed to resemble a treehouse clinging to the trunks of old coconut palms, and the sunny island decor—madras tablecloths, straw and shell handicrafts dangling from the beams, and Haitian murals—captures much of the vibrancy of the region. A big terrace opens onto the sea. Authentic Creole offerings include *lambi* (conch) in zesty tomato stew, and *accras* (cod fritters) in shallot sauce, but you can also find entrecôte in green-peppercorn sauce, veal escalope with fresh morels, and such classic desserts as banana flambé and crème brûlée. The restaurant stages the island's best buffets, featuring such crowd pleasers as roast suckling pig, roast beef, quail, chicken, red snapper, and Caribbean lobster, accompanied by carafes of wine.

Bd. de France. 𝄞 **590/87-50-69.** Reservations required. Main courses 18€– 30€; buffet 42€. AE, MC, V. Mon–Sat 11:30am–3pm and 6–10pm. Closed Sept.

L'Oizeau Rare ★ FRENCH   The "Rare Bird" serves up creative French cuisine in a blue-and-ivory antique house on a green Marigot hillside with a view of a garden and three landscaped waterfalls. Have lunch on the covered terrace, where you can dine

GRAND CASE: foodie HEAVEN

No other town in the Caribbean has as many restaurants per capita as the little village of Grand Case, set near St. Martin's northernmost tip. Don't be put off by the town's slightly tumbledown appearance: Behind the slightly ramshackle Creole facades are French-, Italian-, and American-style restaurants managed by some very sophisticated cooks. Many of these spots open up to lovely beachside settings. Here are some tips on dining in Grand Case:

o **Don't pick the first restaurant you see.** Stroll down the Boulevard de Grand Case; menus are prominently displayed out front, as are the nightly specials. Some restaurants offer $1 = 1€ prices.

o **Drink to the sunset *sur la plage*.** Before you dine, do as the locals do and sip a cool drink as you watch the sunset melt into the sea on Grand Case Beach. One popular spot is **Calmos Café,** 40 bd. de Grand Case (www.calmoscafe. com; ✆ **590/29-01-85**), with candlelit tables in the sand for the nightly sunset ritual. The competition is neighbor **Zen It,** 48 bd. de Grand Case (✆ **590/29-44-84**), where you can sip a beer on the raised wooden porch overlooking the beach. For late-night action, head to the more upscale **Le Moon,** 28 bd. de Grand Case (www.lemoonsxm. com; ✆ **590/51-96-17**), which brings a touch of Miami Beach and the Hamptons to little Grand Case, with melon

on salads and crispy pizzas, or a light tuna tartare with hand-cut French fries. Dinner choices include fresh fish, such as snapper or grouper; beef tenderloin Rossini with foie gras and Marsala sauce; or penne pasta tossed with a shrimp and sea scallop fricassee. There are numerous daily specials, and the wine list features French options at moderate prices. Many guests come here at sundown to enjoy the harbor view over a Kir Royale or the potent house drink, Oizeau Rare: dark rum and tequila with pineapple, orange, and coconut.

Marigot Waterfront. ✆ **590/87-56-38.** Reservations recommended. Main courses 15€–24€ lunch, 18€–25€ dinner. AE, MC, V. Mon–Sat 11:30am–10pm. Closed June.

INEXPENSIVE

La Belle Epoque FRENCH/CREOLE/PIZZA   You won't find a better perch to watch the boats in the Marigot marina than this blue-awning boardwalk cafe. After window-shopping in Marigot, stop by for Belgian beers or a glass of proper rosé, a big salad or fish mojitos on tap, a small pool, and colored lights revving up a seaside lounge.

o **Dress lightly.** Most restaurants are not air-conditioned.

o **Parking area pluses:** The big parking lot near the airport and across from Calmos Café is a great addition for a town that not long ago had traffic going both ways along the little two-lane Boulevard de Grand Case (traffic that had to dodge motorbikes, bicycles, and pedestrians wending their way down the street—*and* had to find parking along said street). Now traffic is one-way from the parking lot area—and cars have a place to park away from the main drag.

o **Parking area minuses:** On the other hand, the parking lot also means more cars and vans. This is a peaceful place that can get overrun with tourist shuttles during the evening hours.

o **Prepare to shop.** Many shops and art galleries along the Boulevard de Grand Case open during the dinner hours to take advantage of the influx of visitors.

o **Don't miss "Grand Case Tuesdays."** It's Carnival every Tuesday evening during high season, when the Boulevard de Grand Case is closed off to vehicular traffic for a street festival featuring musicians, food stands, and a crafts market.

soup, pasta carbonara or a hearty Bolognese, or scrumptious mini-pizzas (8€–19€) with a multitude of toppings. At dinner you can dine on such dishes as shrimp fricassee or duck breast with mango sauce served Creole style with rice and vegetables. A three-course *menu Creole* features saltfish fritters, mahimahi filet, and a fruit salad for 21€. The restaurant is also open for breakfast, serving omelets, pastries, and juices.

Marina Port la Royale. www.belle-epoque-sxm.com. ☎ **590/87-87-70.** Salads, sandwiches, and main courses 14€–24€; grilled lobster 50€. MC, V. Daily 7:30am–11pm (from 5pm Sun).

Grand Case
EXPENSIVE

L'Auberge Gourmande ★★ FRENCH It's worthwhile to dine here if only to spend time in one of the oldest Creole houses in St. Martin. From the burnished wood box-beam ceiling to the arched doorways to a butter-yellow interior, L'Auberge feels like home, if home is a gracious 125-year-old stone and wood cottage warmed by oil lamps and white linen tablecloths. Most people come, however, for the splendidly prepared French cuisine, things like *vol au vent* with scallops, shrimp, and mushrooms in a reduced fish sauce or the whole grilled sole in an almond butter meunière. Even the simple Caesar salad is fresh and delicious. The one downside? It's not on the seaside.

89 bd. de Grand Case. www.laubergegourmande.com. ✆ **590/87-73-37.** Reservations recommended. Main courses 26€–36€. MC, V. Daily 6–10:30pm. Closed Sept–Oct.

Le Bistrot Caraïbes ★★ FRENCH/CARIBBEAN Brothers Thibault and Amaury Mezière, former chefs at Paul Bocuse's restaurant in Lyon, have been cooking at this warm spot for some 17 years. Fresh lobster (choose your own from the circular water fountain out front) and the catch of the day are their specialties. Start with the homemade smoked salmon on toast points or the hot goat cheese in a pastry crust. You can do lobster any number of ways (in butter, simply grilled, or as thermidor) or go for the fisherman's platter in a rich bouillabaisse-style lobster sauce. A classic crème brûlée or homemade profiteroles provide an elegant finish.

81 bd. de Grand Case. www.bistrotcaraibes.com. ✆ **590/29-08-29.** Reservations recommended. Main courses 23€–28€; lobster market price. MC, V. Daily 6–10:30pm. Closed Sat May–Dec.

Le Pressoir ★★ FRENCH One of the prettiest of the Grand Case restaurants, Le Pressoir is set in a restored 19th-century Creole cottage painted yellow and blue. The interior has a whimsical dollhouse charm, with lavender and white napery, mint and red shutters, colorful island paintings (many for sale), carved hardwood chairs, and warm table lamps. The kitchen presents an artful combination of old and new French cuisine. Standout standards include lobster ravioli in a passion-fruit cream sauce, seafood tagliatelle, grilled sea scallops with duck slices and rhubarb, and grilled beef tenderloin in a Camembert sauce. Be sure to cross the street after dinner to admire the restaurant's namesake, a mammoth salt press from the 1800s.

32 bd. de Grand Case. http://lepressoir-sxm.com. ✆ **590/87-76-62.** Reservations recommended. Main courses 19€–38€. AE, MC, V. Daily 6–11pm. Closed Sun in low season and Sept 15–Oct 15.

L'Estaminet ★★ FRENCH On our most recent trip, the name most frequently mentioned by travelers and locals alike as their favorite dining spot in Grand Case was this one. Opened in 2006 in a Creole cottage at the western end of the Boulevard de Grand Case, L'Estaminet has quickly become an essential element of the Grand Case culinary lexicon. The classic French cuisine is innovative and

🎁 Lolos: Local Barbecue Joints

Open-air barbecue stands are a St. Martin institution, dishing out big, delicious helpings of barbecued ribs, lobster, chicken, or fish grilled on split metal drums; garlic shrimp; goat stew; rice and peas; cod fritters; and johnnycakes—all from $10 to $20, a real bargain on pricey St. Martin. In Grand Case, two of the best, **Talk of the Town** (📞 590/29-63-89) and **Sky's the Limit** (📞 690/35-67-84), have covered seating, a waitstaff, and sea breezes ($1 Carib beers don't hurt, either). Several excellent lolo-style Creole restaurants are found in Marigot facing the marketplace and ferry port, including Le Goût and Chez Coco— but our favorite is **Enoch's Place** (📞 590/29-29-88), which serves tasty garlic shrimp (10€), stew chicken (10€), and stew conch (8€); each platter comes with rice and peas, cooked plantains, and salad. Derrick Hodge's **Exclusive Bite** (no phone) is right by the city's scenic cemetery. The Dutch side has its own versions. For lunch try **Mark's Place** (no phone) in Philipsburg's Food Center Plaza parking lot; after 6pm, head for **Johnny B's Under the Tree** (no phone) on Cay Hill Road in Cole Bay.

French St. Martin

bursting with global flavors; sample local fish marinated in a Guyanese masala or vanilla-cigar-smoked pork tenderloin. Fat scallops are stuffed with foie gras and truffle panad to resemble cheeseburgers— imagine that! It may not be on the "water" side of Grand Case boulevard (meaning no sea views), but the atmosphere is fizzy and warm, and the welcome utterly gracious.

139 bd. de Grand Case. www.estaminet-sxm.com. 📞 **590/29-00-25.** Reservations recommended. Main courses 22€–30€. MC, V. Daily 6–10:30pm. Closed Mon in low season.

Le Tastevin ★ FRENCH/CARIBBEAN A warm, candlelit ambience and bewitching sea views have made Le Tastevin a favorite of locals and visitors alike. Daily specials are listed on the blackboard out front, often including fresh fish such as mahimahi, red snapper, or grouper in a classic French- or Asian-infused sauce. The vegetarian dishes are often among the best items on the menu; if it's offered, try the local squash in a curry, potato, black olive, and sun-dried-tomato napoleon. Le Tastevin is known for its extensive and detailed wine list.

86 bd. de Grand Case. www.letastevin-restaurant.com. 📞 **590/87-55-45.** Reservations recommended. Main courses 17€–30€. AE, MC, V. Daily noon– 2pm and 6–10pm. Closed Tues May–Nov.

Spiga ★★ ITALIAN   The affable husband-and-wife team of Ciro Russo (a native of Lecco, Italy) and Lara Bergamasco (second-generation St. Maarten restaurant royalty) have crafted the finest Italian restaurant on the island. Simple elegance reigns, starting with the charming 1914 Creole home in which the restaurant is set. You can dine inside, where darkly stained wooden doors and windows frame salmon-pink walls, or on the candlelit patio. Sample the deeply flavorful tomato and basil lobster bisque and the handmade pappardelle with braised beef-and-mushroom sauce. A hearty cioppino is filled to the brim with shrimp, scallops, and fish in a tomato-crustacean broth. The roast pork tenderloin comes wrapped in smoked pancetta and stuffed with a mushroom ragout. End the evening with a vanilla-bean crème brûlée and raspberry panna cotta, washed down with fiery grappa.

4 rte. de l'Espérance. www.spiga-sxm.com. ✆ **590/52-47-83.** Reservations recommended. Main courses $17–$32. DISC, MC, V. Daily 6–10:30pm. Closed Tues May–Nov.

MODERATE

Sunset Café ★ 🔔 FRENCH/INTERNATIONAL   This open-air restaurant straddles the narrow, rocky peninsula dividing Grand Case Beach and Petite Plage. Tables are set along a breeze-filled terrace that affords sweeping views of the blue sea, Creole Rock, and, of course, the setting sun. It's also a lovely, breeze-filled spot to dine and watch the night waves, the beach below spotlit for extra effect. The chef/operator, Brittany-born chef Alexandre Pele, has a resume that includes cooking stints at the Savoy in London and La Samanna here on French St. Martin. He excels in fresh seafood prepared simply at reasonable prices; sample the tasty red snapper filet *en papillotte* (oven-baked in parchment paper). Breakfast is hearty, and lunch items are basic—sandwiches, burgers, salads—but what's basic about watching herons dive-bombing for fish below?

21 rue de Petit-Plage (in the Grand Case Beach Club). ✆ **590/87-51-87.** Reservations recommended for weekend dinners in winter. Main courses 11€–38€ lunch, 17€–26€ dinner. AE, MC, V. Daily 7am–midnight.

Mont Vernon
MODERATE

Sol é Luna ★★★ 🎁 FRENCH   This gracious family-run Creole *caze* is virtually pillowed in luxuriant greenery, with glittering views from the wraparound terrace of the Mont Vernon hills. Set back from the road, "Sun and Moon" is a jewel box, an ideal spot for a romantic dinner. You might start your meal with lobster bisque or a cocktail of crab. Follow with flambéed sea scallops or an open ravioli of veal sweetbreads in a shiitake morel sauce. Follow up desserts (banana crunchy cake with chocolate mousse) with a minitasting of artisan rums (plum–passion fruit, vanillaginger). The hideaway also offers charming **studios and suites** from $726 a week (low season) or from $860 a week (high season).

61 Mont Vernon (Cul-de-Sac, above Anse Marcel). www.solelunarestaurant. com. ℂ **590/29-08-56.** Main courses 26€–30€. MC, V. Daily 6–10pm. Closed mid-June to mid-July and mid-Sept to Oct.

Baie Nettle & Sandy Ground
VERY EXPENSIVE

Le Santal ★★ FRENCH   The approach to this dazzler is through a ramshackle, working-class Marigot suburb, a sharp contrast to the glam interior filled with mirrors, fresh flowers, ornately carved chairs, Villeroy & Boch china, and Christofle silver. Try to nab one of the coveted oceanfront tables, occupied at one time or another by the likes of Robert de Niro, Brooke Shields, Arab sheiks, and minor royalty. Sadly, you will no longer be greeted by owner Jean Dupont; he passed away in 2005, but his wife and children continue to run the restaurant. The fare is a celebration of the classics. The crepe stuffed with lobster meat, mushrooms, and scallions in a white-wine crawfish butter sauce is a formidable starter; the grilled whole red snapper flambéed in Pastis with fennel beurre blanc is deboned at your table. Superb chateaubriand au poivre is flambéed in aged Armagnac and coated with béarnaise. End your evening with crêpes Suzette, prepared the old-fashioned way: flambéed tableside.

40 rue Lady Fish, Sandy Ground. www.restaurantlesantal.com. ℂ **590/87-53-48.** Reservations recommended. Main courses $38–$49. AE, MC, V. Daily 6–10:30pm.

EXPENSIVE

La Cigale ★★ FRENCH   Celebrating 12 years in the business, this family-run establishment provides a winning combination of innovative French fare, warmth and intimacy, and a romantic lagoon setting. Tucked away behind the Laguna Beach hotel at the end of an alley, Olivier Genet's bistro may be pricey, but it's worth a potential wrong turn or three to find. He recruited his parents from the Loire Valley to help him run the tiny operation. The ambience is relaxed, but chef Mallory Leroux's food is bold and elegant, with sunny island intonations. That sensibility comes to play in dishes like lobster, mushroom, and foie gras ravioli cooked in a lobster bisque soup; or squab rolled in bacon, foie gras, and apricots. La Cigale is meant for lingering by the lagoon, where Olivier will ply you with home-brewed rum *digestifs* and anecdotes of his Sancerre upbringing.

101 Laguna Beach, Baie Nettlé. http://restaurant-lacigale.com. ⓒ **590/87-90-23.** Reservations required. Main courses 30€–49€. MC, V. Mon–Sat 6–10:30pm.

Anse Marcel

C Le Restaurant ★ FRENCH/CARIBBEAN   Perhaps it's the close proximity to such a highly competitive restaurant town (Grand Case, 5 min. away); perhaps the magical setting is an inspiration. For whatever reason, this Radisson restaurant is a surprisingly admirable addition to the local culinary scene. Executive chef Bruno Brazier prepares duck, steak, and lamb with aplomb but has a particularly deft touch with seafood. You might start with mahimahi ceviche, a fish and saffron soup, or even an exemplary Caesar salad, served, whimsically, from a giant martini shaker. Look for such inspired specials as *gambas* (large shrimp) stuffed with crab in a buttery curry sauce with wild rice and vegetables. The attached **Lounge at C** is open till midnight. The setting is bewitching; tables look out over the blue-black waters of Anse Marcel, the sea mirroring the bobbing sailboats, the encircling cliffs, and the glittering lights of Anguilla in the distance. The only thing I would change? The unwieldy name.

Radisson Blu Resort, Marina & Spa. www.c-le-restaurant.com. ⓒ **590/87-67-00.** Reservations recommended. Main courses 21€–35€. AE, DC, DISC, MC, V. Daily noon–3:30pm and 7–10:30pm.

SHOPPING ON ST. MAARTEN/ ST. MARTIN

The island of St. Maarten/St. Martin teems with duty-free bargains ranging from linen to liquor and china to cameras, priced as much as 20% to 40% lower than in the U.S. and Canada. There's an energizing hubbub in **Philipsburg** every morning as cruise-ship passengers scatter eagerly in search of latter-day treasure: The goods displayed in the windows along Front Street are a mind-boggling display of conspicuous consumption, with an emphasis on high-end (gold, diamond, and platinum) jewelry and designer watches.

Philipsburg's inviting French counterpart **Marigot** boasts small boutiques along narrow city streets. Philipsburg encourages you to "shop till you drop"; Marigot murmurs seductively, "Relax, the shops will be open in an hour or two." It's a nice place to savor the salt air, watch the ferries load for Anguilla, and enjoy a steaming cup of café au lait.

THE SHOPPING SCENE
Dutch St. Maarten

Not only is Dutch St. Maarten a free port, but it also has no local sales taxes. Prices are sometimes lower here than anywhere else in the Caribbean, except possibly St. Thomas. Many well-known shops from Curaçao have branches here. Except for the boutiques at resort hotels, the main shopping area is in the center of **Philipsburg. Maho Plaza,** surrounding the Sonesta Maho Beach Resort, is another area for name-brand offerings (and outlets), including branches of Philipsburg's Front Street stalwarts. A five-level concrete mall (topped by 36 luxury apartments), the **Blue Mall** (http://bluemallsxm.com), is a formidable addition to the area around the Porto Cupecoy complex; it's a little off the beaten path but when fully operational should have some 85 shops, plus restaurants.

In general, the prices marked on merchandise are firm, though at some small, personally run shops, where the owner is on-site, some bargaining might be in order.

PHILIPSBURG

Most of the leading shops—from Tiffany to Tommy Hilfiger—are found on and around **Voorstraat (Front Street),** which stretches for about 2km (1¼ miles). The **St. Rose Shopping Mall,** on the beachside boardwalk off Front Street, has such big names as Cartier and Façonnable. The best buys are in electronics, jewelry, watches, and cameras.

Just off Front Street, **Old Street** lives up to its name; here 19th-century houses are now home to specialty stores. More shops and souvenir kiosks sit along the little lanes, known as *steegjes,* that connect Front Street with **Achterstraat (Back Street),** another shoppers' haven.

In general, shops in Dutch St. Maarten stay open from 9am to 6pm.

French St. Martin

MARIGOT

Many day-trippers head to Marigot from the Dutch side just to browse the French-inspired boutiques and shopping arcades. Since St. Martin is also a duty-free port, you'll find some good buys here as well, even at the international boutiques along **rue de la République, rue du Général de Gaulle,** and **rue de la Liberté,** where French luxury items such as Christofle tableware, Vuitton bags, Cartier accessories, and Chanel perfume are sold, as well as *prêt-à-porter* fashion.

At Marigot's harbor side, a lively **morning market** on Wednesday and Saturday hosts vendors selling clothing, spices, and handicrafts. There's a cookie-cutter quality to the crafts, with many of the vendors offering the same (imported) goods, but it's a good spot to pick up spices, colorful and inexpensive children's clothes, and the occasional good-quality craft. The **lolos** (open-air barbecue restaurants) on the market's northern flank make great lunch spots.

In the Marigot heat and humidity, it's a relief to duck into the air-conditioned cool of waterfront **Le West Indies Mall,** Front de Mer (© **590/51-04-19**), with a marble staircase, arches, skylights, and gazebos. Overlooking Marigot Bay, it's a hushed, icily ornate contrast to the steamy, ramshackle market across the street. But it does boast some 22 boutiques selling designer brands.

Les soldes, the twice-yearly official (government-sanctioned) sales seasons, offer big discounts at stores (including designer boutiques) on the French side. The *soldes* generally take place for a month to 5 weeks in May and then again in October. Look for the sign SOLDES in shop windows.

Smaller complexes include **Galerie Périgourdine** and **Plaza Caraïbes,** which houses Cartier and Longchamp outposts.

In the middle of town, mornings are bustling in the **Marina Port la Royale:** Boats board guests for picnics on deserted beaches, and a dozen restaurants ready for the lunch crowd. Marina Royale is peppered with narrow warrens and alleyways where boutiques sell everything from designer clothes to jewelry.

Prices are quoted in euros or U.S. dollars, and most salespeople speak English. Credit cards and traveler's checks are generally accepted.

Tip: Keep in mind that most shopkeepers in French St. Martin close to take an extended lunch break from around 12:30 to around 2pm. French St. Martin stores open around 9am and close around 7pm.

GRAND CASE

Several clothing boutiques and galleries fight for scraps of space between the bistros along the main drag of St. Martin's "second" city, **Grand Case,** nicknamed "Caribbean Restaurant Row." They keep unusual hours: Most are shuttered during the day but fling their doors open come evening for pre- and post-dinner strollers.

SHOPPING A TO Z
Art

The island's charming local scenes and resplendent light have inspired such renowned artists as Romare Bearden over the years. I generally find the galleries on the French side more sophisticated; curious shoppers can also visit various ateliers.

DUTCH ST. MAARTEN

Planet Paradise ★ Also known as the Island Arts of the Yoda Guy, this nonprofit museum is the playpen of the wildly creative Nick Maley, an artist/special-effects designer who was instrumental in fashioning *Star Wars*'s resident gnome and contributed to other blockbusters from *Superman* to *Highlander*. John Williams's iconic theme music wafts through the air as you examine rare Lucasfilm prints, posters signed by the director himself, and Nick's own island-themed artworks. Check out Nick's new **Yoda Guy Movie Exhibit,** a collection of film memorabilia including the faces of Hollywood stars and characters, as well as movie story-boards. There's a second location at 106 Old St. 19A Front St. www.netdwellers.com/mz/planetp. ✆ **721/542-4009.**

FRENCH ST. MARTIN

Antoine Chapon ★   Painter Andrew Wyeth once lauded this Bordeaux-born painter's ethereal watercolors of serene island scenes. Chapon's watercolors are bathed in light and depict the interplay of blue sky and blue seas; his oils have a denser, earthier feel. Chapon, who has lived in St. Martin since 1995, offers limited-edition high-definition archival prints—giclees—at excellent prices. 1 Les Terrasses de Cul-de-Sac. http://chaponartgallery.com. ✆ **590/52-93-75.**

Dona Bryhiel   Now open by appointment only, the atelier of Dona Bryhiel reveals the whimsical Fauvist sensibility the artist brings to her decorative paintings of St. Maarten and her native Provence. 9 Residence Lou Castel, Oyster Pond. www.donabryhiel.com. ✆ **590/87-43-93.**

Escale des îles ★   This art gallery in a vintage Creole *maison* opposite the Marigot Market holds the works of many of the island's top artists, including the stunning wood marquetry of Jean-Pierre Straub. It's lined with a nicely curated collection of paint-ings, ceramics, handicrafts, and jewelry. 23 Bd. de France, Marigot. ✆ **590/87-26-08.**

Francis Eck ★   Francis Eck commands high prices for his intense, color-saturated abstract landscapes and seascapes. Their jazzy, Rothko-esque riffs of primary color and bold impasto (exe-cuted with knife and trowel) enable him "to explore the intersec-tion of figurative and abstract." His atelier is open by appointment only. You can also see his work on display on the walls of Bistro Nu and Mario's Bistro in Marigot, and Restaurant Le Soleil and Bistro Caraïbes in Grand Case. Hotel le Flamboyant, Baie Nettlé. www.francis-eck.com. ✆ **690/59-79-27.**

Galerie Gingerbread ★   Gingerbread Gallery exhibits vivid, powerful Haitian art, including works by such modern masters as Françoise Jean and Profil Jonas. 14 Marina Royale, Marigot. www.ginger bread-gallery.com. ✆ **590/51-94-95.**

Minguet Gallery ★   Another highly regarded French expat, Alexandre Minguet (1937–96) was an accomplished painter and watercolorist whose vibrantly colorful canvases recall Matisse and

Dufy; his gallery lies 2 minutes west of Grand Case. Rambaud Hill, btw. Marigot and Grand Case. ✆ **590/87-76-06.**

NOCO Art Gallery ★ NOCO Art was founded in 2004 by German sisters Norma and Corinne Trimborn, whose work couldn't be more different. Norma's paintings are figurative with abstract expressionist elements; her delightful Impressionistic still lifes call to mind Cezanne. Corinne paints unsettling neo-surrealist works in striking color fields. 39 Falaise des Oiseaux, Terres Basses (near Plum Bay). www.nocoart.com. ✆ **690/45-67-91.**

Roland Richardson Gallery ★ Known for luminous *plein air* landscapes, portraits, and still lifes, Roland Richardson's clearest influence is the 19th-century Barbizon School of Impressionists. A native of St. Martin and one of the Caribbean's premier artists, he has exhibited in more than 100 one-man and group shows in museums and galleries around the world. Celebrity collectors have ranged from Martha Graham to Jackie Kennedy Onassis, and from the Getty family to Queen Beatrix of the Netherlands. Richardson's carefully restored landmark West Indian home holds a court-yard garden and art gallery dating back to the 1700s. Richardson is also the resident artist at the resort **La Samanna** (p. 77), where he has a changing collection of works. 6 rue de la République, Marigot. www.rolandrichardson.com. ✆ **590/87-32-24.**

Clothing
DUTCH ST. MAARTEN

Del Sol St. Maarten This shop sells men's and women's sportswear. Embedded in the mostly black-and-white designs are organic crystals that react to ultraviolet light, which transforms the fabric into a rainbow of colors. Step back into the shadows, and your T-shirt will revert to its original black-and-white design. The same technology is applied to yo-yos, which shimmer psychedelically when you rock the baby or walk the dog. 55 Front St., Philipsburg. www.delsol.com. ✆ **721/542-8784.**

Rima Beach World Crave ticky-tack souvenirs and generic beach paraphernalia? Cut out the middleman by coming to what is essentially a resort-wear factory outlet stocked to the rafters with any and every beach accessory you need, from peasant skirts to pareos, flip-flops to kids' beachwear, and shellacked shells to beach toys, much of it in electric tropical hues. 41 Nisbeth (Pondfill) Rd., just north of Philipsburg. ✆ **721/542-1424.**

FRENCH ST. MARTIN

Act III If you've been invited to a reception aboard a private yacht, this is the place to outfit yourself. Act III prides itself on its designer evening gowns and chic cocktail dresses. Designers include Christian Lacroix, Cavalli, Armani, Lanvin, Versace, and Gaultier. The bilingual staff is accommodating, tactful, and charming. 3 rue du Général de Gaulle, Marigot. ✆ 590/29-28-43.

Havane Boutique This boutique is a hyper-stylish clothing store for men and women, selling designer clothes from Armani to Zegna. 50 Marina Royale, Marigot. www.havaneboutique.com. ✆ 590/87-70-39.

L'Atelier ★ L'Atelier showcases clothing and accessories (shoes, belts, and bags) from well-known European designers, and the store is stocked with the latest Paris fashions. 28 Marina Royale, Marigot. ✆ 590/87-13-71.

MaxMara This, the first Caribbean franchise for the Italian Maramotti empire, carries every line, from the more casual, lower-priced SportMax and Weekend to the dressy Pianoforte. 33 rue du Président Kennedy, Marigot. ✆ 590/52-99-75.

Pomme Boutique ★ This children's clothing store has been selling top-quality kids' brands for more than 23 years. Look for darling frocks by Petit Bateau, Lili Gaufrette, Sucre d'Org, and Berlingot. 6 rue de l'Anguille, Marigot. ✆ 590/87-87-20.

Serge Blanco "15" Boutique Although a relatively unknown name in North America, Blanco is revered in France as one of the most successful rugby players of all time. His menswear is sporty, fun, and elegant. Clothes include polo shirts, shorts, shoes, and latex jackets. Marina Royale, Marigot. ✆ 590/29-65-49.

Vie Privée This shop offers belts with elaborate buckles in leather and various exotic skins from ostrich to crocodile. It also sells bags and luggage. Marina Royale, Marigot. ✆ 590/87-80-69.

Cosmetics & Perfume

Lipstick This is a Caribbean chain noted for its top-notch selection of scents and cosmetics, from Clarins to Clinique, Chanel to Shalimar. Stylists here do makeovers, touch-ups, skin-care sessions, and even facials utilizing primarily Dior products. There's a Dutch side branch at 31 Front St. (✆ **721/542-6051**). Rue de Président Kennedy, Philipsburg. ✆ 590/87-73-24.

Pharmacie Centrale ★ I love browsing in pharmacies on French St. Martin. The French are famous for the quality of their creams and potions, and even basic toiletries—deodorants, toothpastes—are fashioned with French flair and care. At Pharmacie Centrale, you can find highly touted French brands at duty-free (and tax-free) prices: La Roche-Posay, Vichy, Carita, and more. 10 Rue du Général de Gaulle, Marigot. ✆ 590/51-09-37.

Tijon Parfumerie & Boutique ★★ 🎁   Looking for that certain something you won't find anywhere else? This boutique *parfumerie* and skin-care manufacturer makes all its wonderfully scented products right here at its headquarters in Grand Case. And you can make your own scents in the Tijon laboratory: More than 5,000 people have crafted custom-made perfumes since the boutique opened 5 years ago. The creams are divine, never overpowering, and built around the natural scents of the Caribbean. 1 rue de L'Esperance, Grand Case. http://tijon.com. ✆ **590/52-08-12.**

Food, Drink & Cigars

In addition to the usual upmarket single malt and stogie culprits (remember that Cubanos are illegal in the U.S.), the island produces its own concoctions. Though the base rums are imported from Guadeloupe, local distillers blend or infuse them creatively. Look for Rum Jumbie, whose flavored varieties include coconut, mango, vanilla, and pineapple. But the trademark libation is guavaberry liqueur (incorporating citrus, spices, and passion fruit), the traditional Christmas drink of St. Maarten.

DUTCH ST. MAARTEN
The Belgian Chocolate Box ★   All ages will savor the delicious chocolates sold here, including such specialties as Grand Marnier butter-cream truffles. It's always bustling, especially when the cruise ships are in. Another shop is located at Harbor Village in Point Blanch. 109 Old St. http://thebelgianchocolatebox.com. ✆ **721/542-8863.**

Cigar Emporium   This place has one of the Caribbean's largest selections of Cuban cigars under one roof. The smoking lounge is often filled with would-be CEOs puffing out their chests while puffing on Partagas. The shop also carries countless cigar and pipe accessories, cutters, and cases. 66 Front St. www.cigaremporium.biz. ✆ **721/542-2787.**

Guavaberry Emporium ★★   Guavaberry Emporium sells the rare "island folk liqueur" of St. Maarten, which for centuries was made only in private homes and is the island's traditional celebratory Christmas drink. Sold in square bottles, this rum-based liqueur is flavored with guavaberries, grown on the hills in the center of the island. (Don't confuse the yellow guavaberries with guavas—they're quite different.) The liqueur has a fruity, woody, smoky, bittersweet tang. Some people prefer it blended with coconut as a guavaberry colada or splashed in a glass of icy champagne. You can sample the line of liqueurs at the counter. The charming 18th-century Creole cottage also contains exotic natural perfumes and hot sauces (such as habanero-lime or Creole chipotle). The elegant hand-crafted specialty bottles and hand-carved wooden boxes make especially nice gifts. 8–10 Front St. www.guavaberry.com. ✆ **721/542-2965.**

FRENCH ST. MARTIN

Busco ★★   If the heavenly smells in this little shop don't seduce you, you may be olfactorily challenged. The company sells high-quality jams, condiments, spices, sugars, fruit punches, and rhum agricole—the agriculturally produced rum made from pure sugar-cane juice, with a deceptively elegant perfume and a toe-curling 70-proof kick. Everything is made in Guadeloupe and is brilliantly packaged. Rue The Bloudy, Concordia. ✆ **590/87-78-89.**

Le Goût du Vin ★★   This is one of the island's top sources for wines (as well as brandies and rare aged rums). The inventory of 300,000 bottles showcases the best of France, but thoughtfully includes intriguing offerings from around the globe. It now has locations in Anguilla and St. Barts. Rue de l'Anguille. http://french-wines-west-indies.grands-vins-de-france.eu. ✆ **590/87-25-03.**

Ma Doudou ★ 🎁   Ma Doudou occupies a tiny shack virtually obscured by overgrown foliage in the town of Cul-de-Sac. Call ahead unless you're in the neighborhood, as the shop keeps irregular hours. Ma Doudou means "my darling" in Creole patois. "Darling" certainly describes the collectible hand-painted bottles garnished with madras clippings. The products—rum-filled candies, spices, jams, and 20 flavored rums—practically overflow the shelves in the cramped space. The owners often throw in a free bottle with a minimum purchase. Cul-de-Sac. ✆ **590/87-30-43.**

Vinissimo   This wine boutique, which also has locations in Anguilla and St. Barts, is one of the island's top places to buy wines from around the world. 1 Rue de Low Town, Marigot. ✆ **590/87-70-78.**

Handicrafts & Gifts
DUTCH ST. MAARTEN

Blooming Baskets by Lisa   Blooming Baskets showcases the talents of two sisters from Harrisburg, Pennsylvania. The baskets are actually straw-and-raffia handbags in various sizes adorned with silk flowers duplicating not just island blossoms but a virtual botanical garden, from irises to sunflowers. Their hand-mixed dyes ensure no two bags are ever quite alike. Note that Blooming Baskets has moved its stores to the Porto Cupecoy shopping/residential complex in Cupecoy Beach. Marina Village of Porto Cupecoy, Cupecoy Beach. www.bloomingbasketsbylisa.com. ✆ **721/586-7055.**

Linen Galore ★ The beautiful tablecloths, napery, place mats, towels, fine lace, and runners on sale here are carefully sourced from Europe (Belgian tapestries, Battenburg lace) and Turkey. 45D Front St., Philipsburg. http://linengalore-sxm.com. ✆ **721/542-4590.**

Sint Maarten National Heritage Foundation Shop ★ Museum gift shops often have the most original gift items around, and this modest store, set amid generic jewelry shops between Front Street and the beachside boardwalk, is no exception. It stocks interesting crafts by local artists, including Christmas ornaments, as well as books, maps, and helpful guides to historic Philipsburg. 7 Front St., Philipsburg. www.museumsintmaarten.org. ✆ **721/542-4917.**

FRENCH ST. MARTIN
Les Exotiques ★ This is the workshop and showroom of Marie Moine, a ceramicist who fires charming local scenes onto plates: Creole houses, birds flying over Monet-like ponds, and tiny Antillean figures in traditional dress. 76 rue de la Flibuste, Oyster Pond. www.ceramexotic.com. ✆ **590/29-53-76.**

The Perfect Ti Pot ★ This little shop at the foot of the Hotel L'Esplanade showcases the handmade pottery of Cécile Petrelluzzi. Her lovely pieces deftly balance art and function. The shop is open at irregular hours; call Petrelluzzi to make an appointment to see her wares. 6 Rte. de Petit-Plage, Grand Case. ✆ **690/61-90-48.**

Jewelry

Front Street can seem like one jeweler after another (not unlike New York's W. 47th St. Diamond Exchange). All sell loose stones as well as designer items. Many stores operate branches on both sides of the island. *Note:* Beware unscrupulous hucksters selling loose "gems" like alleged emeralds and diamonds on the street.

DUTCH ST. MAARTEN
Hans Meevis Jewelry ★ Hans Meevis is a master goldsmith who works brilliantly in miniature. He loves using inlays, such as larimar in ebony, or fashioning mosaics of tiny gems. Signature items include dolphin rings and pendants, and remarkable keepsake blued titanium disks with intricate reliefs of the island in burnished white gold—right down to salt ponds and isthmuses. But Hans is also happy to customize all manner of decorative pieces (including bric-a-brac) on-site. 65 Airport Blvd., Simpson Bay. www.meevis.com. ✆ **721/522-4433.**

Shiva's Gold & Gems ★ Locals highly recommend this family business selling designer and custom-made jewelry as well as a fine collection of diamonds and diamond jewelry. The family also owns **Trident Jewelers** at 70 Front St. (© 721/542-5946). 75 Front St., Philipsburg. www.trident-shivas.com. © **721/542-5946.**

Zhaveri Jewelers Zhaveri carries the spectrum of certified loose gems, as well as genuine cultured pearls, brand-name watches, and handsomely designed necklaces, rings, bracelets, and brooches. 53A Front St., Philipsburg. www.zhaveri.com. © **721/543-1075.**

FRENCH ST. MARTIN

Art of Time This store carries extravagantly designed and priced jewelry and watches, ranging from garish to utterly ravishing. Featured individual designers and brands include David Yurman, Mikimoto, Fabergé, Scott Kay, Van Cleef & Arpels, Piguet, and Girard-Perregaux. More inventory is available in the two Philipsburg stores, **Artistic Jewelers,** 61 Front St. (© 721/542-3456); and **Art of Time,** 26 Front St. (© 721/542-2180). 3 rue du Général de Gaulle. www.artoftimejewelers.com. © **590/52-24-80.**

Goldfinger Goldfinger is the island's official Rolex agent, but it also stocks designs by watchmakers like Tag Heuer and Tissot. Other high-ticket items include designer jewelry, art glass (Kosta Boda, Orrefors, Waterford), tableware (Christofle, Daum), and porcelain (Herend, Lladró). You can also stop by locations on Rue de la République (© 590/87-55-70), at Marina Royale (© 590/87-59-96), and at 79 Front St. in Philipsburg (© 721/542-4661). Le West Indies Mall, on the waterfront. © **590/87-00-11.**

Technology & Cameras

Boolchand's ★ Need a digital camera, stat? Locals recommend this shop in Dutch St. Maarten as the place to go for all your electronics needs, with an au courant (and competitively priced) array of cameras, binoculars, cellphones, computers, jewelry, and watches. 12 and 50 Front St., 5 Harbor Point Village, Philipsburg. www.boolchand.com. © **721/542-2245.**

ENTERTAINMENT & NIGHTLIFE ON ST. MAARTEN/ ST. MARTIN

egend has it that the French/Dutch border was drawn in an 18th-century drinking contest. How fitting, then, that St. Maarten/St. Martin arguably contains more bars per capita than any other Caribbean island. Or maybe it just seems that way, given the myriad sunset booze cruises and barefoot beach bars.

This is a friendly, good-time place, where after-dark activities begin early—usually a sundowner overlooking one of the island's celebrated white-sand beaches. Nightlife choices range from salvaged scows to glitzy discos to rum shacks and, of course, casinos—all 14 of them located on the Dutch side of the island. In fact, the Dutch side at times feels like a perpetual spring break, with rolling happy hours at beach bars and club lounges. Free entertainment abounds. Many restaurants (notably at Simpson Bay; see chapter 3) and beach bars (especially on Orient Bay) host live music at least once a week, not to mention joyous happy hours. Hotels sponsor beachside barbecues with string bands.

Then there are the regular community jump-ups. On Friday nights, the Philipsburg boardwalk along Front Street percolates with activity, as does Marigot's waterfront market on Wednesdays and Sundays in season. Tuesdays from January to May, the "Mardi de Grand Case" (aka Harmony Night) in St. Martin's northern fishing village explodes with color and sound: music, dancers, crafts booths, and barbecue.

To find out what's on during your stay, get the **Thursday edition** of *The Daily Herald*, which runs an "Out and About" section and lists of upcoming events.

Look for appearances around the island by soca musician **T-Mo** (full name: Timothy King T-Moi van

Heyningen)—a six-time winner of the title of "Soca Monarch." Eleven-time Calypso Monarch **Beau Beau** can be seen most nights singing and dancing with the Beaubettes at his eponymous seafood restaurant at the Oyster Bay Beach Resort (www.oyster baybeachresort.com/the-resort/beau-beaus; © **721/543-6049**).

CLUBS & LOUNGES

Both sides of the island boast sexy lounges and clubs where you can move to great DJ mixes. The action usually starts at 10pm (though the beachfront discos throw afternoon theme parties). Most of the clubs charge a small cover (around $10 per person) after 10 or 11pm, but look for flyers or free-admission coupons in local magazines.

Dutch St. Maarten

Bliss ★ Conveniently located within walking distance of the Maho strip, this Miami Beach–style open-air nightclub on Maho Beach has a sizzling state-of-the-art lighting and sound system and new management. Big-time DJs keep the dance floor jumping. Sample a "Blisstini"—designer martinis flavored with espresso, watermelon, passion peach, and more—or take a dip in the heated pool. 2 Beacon Hill Rd. (at Caravanserai Resort), Maho Beach. http://bliss-sxm.com. © **721/545-3996.**

Privé Hookah and Sky Lounge ★ Simpson Bay's newest club is a double threat, with an open-air rooftop terrace and an indoor lounge. Mega Yacht Mall, above Market Garden, Simpson Bay. © **721/581-7658.**

Tantra ★ Formerly the Q-Club, this is the island's closest thing to a big city disco, featuring multilevel dance floors, wraparound catwalks, and go-go dancers. International DJs spin hip-hop, house, mash-ups, funk, and R&B (courtesy of a state-of-the-art sound system). It's jammed and jamming on weekends. Open Wednesday, Friday, and Saturday at 10:30pm. Casino Royale, Sonesta Maho Beach Resort. www.tantrasxm.com. © **721/545-2861.**

French St. Martin

Club One Formerly known as In's Club/L'Alibi, this *boîte* lies among the hotbed of cool joints peppering the marina that bop until dawn. DJs heat up the crowd with sizzling house mixes. Alberge de la Mer, Marina Royale, Marigot. © **590/27-13-11.**

5

Clubs & Lounges

ENTERTAINMENT & NIGHTLIFE

BEACH BARS & CLASSIC HANGOUTS
Beach Bars & Shacks

For many people, the best island nightlife revolves around the blessedly laid-back days at barefoot **beach shacks,** where it's limin' time: swimming, sunbathing, hanging in a hammock beneath a waving palm tree, listening to music, and sampling island rum and fresh lobster or barbecue ribs hot off the grill. Keep in mind that most of the following serve food and drink during the day but shut down at sunset. Some offer special nighttime events, like the Full Moon parties at Kali's Beach Bar and the New Year's Eve fireworks party at Waïkiki Beach.

DUTCH ST. MAARTEN

At **Dawn Beach, Mr. Busby's Beach Bar** ★ (✆ 721/543-6828) is a great place to kick back and even take a dip in the sea during the day; it turns into Daniel's by the Sea at night. **Beau Beaus's at Oyster Bay** (✆ 721/543-6040) is the Oyster Bay Beach Resort's beachfront bar, offering tropical drinks, music, and food, and nightly cabarets starring local calypso king Beau Beau.

FRENCH ST. MARTIN

At **Baie Rouge (Red Beach),** you have two beach bars to sample: **Gus'** (no phone) and **Chez Raymond** (✆ 690/30-70-49). The latter cooks up blistering barbecue and delivers a knockout punch with Raymond's Special, a blend of six rums; hear reggae on weekends. On **Baie Nettlé (Nettle Bay),** Laurent Maudert's **Ma Ti Beach Bar** (✆ 590/87-01-30) and **Layla's** (✆ 590/51-00-93) are lively beach bars with French and Creole specialties, respectively.

On isolated **Anse des Pères (Friar's Bay Beach), Friar's Bay Beach Café** (no phone) sells Laurent's sublime stuffed mussels. The competitor is **Kali's Beach Bar** (✆ 590/49-06-81), a thatched bamboo hut splashed in Rasta colors, where Kali serves some of the island's best barbecue. Kali hosts Full Moon parties, featuring reggae bands on the beach, a bonfire, and plenty of drinks.

Happening (and clothing-optional) **Baie Orientale (Orient Beach)** has full-service beach bars that offer not only food, but also beach chairs and umbrellas, live music, boutiques, massages, parasailing, jet-ski rentals, kiteboard instruction, and more. Full nudity is more prevalent on the beach's southern end, home to the famous Club Orient Naturist Resort. Most of the beach bars at Orient offer chairs and umbrellas for 20€ for the day. **Waïkiki Beach** (www.waikikibeachsxm.com; ✆ **590/87-43-19**) has beach lounges and a restaurant and snack bar—and, for its annual New Year's Eve party, features dinner, a dance show (featuring Parisian DJs), and one of the biggest fireworks displays in the Caribbean. **Kontiki** (kontiki-sxm; ✆ **590/87-43-27**) has two sections: the main eatery and the Tiki Hut, serving a mix of dishes from jerk chicken to sushi; it's famous for its Sunday-night parties. **Kakao** (www.kakaobeach.com; ✆ **590/87-43-26**) is an all-purpose beach bar that has watersports rentals; beach chairs and umbrellas; a boutique selling Kakao-labeled T-shirts, towels, and more; and a menu of grilled meats, pizzas, and fresh lobster. **Bikini Beach** ★ (www.sxm-orientbeach.com/bikinibeach; ✆ **590/87-43-25**) is a beachside bar and grill that also sells fresh fruit smoothies (along with more hard-core drinks). It has a full watersports facility, a boutique, and even a children's playground.

At **Baie de l'Embouchure,** embracing **Le Galion** and **Coconut Grove beaches,** tiki carvings and blue umbrellas mark the appealing **Chez Pat** (www.sxm-orientbeach.com/chezpat; ✆ **590/87-37-25**). Locals love this laid-back spot; many families come to swim the calm seas and make charcoal pits in the sand for impromptu barbecues.

On the island of **Pinel,** a short boat ride from Orient Beach, you'll find two delightful beach bistros, each with its own section of beach chairs and umbrellas. Among them, **Karibuni** ★ (✆ **690/39-67-00**) is the country's longest-running beach bar.

Classic Hangouts
DUTCH ST. MAARTEN

Bamboo Bernies ★   On the second floor at Sonesta Maho Beach Resort, Bamboo (also known as Bamboo Bernies) remains an updated homage to the Trader Vic tiki bar. It's a sushi bar, grill, and lounge and a veritable United Nations of Buddhas, African masks, Chinese paper lanterns, totem poles, Indian tapestries, torches, painted wood barrels, and transparent glowing tiki gods. Inside Bernies, the **Buddha Lounge,** as the owners say, "may very well be the only place in St. Maarten where one can relax, chill out, and actually have a conversation and hear the other person while conversing." It serves food and drinks into the wee hours. Sonesta Maho Beach Resort, Rhine Rd. www.bamboobernies.net. ✆ **721/545-3622.**

Buccaneer Beach Bar   Head here any time of day or night for a sublimely mellow setting and kick back over pizzas or burgers and knockout rum punches. The Triple B is less frenzied than many of the other Simpson Bay and Maho beach bars, with an open-air bar and picnic tables under thatched umbrellas and palm trees, but it occupies a nice perch above the beach for sunset-watching. Beach chairs and umbrellas are free. Kim Sha Beach, next to Atrium Hotel and Simpson Bay Bridge. www.buccaneerbeachbar.com. ✆ **721/522-9700.**

The Greenhouse ★   This big, breezy, plant-filled, open-air eatery at the end of the Philipsburg boardwalk has views of the marina, Great Bay, and the massive cruise ships that dock nearby. It's a favorite among locals and island regulars who swarm the place during happy hours (4:30–7pm), downing two-for-one drinks and discounted appetizers from conch fritters to jalapeño poppers. Wednesday's Crab-a-ganza and Friday's Lobster Mania sate anyone's crustacean cravings. But the food at the Greenhouse is a great value at any time (especially the certified Angus steaks, mango chicken, and such seafood specials as baked stuffed swordfish). A second Greenhouse opened in the Simpson Bay area in 2009 (✆ **721/544-4173**). Bobby's Marina, Front St., Philipsburg www.thegreenhouserestaurant.com. ✆ **721/542-2941.**

Lady C Floating Bar & Grill   Although the rickety 1938 craft barely seems seaworthy, *Lady C* cruises Simpson Bay lagoon Wednesday and Sunday afternoons. The deceptively decorous-sounding *Lady Carola* remains berthed otherwise, basically a bar on a docked boat. Welfare Rd., #88, Simpson Bay. ✆ **721/544-7499.**

Sky Beach ★   High above Maho Beach on the rooftop of the Sonesta Maho, this 1858-square meter (20,000-square-foot) alfresco space has a sumptuous roominess. You can sprawl about on a linen-draped daybed and sip custom cocktails to relaxing music. You can admire the views or dig your toes into real Caribbean sand. Sky Beach serves a light menu of tapas and panini, and features live jazz on the weekends. Closed Monday and Tuesday. Sonesta Maho Beach Hotel & Casino. www.theskybeach.com. ✆ **721/545-3547.**

Sunset Bar & Grill ★   This popular beach bar is set directly on the beach and often mobbed—it's the place to be on Sunday afternoons. No one seems to mind the roar of airplane engines from aircraft that zoom by just a few dozen feet overhead (so close that the planes' exhaust perfumes the air). The day's flight schedule is posted on a blackboard on the beach. A live band plays reggae or calypso music evenings and weekend afternoons—expect a good-time party atmosphere. It's noisy, crowded, and silly, but where else can you get buzzed by 757s and kamikazes? 2 Beacon Hill Rd. www.sunsetsxm.com. ✆ **721/545-2084.**

Taloula Mango's Caribbean Café ★ Facing Great Bay Beach, Taloula Mango's offers views of the harbor and fresh sea breezes. The handsome colonial-style room (with ceiling fans and plantation shutters) is a fine place to sample creative cocktails and delicious pub grub (burgers, pizza, tapas, salads) as well as island specialties, such as fish prepared Creole style and Caribbean conch and dumplings. Look for live music on weekends. On the Boardwalk, Great Bay Beach, Front St., Philipsburg. http://taloulamango.com. ✆ **721/542-1645.**

FRENCH ST. MARTIN

Bali Bar ★ A bohemian crowd bellies up to Bali's bar for cocktails and global tapas—grilled chorizo, shrimp tempura, chicken Chinese rolls, and sautéed mushrooms. It's a fun, sexy spot, with mauve drapes, Indian embroidered silk wall hangings, and carved teak chairs. Smoky soca and jazz chanteuses occasionally animate the proceedings. Marina Royale, Marigot. ✆ **590/51-13-16.**

Calmos Café ★ Varnished-wood picnic tables beneath a beamed wooden roof lead to a white-sand beach with chairs and chaises in the sand. The crowds—hipsters, families, locals, and tourists—gather for hearty lunches and to watch the epic sunsets over Grand Case Bay. Sundays are Sunset Reggae celebrations. 40 bd. de Grand Case, Grand Case. http://lecalmoscafe.com. ✆ **590/29-01-85.**

Le Moon Le Moon brings a touch of Miami Beach and the Hamptons to little Grand Case. Sip melon mojitos by the small pool or dance the night away. 28 bd. de Grand Case, Grand Case. www.lemoonsxm.com. ✆ **590/51-96-17.**

The Tree Lounge ★ This lounge high up in the trees at the Loterie Farm reserve is a refreshing switch from the beach-bar scene—you'll be nestled in greenery as you relax over a cocktail and tapas with fellow grown-ups. Sample a frozen concoction made with fruit plucked from the reserve's trees. The lounge is perched atop the farm's original 19th-century milk shed. 103 Rte. de Pic Paradis, Loterie Farm. ✆ **590/87-86-16.**

Zen It ★ This and neighboring Calmos Café share a similar laid-back, beach-bar ethos. While Calmos Café is firmly rooted in the beach sand, however, Zen It enjoys a sunset vantage point from a raised wooden porch that feels more Cape Cod than Caribbean. It's a wonderfully breezy spot to have a beer and a bite at the day's end. 48 bd. de Grand Case, Grand Case. ✆ **590/29-44-84.**

LIVE MUSIC
Dutch St. Maarten

Cheri's Café ★ American expat Cheri Batson opened this cherished institution in 1988. The rare tourist trap that even appeals to locals, Cheri's is outfitted in an irrepressible color scheme of scarlet, hot pink, and white. Everybody from rock bands to movie stars, casino high rollers to beach bums, makes a pit stop at this open-air pavilion. The surprisingly good, relatively cheap food (think burgers, steaks, pastas, and fresh fish) is a bonus, but most come for flirting and dancing to an assortment of live acts 6 nights a week. Don't miss such regulars as Sweet Chocolate Band, if only to watch the guys don wigs and falsies. Rhine Rd. #45, Maho Beach. www.cheriscafe.com. © **721/545-3361.**

Pineapple Pete Pete co-opts most of an alley between the lagoon and the main drag. T-shirts dangle from the rafters in the main room (with dart boards, arcade games, and eight pool tables), where yachters, local businesspeople, and timeshare owners marinate and get chummy. The fairly priced fare is quite good—signature dishes include crab-stuffed shrimp, lobster thermidor, and dark rum crème brûlée. Nightly live music keeps things rocking. Airport Rd., Simpson Bay. www.pineapplepete.com. © **721/544-6030.**

Red Piano Bar The grand piano is indeed quite red, and patrons are often red-faced from the killer cocktails. The performers, professional or otherwise, are variable, but the place continues to be a popular spot to listen to live entertainment. Pelican Resort, Billy Folly Rd., Simpson Bay. www.theredpianosxm.com. © **721/544-6008.**

Sopranos Piano Bar This piano bar delivers a soigné ambience without thematic overkill (other than the signature Bada Bing merchandise for sale). The photos of musicians posed as Mafiosi and giant poster of James Gandolfini (aka Tony Soprano) glaring down at the grand piano are witty, and the dim lighting, intimate banquettes, and red-and-black color scheme set the right tone. Sonesta Maho Beach Resort & Casino. www.sopranospianobar.com. © **721/545-2485.**

French St. Martin

Blue Martini Although it doesn't have beach access, this place more than compensates with an enchanting garden, the perfect place to savor specialty cocktails and tasty food. It stirs things up with live bands Thursday through Saturday. 63 bd. de Grand Case, Grand Case. www.bluemartinisxm.com. © **590/29-27-93.**

ENTERTAINMENT & NIGHTLIFE

Live Music

FOR ADULTS ONLY

Dutch St. Maarten has its share of adults-only entertainment, from topless lounges to gentlemen's clubs.

Golden Eyes Offering what it calls "upscale topless entertainment," Golden Eyes has weekly theme parties and VIP champagne and bottle service. In an effort to be inclusive, it welcomes couples and women. The club itself is handsomely appointed, and an outdoor terrace offers lovely marina views. 12 Airport Rd., Simpson Bay. www.goldeneyesclub.com. 🕐 **721/527-1079.**

Platinum Room The gold standard of gentlemen's clubs, this place cultivates an air of class: neocolonial arches and colonnades, inlaid woods, knockoffs of Michelangelo's *David* and Grecian urns, sequined curtains, and cheery turquoise banquettes. It crowds up quickly and stays open till 5am. Maho Village. www.theplatinumroom. com. 🕐 **721/587-0055.**

CASINOS

Gambling is currently legal only on the Dutch side. This is no Caribbean Vegas, but that's not necessarily a bad thing. Think low-key, laid-back gaming, played to a lilting calypso beat. The 12 casinos offer free live theater, with everyone from blue-haired fanny packers to dreadlocked Rastas feeding the maw of the

---

ST. MAARTEN'S RED-LIGHT DISTRICT

The Dutch are notoriously liberal and have cultivated a permissive attitude regarding prostitution on St. Maarten. This box is neither an endorsement nor an encouragement; it merely offers some enlightenment on a big element of St. Maarten nightlife. Brothels operate around the island and must purchase a permit and supply affidavits on their employees, who must submit to monthly medical checkups.

It all started with the **Seaman's Club,** 79 Sucker Garden Rd. (🕐 **721/542-2978**), known to the locals as the "Japanese club." It was founded in the 1940s to service Japanese tuna fishermen who'd been at sea for months at a time. These single men needed a place to carouse, and the government didn't want them hassling local girls, so a tradition was born.

Note: One big difference from Amsterdam's red-light district is that possession of marijuana is not tolerated here. An infraction could lead to stiff fines or even imprisonment.

machines. If you indulge, just remember that the odds always favor the house. Hours vary, but most casinos are open from 1pm to 6am. Here is a sampling.

Atlantis World Casino ★   This is St. Maarten's most Vegas-style venue, if only for adopting that destination's gourmet aspirations. The owner/developer cleverly attracted top restaurateurs by offering competitive rents. The interior appears fairly posh if you don't look too closely: mirrored ceilings, Christmas lights, faux plants, lipstick-red accents, and murals and frescoes, mostly depicting cherubs cavorting in azure skies or surreal encounters between Renaissance figures and islanders. Atlantis features all the major table games, as well as more than 500 slot and video poker machines. It tends to attract a more mature, settled crowd. 106 Rhine Rd., Cupecoy. www.atlantisworld.com. ℂ **721/545-4601.**

Casino Royale ★   St. Maarten's largest, glitziest, and supposedly ritziest gaming emporium, Casino Royale's splashy exterior of illuminated fountains and its huge multihued neon sign spitting lasers almost approximates the gaudy best (and worst) of Vegas. Despite the upscale pretensions, most people ignore the rarely enforced dress code (no shorts or tank tops). The casino offers games from blackjack to baccarat and more than 450 slot machines. The 800-seat **Showroom Royale** is the island's largest, most technologically sophisticated theater; its glittery shows change every few months, but might include acrobatics, jugglers tossing bowling pins, and/or magicians with the usual large-scale tricks up their sleeves. Upstairs is the island's loudest dance spot, **Tantra** (see "Clubs & Lounges," earlier in this chapter). Rhine Rd. #1, Maho Bay. ℂ www.playmaho.com. ℂ **721/545-2590.**

Hollywood Casino   The Hollywood Casino does make some half-hearted stabs at playing up its name: How about "Oscar" door handles, movie stills (*Pulp Fiction* and *Planet of the Apes*), fake stars in the ceiling, klieg lights, and a wall devoted to Marilyn Monroe? It does offer a panoramic view of the bay, roulette, black-jack, stud poker, Let It Ride, progressive jackpot bingo, 150 slot machines, and bingo, plus island shows featuring Caribbean bands. Pelican Resort, 37 Billy Folly Rd., Simpson Bay. www.casinosxm.com. ℂ **721/544-4463.**

Jump Up Casino   A Carnival-themed casino, Jump Up has several ornate costumes on display. Live late weekend shows (11pm–2am) showcasing local bands (Playstation, Jump Up Stars, Explosion, Impact) are the best reason to visit. Emmaplein #1 (end of Front St.), Philipsburg. www.jumpupcasino.com. ℂ **721/542-0862.**

Princess Casino ★   This place wins the prize for overall elegance, as evidenced by the dressier crowd and handsome neoclassical design (columns, arches, domes, and frescoes galore). Princess has more than 650 one-armed bandits and 20 table games, from craps to blackjack. Dining options include the Peg Leg Pub, a fine buffet, and a sushi bar. The live shows are spectacularly mounted (by island standards). Princess Port de Plaisance Resort, Cole Bay. www.princessportdeplaisance.com/casino/casino.htm. ② 721/544-4311.

Rouge et Noir   This joint is all red and black inside, just like a roulette wheel, with a vaguely futuristic design. It offers slot machines, roulette, blackjack, bingo, and Antillean and 3-card poker. 67 Front St., Philipsburg. ② 721/542-2952.

WHERE TO STAY ON ST. MAARTEN/ ST. MARTIN

Despite its small size, St. Maarten/St. Martin offers a range of accommodations: large high-rise resorts, small "bourgeois" hotels, and locally owned guesthouses ranging from boutique to budget, not to mention villas and apartments. But timeshares comprise some 60% of the St. Maarten accommodations market. What this means is that you may be competing for rooms with timeshare owners, who generally get first dibs.

DUTCH ST. MAARTEN

The winding two-lane roads in Dutch St. Maarten are beginning to look like high-rise alleys, particularly along those densely developed sections of Maho Bay, Simpson Bay, and, now, Cupecoy, with its sprawling Porto Cupecoy complex. These three areas are where the action is—where most of the casinos, clubs, and beach bars are located—so if you prefer a little peace and quiet, head to the Oyster Pond/Dawn Beach section of the island, which despite a handful of big resorts (the Westin, Princess Heights, and Oyster Bay Beach Resort) still has a getaway feel. Or book a room at little guesthouses like Horny Toad or Mary's Boon, which manage to feel like serene beachside havens in spite of their proximity to the airport and the bustle of Simpson Bay.

Keep in mind that a government tax of 5% will be added to your hotel bill. On top of that, many resorts tack on a service charge of between 10% and 15%. Ask whether taxes are included in the original rates you're quoted.

Expensive

Divi Little Bay Beach Resort ★ 🔥 Built on a slender peninsula about a 10-minute drive east of the airport, this timeshare resort/hotel originated as a simple guesthouse in 1955 and soon became famous as the vacation home of the Netherlands' Queen Juliana, Prince Bernhard, and Queen Beatrix. It's been beaten and battered by hurricanes over the years—its beach bar, **Gizmo's,** was wiped out in 2008 by Hurricane Omar—but it remains the stalwart flagship of the Divi chain. The rooms and public spaces have been renovated and freshened up. The architecture evokes a European seaside village, with stucco walls and terra-cotta roofs, and some Dutch colonial touches. In the upper reaches of the property are the ruins of Fort Amsterdam, once Dutch St. Maarten's most prized military stronghold and today a decorative historical site. Gardens are carefully landscaped, and Divi built up the nearby beach after it suffered erosion. Divi also has a shopping promenade and an art gallery.

Accommodations are airy, accented with ceramic tiles and pastel colors, and each has its own private balcony or patio; suites and studios have fully equipped kitchens—the only units that don't have kitchens are the beachfront doubles. The luxury Casita one-bedroom suites have iPod docking stations. The resort offers a variety of meal plans, including an all-inclusive option.

Little Bay Rd. (P.O. Box 961), Philipsburg, St. Maarten. www.divilittlebay.com. © **800/367-3484** in the U.S., or 721/542-2333. Fax 721/542-4336. 225 units. Winter $230–$288 double, $272–$328 1-bedroom suite, $475 2-bedroom suite; off season $150–$160 double, $179–$199 1-bedroom suite, $379 2-bedroom suite. Children 12 and under stay free in parent's room. AE, DC, MC, V. **Amenities:** 3 restaurants; bar; activities coordinator; babysitting; dive shop; grocery shopping; gym; Internet (in Bayview Café); 3 outdoor pools; spa; 2 lit tennis courts; watersports center and watersports equipment (extensive). *In room:* A/C, TV (DVD in studios and suites), CD player (in studios and suites), Jacuzzi (in studios and suites), kitchen (in studios and suites), MP3 docking station (in Casita suites).

Holland House Beach Hotel ★ The lobby of this polished, well-run "city" hotel runs practically uninterrupted from bustling Front Street to Great Bay Beach. Creamy adobe walls in the stylish public areas are hung with rotating local and Dutch artworks. The global clientele appreciates the smart little touches (free international newspapers, beach chairs, and freshwater beach shower). Most rooms have gorgeous polished hardwood floors and large, arched balconies. The one-bedroom penthouse includes a kitchenette, a large-screen TV, a DVD player, and a fax machine. The $36 surcharge is well worth it for the popular oceanview rooms, but weekly stays in any unit lasso huge savings.

Crowned by a billowing white tent, the **Ocean Lounge** beachfront restaurant and bar is a beautiful spot to dine or sip a cocktail with the sea breeze wafting in from Great Bay. Fresh seafood is the Dutch chef's specialty.

43 Front St. (P.O. Box 393), Philipsburg, St. Maarten. www.hhbh.com. © **800/223-9815** in the U.S., or 721/542-2572. Fax 721/542-4673. 54 units. Winter $229–$310 double, $425 1-bedroom suite, $650 penthouse; off season $175–$310 double, $295 1-bedroom suite, $560 penthouse. Weekly rates available. AE, MC, V. **Amenities:** Restaurant; bar; watersports equipment. In room: A/C and ceiling fan, TV, fridge, Wi-Fi (free).

Princess Heights ★   In the hills above Dawn Beach, just across the road, this boutique all-suites condo hotel has heart-stopping panoramic views. Princess Heights is reached after a 10-minute drive from Philipsburg. The large suites are tastefully furnished, each containing one or two bedrooms, with separate living rooms opening onto balconies with views of St. Barts in the distance. Living rooms have not only foldout sofas but foldout chairs as well. The suites are well-appointed: Granite-topped counters, clay-tiled terraces, marble floors throughout, and well-crafted, fully equipped kitchens make for a comfortable stay. The hillside location spells privacy—although to reach Dawn Beach, you'll have to walk 5 minutes down a steep path or drive (most guests have rental cars). The 36 oceanview deluxe suites on the hillside slightly above the original building are the hotel's spiffiest (and newest) units.

156 Oyster Pond Rd., Oyster Pond, St. Maarten. www.princessheights.com. © **800/881-1744** in the U.S., or 721/543-6858. Fax 721/543-6007. 51 units. Winter $285 studio, $350–$450 suite; off season $160–$210 studio, $225–$375 suite. Children (2 maximum) 11 and under stay free in parent's room. Extra person $35–$45. AE, DISC, MC, V. **Amenities:** Babysitting; gym; Internet; outdoor pool. In room: A/C, flatscreen TV, Wi-Fi (in newer building only; free), Jacuzzi, kitchen (in suites), kitchenette (in studios), minibar, washer/dryer (in some).

Sonesta Great Bay Beach Hotel & Casino ★ ☺   Built in 1968, the second-oldest hotel in St. Maarten (after Divi) is ideally located a few minutes' walk from downtown Philipsburg. Newly refurbished interiors have done much to brighten things up, but the old girl is still creaky in spots. No matter: Public spaces, pools, beaches, and bars are always buzzing with activity—and the setting inside a sexy curve of Great Bay Beach forgives many sins. You get killer views virtually anywhere and everywhere you plop yourself, whether you're breakfasting in the alfresco **Bay View** restaurant, sunning beside the infinity pool, or having dinner at the **Molasses** restaurant, with the lights on the harbor shimmering like diamonds. The rooms feature standard decorative tropical trappings, but budget travelers can save money by choosing a room with a "mountain view" (St. Maarten hills, some shrubbery, a parking lot) over one with ocean views. Suites include kitchens and sofa beds. Friendly management, extensive watersports, and an enviable location make this a terrific choice for families. The **Golden Casino** offers a little action for the grown-ups. *Tip:* Save big on advance-purchase rates.

19 Little Bay Rd. (P.O. Box 910), Philipsburg, St. Maarten. www.sonesta.com/greatbay. © **800/766-3782** in the U.S., or 721/542-2447. Fax 721/544-3859. 257 units. Winter $300–$420 double, $425–$595 suite; off season $215–$335 double, $540–$700 suite. Special rates for Caribbean residents. Ask about all-inclusive rates. AE, DC, DISC, MC, V. **Amenities:** 3 restaurants; 4 bars; babysitting; casino; children's program; dive shop; fitness center; Internet cafe; 2 Jacuzzis; 3 outdoor pools; spa; lit tennis court; watersports equipment (extensive). *In room:* A/C and ceiling fan, satellite TV, fridge (in some), kitchens (in suites), kitchenette (in some), Wi-Fi ($18/day or $55/week).

Sonesta Maho Beach Hotel & Casino ★ Separated into three distinct sections, this modern megaresort is the island's largest hotel and practically a self-contained village. It's the closest thing on either the Dutch or French side to a Vegas-style blockbuster resort, and it's right in the thick of the Maho Bay action. While it's often swarming with conventioneers and tour groups, the resort undergoes ongoing refurbishment. Set on a 4-hectare (10-acre) tract that straddles the busy—and often congested—coastal road adjacent to the crescent-shaped Maho Beach, the hotel's scattered structures are painted a trademark cream and white. Rooms in the Ocean Terrace building are large and comfortably furnished. Inside the main building, the premier rooms on floors six through nine are done in pleasing hues of dusty lavender/rose and orange-browns. Suites have ocean views and Jacuzzi tubs that open onto the bedroom. Each has Italian tiles, plush upholstered furniture, a walk-in closet, and good soundproofing (important, since planes taking off at the nearby Princess Juliana airport come thundering by several times a day).

The hotel has several restaurants. The newest, **Brother Jimmy's BBQ,** is a transplant from New York, where it has a popular and family-friendly chain of Southern-fried restaurants. The **Point** is good for steak and seafood; the open-air **Palms** is a casual beachfront cafe; the **Ocean Terrace** has all-day buffets. Up on the rooftop, the cocktail crowd gathers at **Sky Beach,** with stupendous views of beach and sea. On the resort's street front, the **Maho Promenade** is filled with several dozen shops open late, restaurants (including Cheri's Café), a scuba-diving center, a dance club, even a gentleman's club. The glitzy **Casino Royale** is just across the street from the resort. *Tip:* Save big on advance-purchase room rates.

Maho Beach, 1 Rhine Rd., St. Maarten. www.sonesta.com/mahobeach. ℰ **800/766-3782** in the U.S., or 721/545-2115. Fax 721/545-3180. 537 units. $135–$470 double, $280–$620 suite. AE, DC, DISC, MC, V. **Amenities:** 4 restaurants; coffee bar; lounge; swim-up bar; babysitting; casino; children's program; fitness center; 2 outdoor pools; room service; spa; 4 tennis courts. *In room:* A/C, TV, fridge (in some), Wi-Fi ($18/day or $55/week).

Westin St. Maarten Dawn Beach Resort & Spa ★ ☺ This

hotel's colonnaded beachfront facade is much more elegant than its character-free backside, and its huge freshwater infinity pool fronting Dawn Beach is beautiful. In fact, this is Dutch St. Maarten's top lodging option, and the 310 mostly oceanview guest rooms (and 15 suites) have all the state-of-the-art trappings you'd expect from a Westin, including the trademark Heavenly Bed mattresses—heavenly indeed. Rooms and rates cover a range of budgets. The lobby has a spiffy Frank Lloyd Wright feel, although it's joined at the hip by a garish casino that clangs away night and day. Facilities include the European-style **Hibiscus Spa,** a fitness center, duty-free retail shops, two oceanfront restaurants, watersports, and meeting facilities. Kids get the royal treatment at Westin Kid's Club, Camp Scallywag. The Westin has a popular **Sunday champagne brunch** in the **Ocean** restaurant (noon–3pm; $40 per person plus 15% service charge).

144 Oyster Pond Rd., St. Maarten. www.westinstmaarten.com. ℰ **800/WES-TIN-1** (937-8461) or 721/543-6700. Fax 721/543-6004. 325 units. Winter $325–$525 double; off season $190–$355 double. Ask about suite rates. AE, MC, V. **Amenities:** 3 restaurants; 2 lounges; babysitting; casino; concierge; fitness center; outdoor pool; room service; spa; Wi-Fi (free, in lobby). *In room:* A/C, TV, minibar, Wi-Fi ($15/day or $50/week).

Moderate

La Vista Hotel/La Vista Beach These two small hotels lie at the foot of Pelican Cay. For a fee, guests can use the more elaborate facilities of the nearby Pelican Key timeshare resort, with its casino, shops, and spa. The two hotels are La Vista Hotel, a 2-minute walk from a good sandy beach, and La Vista Beach, whose units open directly onto the beach with studios and two-bedroom apartments. Rooms with a view come in seven different categories, including a junior suite, deluxe suite, and penthouse. Accommodations feature fully equipped kitchenettes or kitchens. A one-bedroom Antillean cottage comes with its own front porch and sleeps four.

The **Hideaway Bar & Restaurant** serves well-prepared French cuisine adjacent to the pool, with live entertainment several nights a week.

53 Billy Folly Rd. (P.O. Box 2086), Pelican Cay, St. Maarten. www.lavistaresort. com. ℰ **721/544-3005.** Fax 721/544-3010. 52 units. Winter $260 studio,

$180–$210 junior and deluxe suites, $235–$330 suites for 4, $270–$300 penthouse, $210 cottage; off season $135–$200 studio, $140–$160 junior and deluxe suites, $175–$225 suites for 4, $200–$215 penthouse, $160 cottage. Extra person $20. Children 11 and under stay free in parent's room. AE, DISC, MC, V. **Amenities:** Restaurant; bar; outdoor pool; Wi-Fi (free). *In room:* A/C, TV, kitchen or kitchenette, Wi-Fi (fee).

Mary's Boon Beach Resort ★

Mary's Boon is one of those endearing places that draw loyal guests year after year. It's the kind of laid-back spot where people not only *talk* to other people, they get downright chummy. The small, convivial bar has a fizzy happy hour, drawing local businessfolk from nearby Simpson Bay. In business for 40-plus years, Mary's Boon enjoys direct access to one of the nicest beaches on St. Maarten: an uncrowded stretch with powdery white sand. Even better, its owner has upgraded and beautified the rooms and added spa services. He has succeeded in substantially spiffing up the place without undermining the charming, offbeat ambience.

Mary's Boon is right near the airport, so guests have to deal with the plate-rattling sounds of jets taking off at various times during the day. But it's also minutes from casinos, shops, and restaurants. Each room varies architecturally, but all have verandas or terraces; a number have big cherrywood beds and Balinese woodcarvings. Those facing the sea directly are high-ceilinged and wonderfully breezy. Renovated rooms are equipped with full fridges, granite countertops, stainless-steel appliances, and flatscreen TVs. Upstairs, nos. 201 through 205 are particularly spacious, opening up to the sea on one side and the garden on the other. **Tides,** the modest beach restaurant and bar, offers satisfying, good-value food that reveals a sure hand in the kitchen (it should—the head chef, Leona, has been cooking here for almost 40 years!), and its perch over the beach, with the sea breeze wafting in, is tonic for whatever ails you.

117 Simpson Bay Rd., St. Maarten. www.marysboon.com. ☎ **877/260-7483,** 305/677-3833, or 721/545-7000. Fax 721/545-3403. 37 units. Winter $135–$335 double (studios and 1-bedroom suites), $250–$425 2-bedroom suites; off season $75–$300 double, $135–$425 2-bedroom suites. Extra person $35. MC, V. Take the first right turn as you head from the airport toward Philipsburg; follow the signs to Mary's Boon. **Amenities:** Restaurant; bar; babysitting; outdoor pool; room service; spa; Wi-Fi (free, in lobby). *In room:* A/C and ceiling fan, TV, kitchen or kitchenette.

Oyster Bay Beach Resort ★

At the end of a twisting, scenic road, a 1-minute walk from Dawn Beach, this retreat was originally designed for vacationers who don't like overly commercialized megaresorts; now it's largely a timeshare. Once an intimate inn, it's been growing by leaps and bounds, having witnessed a five-fold increase in size since it was established in the 1960s. It can't be considered intimate anymore, but it's still not overwhelming. On a circular harbor on the eastern shore, near the French border, the fortresslike structure stands guard over a 14-hectare (35-acre) protected marina. There's a central courtyard and an alfresco lobby.

More than half the units have kitchens, and most have West Indian decor with lots of rattan and wicker. The bedrooms offer balconies overlooking the pond or sea; the deluxe and superior rooms are preferable to the tower suites. Rooms are airy and fairly spacious, and suites have a bathroom with a tub and a shower. Each of the five penthouses in the Mainsail Pavilion has its own deck, small pool, and outdoor kitchen.

The resort restaurant, **Infinity,** serves international food for breakfast, lunch, and dinner. The newly renovated **Beau Beau's,** facing the beach, serves seafood and Caribbean fare at lunch and dinner, and offers nightly entertainment and musical cabarets from local calypso king Beau Beau. Just next door is one of the island's most popular beach bar/restaurants, **Mr. Busby's on the Beach.**

10 Emerald Merit Rd. (P.O. Box 239), Oyster Pond, St. Maarten. www.oyster baybeachresort.com. ✆ **866/978-0212** in the U.S., or 721/543-6040. Fax 721/543-6695. 178 units (153 are timeshares). Double $150–$325; suite $390–$675; deluxe loft $250–$300; Mainsail penthouse $690–$898. Extra person $50–$60. Children 11 and under stay free in parent's room. Ask about meal plans. AE, DISC, MC, V. **Amenities:** 2 restaurants; 2 bars; babysitting; fitness center; outdoor pool; spa; 4 tennis courts. *In room:* A/C, TV/DVD, Internet, kitchen or kitchenette (except for Superior rooms).

Inexpensive

The Horny Toad Guesthouse ✦ This homey, welcoming place is run by an expatriate from Maine, Betty Vaughan. The hotel is near the airport, but the roar of jumbo jets is heard only a few times a day. Children 7 and under are not allowed, but families with older children often come here to avoid the megaresorts, and repeat visitors quickly become part of the Horny Toad family. Seven well-maintained units lie in an amply proportioned beach-side house originally built in the 1950s as a private home by the island's former governor. The eighth room is in half of an octagonal "round house," with large windows and views of the sea. Guest rooms range from medium-size to spacious, and each has a fully equipped kitchen and a king-size bed. The guesthouse has no pool, no restaurant, and no organized activities of any kind, but the beach is just steps away, the island of Saba floats tantalizingly off in the distance, and guests enjoy impromptu get-togethers in the outdoor barbecue pavilion.

2 Vlaun Dr., Simpson Bay, St. Maarten. www.thehornytoadguesthouse.com.
(C) **800/417-9361** in the U.S., or 721/545-4323. Fax 721/545-3316. 8 units.
Winter $218 double; off season $118 double. Extra person $40 in winter, $25
off season. MC, V. Children 7 and under not allowed. **Amenities:** Smoke-free
rooms. *In room:* A/C and ceiling fan, kitchen, Wi-Fi (free).

Pasanggrahan Royal Guest House ★ 🔥 This charming,
vintage West Indian–style guesthouse, once the summer home of
the Dutch Queen Wilhelmina, is one of the rare St. Maarten
accommodations that has real character and good bones. A handsome relic from another era, the inn enjoys a prime spot on the
beach in Philipsburg, sandwiched between bustling Front Street
and the harborside boardwalk, and set back under shady tall trees.
The public spaces have a gracious Victorian feel, with peacock
bamboo chairs, Indian spool tables, and a gilt-framed oil portrait of
her majesty. A new West Wing addition has 10 spiffy new rooms,
furnished in plantation style. The older small- to medium-size
accommodations have queen-size, double, or king-size beds with
four-poster designs; some are in the main building and others are
in an adjoining annex. The finest have genuine colonial flair, with
antique secretaries and four-posters swaddled in mosquito netting,
madras valances, hand-stitched quilts, beamed ceilings, and still-
life paintings. The worst have a tired, somewhat shabby feel.

Set among lush palms is the harborfront **Pasanggrahan Restaurant ★,** which specializes in fresh fish caught by the hotel's
own deep-sea charter fishing boat, and grilled lobsters caught on
the nearby island of Saba. Even if you aren't staying here, this is a
peaceful, shady oasis for lunch or a drink after a day wrestling the
cruise-ship hordes in downtown Philipsburg. The food is good and
fresh, and the view of the harbor from the old wooden veranda,
with Fort Amsterdam in the distance, never quits.

19 Front St. (P.O. Box 151), Philipsburg, St. Maarten. www.pasanroyalinn.com.
(C) **721/542-3588.** Fax 721/542-2885. 30 units. Winter $175–$250 double;
off season $98–$250 double. Extra person $45. DISC, MC, V. Closed Sept.
Amenities: Restaurant; 2 bars; Internet (free). *In room:* A/C and ceiling fan,
TV, fridge, kitchenette (in some).

Turquoise Shell Inn 🔥 This trim yellow-and-white apartment
complex steps from Simpson Bay Beach, and the price is right.
Each of the 10 one-bedroom suites has a fully equipped kitchen,
though the restaurants and bars along the Simpson Bay strip are
within easy walking distance (though the walk home is not recommended if you're alone after a night's carousing). The plumbing can
be noisy, the shower-only bathrooms cramped, and the decor unassuming, but the friendly, obliging management keeps everything
tidy. Children 5 and over are allowed; no children 4 and under.

34 Simpson Bay Rd., Simpson Bay, St. Maarten. www.tshellinn.com. ✆ **721/ 545-2875.** Fax 721/545-2846. 10 units. Winter $145 double; off season $115 double. Extra person $25–$35. Rates include tax and service charges. MC, V. No children 4 and under. **Amenities:** Pool. *In room:* A/C and ceiling fan, TV, Wi-Fi (free).

FRENCH ST. MARTIN

Unlike Dutch St. Maarten, French St. Martin has no high-rise hotels; accommodations on this side of the island are small-scale and trend toward boutique. Many, like La Samanna and the Grand Case Beach Club, are smack-dab on the beach; others, like Hotel L'Esplanade and Hotel La Plantation, are tucked into rugged green slopes above the sea. The largest French St. Martin hotel by far, the Radisson Blu, is nestled inside a protected cove, where it maintains a serene and unobtrusive presence.

Hotels on French St. Martin add a 10% service charge and a *taxe de séjour.* This local room tax is 4% to 5%. Expect higher rates during Christmas week. *Note:* Rates are quoted in either euros or dollars, depending on how establishments quoted them at press time.

Very Expensive

La Samanna ★★★ With whitewashed Mediterranean-style villas nestled atop one of St. Martin's finest beaches, La Samanna is easily the island's top luxury hotel. An Orient-Express hotel, the 22¼-hectare (55-acre) resort oozes understated posh, and rates are correspondingly high-end. Despite the price tag, La Samanna isn't stuffy; here in the laid-back West Indies, everyone gets the royal treatment. Most rooms, regardless of size, have private terraces. The colonial-style lobby and bar are handsomely atmospheric. Suites and villas come with spacious bedrooms with luxurious beds, fully equipped kitchens, living and dining rooms, and large patios. Bathrooms are big and well designed, with bidets and hand-painted Mexican tiles. State-of-the-art specialty suites have private terraces with sumptuous Baie Longue views. For the ultimate in luxury, book one of the eight three- or four-bedroom villas with private wraparound infinity pools and rooftop terraces—views are magnificent. The villas come with private concierge service, private beach cabanas, and VIP airport transfers.

At **Le Reservé,** the resort's main restaurant, guests dine on a candlelit terrace spectacularly perched above Baie Longue—the ambience is pure French Riviera. (*Note:* Children requiring a high chair are not permitted in Le Reservé for dinner.) Enjoy a private dinner in the wine cellar, **Le Cave,** amid the hotel's award-winning collection of international wines. The poolside **Grill** serves drinks and tapas nightly. If you can't make dinner at Le Reservé, you can enjoy the same great views at the restaurant's **buffet breakfasts** ★, as delicious as the setting (and included in the room rates). With the curve of Baie Longue stretched out before you, it's a mighty fine way to start the day.

Baie Longue (B.P. 4077), 97064 St. Martin CEDEX, F.W.I. www.lasamanna.com. ℂ **800/957-6128** in the U.S., or 590/87-64-00. Fax 590/87-87-86. 83 units. Winter $995 double, $2,025–$5,475 suite; $9,000–$9,500 villa; off-season $395–$445 double, $521 and up suite; call about villa rates. Extra person $75. Children 11 and under stay free in parent's room. Rates include full buffet breakfast. Meal plans available. AE, MC, V. Closed Sept 1 to Nov 1. **Amenities:** 2 restaurants; 2 bars; babysitting; fitness center; 2 freshwater outdoor pools; room service; spa; 3 lighted tennis courts; watersports equipment (extensive). *In room:* A/C and ceiling fan, TV/DVD, CD player (in some), minibar, plunge pool (in some), Wi-Fi (free).

Expensive

Alamanda Resort ★   Small and intimate, like a European beachfront inn, the Alamanda opens onto Orient Bay's golden sands. The resort is a cluster of Creole *cazes,* or little houses, surrounding a lushly landscaped outdoor pool quite near the beach. The Alamanda has a few drawbacks, one being that not all rooms have ocean views. Bedrooms are spacious and done up in soothing earth tones, with pineapple patterns or decorative accents in bold colors, from sunflower yellow to tomato red. The king-size beds are elegantly carved, often four-posters. The best accommodations are the two-bedroom duplexes with a second bathroom. My favorite place to dine here is at the beachfront restaurant **Kakao Beach,** which features both Creole and European specialties in a laid-back Caribbean atmosphere. A less expensive choice, **Cafe Alamanda,** serves an inventive island cuisine poolside.

Parc de la Baie Orientale (B.P. 5166), 97071 St. Martin, F.W.I. www.alamanda-resort.com. ℂ **590/52-87-40.** Fax 590/52-87-41. 42 units. Winter $375–$490 double, $600 2-bedroom duplex, $710–$790 suite; off season $270–$340 double, $440 2-bedroom duplex, $450–$500 suite. Extra person in suite $50. Up to two children 11 and under stay free in parent's room. AE, MC, V. Closed Sept. **Amenities:** 2 restaurants; 2 bars; babysitting; concierge; gym; outdoor pool; room service; 2 tennis courts; watersports equipment. *In room:* A/C and ceiling fan, TV, kitchenette, Wi-Fi (free).

Esmeralda Resort ★   This hillside housing development gives the appearance of a sprawling, well-maintained low-rise village, where Creole-inspired villas are interspersed with lush gardens. Opening onto Orient Beach, the Esmeralda blossomed into a full-scale resort in the early 1990s, offering views over Orient Bay and a decidedly French flavor. Each of the 18 Spanish Mission–style tile-roofed villas can be configured into four separate units. Each individual unit contains a king-size or two double beds, a kitchenette, a terrace, and a private entrance. The creamy palette is pleasing, with tile floors and splashes of earthy color. Each villa has its own communal pool, which creates the feeling of a private club. The suites (one to five bedrooms) are quite spacious.

The **Astrolabe** serves fine French-Caribbean specialties at breakfast and dinner daily (main courses 20€–33€). The hotel issues an ID card that can be used for lunch discounts at any of a half-dozen restaurants along Orient Bay.

Parc de la Baie Orientale (B.P. 5141), 97071 St. Martin, F.W.I. www.esmeraldaresort.com. ⓒ **590/87-36-36.** Fax 590/87-35-18. 65 units. Winter $375–$550 double, $690–$2,870 suite; off season $270–$370 double, $440–$1,740 suite. Extra person 12 and over $80; children 11 and under stay free in parent's room. AE, MC, V. Closed Sept. **Amenities:** 2 restaurants; bar; babysitting; horseback riding (nearby); 18 outdoor pools; room service; 2 tennis courts; watersports equipment (extensive). *In room:* A/C and ceiling fan, TV, fridge, Internet, kitchenette.

Grand Case Beach Club ★ ☺ This bundling of bougainvillea-draped buildings sits between two beaches just a short stroll from the action in "downtown" Grand Case. All rooms have well-stocked kitchens with granite counters and private balconies or patios (the best offering smashing views of Anguilla). The property is constantly updating the rooms, and you can't beat the views. Families will particularly appreciate the gated entrance (making the lovely Petite Plage—a wonderful beach for children—practically private) and 24-hour security guard and video surveillance. Little extras include a sampling of island CDs and a bottle of wine at check-in. The general manager is conscientious, cordial, and helpful, qualities he inculcates in the staff.

The **Sunset Café** (p. 46), set spectacularly on the rocks overlooking the water, serves hearty French food at reasonable prices for breakfast, lunch, and dinner daily.

Grand Case, 97150 St. Martin, F.W.I. www.grandcasebeachclub.com. ⓒ **800/344-3016** in the U.S., or 590/87-51-87. Fax 590/87-59-93. 73 units. Winter $335–$415 studio double, $415–$550 1-bedroom suite, $545–$585 2-bedroom suite; off season $165–$195 studio double, $195–$295 1-bedroom suite, $295–$310 2-bedroom suite. Rates include continental breakfast. Children 12 and under stay free in parent's room. Rates for 2-bedroom suites cover 4 people; extra person $35. AE, MC, V. **Amenities:** Restaurant; bar; fitness center; outdoor pool; tennis court; watersports equipment (extensive). *In room:* A/C and fan, TV, CD player, kitchen.

Hotel Beach Plaza This is the best hotel within a reasonable distance of Marigot's commercial heart—and it even has its own white-sand beach. A three-story building that centers on a soaring atrium festooned with live banana trees and climbing vines, it's within a cluster of buildings mostly composed of condominiums. Built in 1996 and painted in shades of blue and white, it's set midway between the open sea and the lagoon, giving all rooms water views. The white interiors are accented with tile floors and a tropical motif. Each room contains a balcony, tile floors, native art, and simple hardwood furniture, including a writing desk and comfortable beds. Connecting rooms are available for families. The hotel's French-Caribbean restaurant, **Le Corsaire,** resides poolside, with glittering harbor views.

Baie de Marigot, 97150 St. Martin, F.W.I. www.hotelbeachplazasxm.com. ℭ **800/221-5333** in the U.S., or 590/87-87-00. Fax 590/87-18-87. 144 units. Winter 204€–464€ double, 464€ suite; off season 150€–341€ double, 341€–394€ suite. One child 11 and under stays free in parent's room. Rates include nightly shuttle to the casino. AE, MC, V. **Amenities:** Restaurant; 2 bars; babysitting; bikes; outdoor freshwater pool; room service; watersports equipment (extensive). *In room:* A/C, TV, fridge, Wi-Fi (free).

Hôtel L'Esplanade ★★ This charming, beautifully managed small hotel just gets better and better. Along with its sister hotel, **Le Petit** (see below), it's easily one of the top places to stay on island. Everything is meticulously maintained; you won't see a tatter here or a loose thread there. With a collection of suites terraced on a steeply sloping hillside above the village of Grand Case, the hotel has a summer-in-the-French-Alps feel. Flowered vines frame tiled terraces with views of the village and sea below. The resort is connected by a network of steps and lush gardens; cascades of bougainvillea drape walls accented with hand-painted tiles and blue slate roofs. The lovely pool is just steps down the hill, and access to the beach and town is via a 5-minute walk down a lighted pathway. There's no restaurant, but a light lunch is served by the pool in high season, and the village of Grand Case is a virtual smorgasbord of seaside bistros.

All guest rooms have private terraces that angle out toward the sea and the sun setting behind Anguilla. Each individually decorated unit contains a kitchen with cookware, Italian porcelain tile floors, Balinese furniture, and supremely comfortable queen- or king-size beds (many four-poster). Slate and tumbled marble bathrooms are beautifully equipped, with big, pebble-surfaced showers. The loft suites on the upper floors include a sofa bed downstairs, an upstairs master bedroom with a king-size bed, and a partial bathroom downstairs. If utter privacy is what you crave, the **ocean-view villa** perched high on the hill has three bedrooms, three bathrooms, and a gourmet kitchen ($4,830–$6,930/week). The cordial owners, Marc and Kristin Petrelluzzi, keep the place looking effortlessly au courant.

Grand Case (B.P. 5007), 97150 St. Martin, F.W.I. www.lesplanade.com.
📞 **866/596-8365** in the U.S., or 590/87-06-55. Fax 590/87-29-15. 24 units.
Winter $395 studio, $445–$495 loft, $495 suite; off season $245 studio, $295–
$345 loft, $345 suite. Extra person $70 winter, $50 off season. MC, V. **Amenities:** Bar (winter); babysitting; outdoor pool. *In room:* A/C and ceiling fan, TV/
DVD, CD player, Internet (free), kitchen, minibar, MP3 docking station.

Le Domaine de Lonvilliers ★   This attractive resort sprawls
over 60 hectares (148 acres) of palm-fringed gardens, and follows
the lovely curve of the beach at Anse Marcel. It and the neighboring Radisson (originally one hotel) are the only inhabitants of this
beguiling secluded cove. The comfortable rooms are done in cool
creams and browns or bold reds set against ivory walls and white
tile floors. All have spacious bathrooms and either a private balcony
or terrace. The hotel's beachside restaurant, **La Table du
Marché,** is the Caribbean twin to its St-Tropez sister, serving
French classics with Caribbean influences. The hotel can arrange
boat transfers from the airport to the resort (80€ per person
round-trip), a very nice way to arrive.

Anse Marcel, 97150 St. Martin, F.W.I. www.hotel-le-domaine.com. 📞 **590/52-
35-35.** Fax 590/29-10-81. 145 units. Winter 370€–430€ double, 630€–870€
suite; off season 330€–400€ double, 590€–800€ suite. Extra person 60€. One
child 11 and under stays free in parent's room. Rates include buffet breakfast.
MC, V. **Amenities:** Restaurant; beach bar; lounge; fitness center; outdoor
pool; room service; spa; 2 tennis courts; watersports equipment (extensive).
In room: A/C, TV, kitchen (in some), Wi-Fi (free).

Le Petit Hotel ★★ 🎁   This beautifully managed, Mediterranean-style hotel opens directly onto the sands of Grand Case
Beach. It shares the same strong management, meticulous attention to detail, and sense of stylish comfort that distinguishes its
splendid sister property, L'Esplanade (see above). Furnishings and
accents are sourced from around the globe, including hand-
painted tiles and Balinese teak and Brazilian mahogany. Supremely
comfortable "Celestial Beds" are sheathed in white down duvets.
Luxurious touches include Frette linens and Damana toiletries.
Each has a huge, beautifully appointed terrace or balcony overlooking the sand. Studios have kitchenettes; the one-bedroom suites
have fully equipped kitchens. The overall effect is of serene sanctuary. Though there's no restaurant, the gracious staff offers advice
on the town's superb dining options.

248 bd. de Grand Case, Grand Case, 97150 St. Martin, F.W.I. www.lepetit
hotel.com. 📞 **590/29-09-65.** Fax 590/87-09-19. 10 units. Winter $415–$455
double, $525 suite; off season $265–$305 double, $375 suite. Extra person in
suite (including children) $50–$70. Rates include continental breakfast. MC, V.
Amenities: Babysitting. *In room:* A/C and ceiling fan, TV/DVD, CD player,
fridge, kitchenette (studios), kitchen (suites), MP3 docking station, Wi-Fi (free).

Radisson Blu Resort Marina & Spa, St. Martin ★ ☺   This is the only resort on the island with direct access to a full-service marina. The setting is a real beaut, tucked inside a half-moon cove at Anse Marcel, with the lights of Anguilla twinkling across the sea. It's a full immersion in tropical flora and fauna: White egrets flutter in the folds of mossy hills rising above the cove, and lizards skitter along pathways. This property had a couple of incarnations before Radisson gave it a big-time face-lift in 2008. Its location inside this secluded cove and the property's sheer sense of space (7 hectares/17 acres) give it a real getaway feel. At 93m (305 ft.), the zero-entry infinity pool is the largest freshwater pool on the island. The hotel is suite-heavy (63 suites), and most of the units face the flower-filled courtyard; if you want a full ocean view from your patio, ask for a room at the end of the East and West buildings. Every room has a patio/balcony and the trademark Radisson "Sleep Number" Bed, with remote controls to harden or soften the bed to your liking.

C Le Restaurant (p. 48) is the resort's main restaurant; it's set alongside the Baie des Froussards, where sailboats are silhouetted against the starry sky. (The food is so good you may not want to head to Grand Case, 5 minutes away, for dinner—but you should, at least once.) The full breakfast buffet in the cheerful **Le Marché** is copious (and included in the rates). Radisson will arrange watersports excursions that leave straight from the resort marina—you don't have to go through St. Maarten. **Le Spa** has five treatment rooms and two full cabanas for outside treatment; you can choose the color of your lighting. You can get to the Radisson the prosaic way (by taxi) or the exhilarating way: by **water taxi** (round-trip $120 adult, $90 children 3–12), a 30-minute scenic trip that delivers you straight from the airport to the resort.

Anse Marcel (B.P. 581), 97056 St. Martin, F.W.I. www.radissonblu.com/resort-stmartin. ℂ **800/967-9033** in the U.S. or Canada, or 590/87-67-00. Fax 590/87-30-38. 252 units. Winter 359€–482€ double, 569€–719€ suite; off season 229€–309€ double, 389€–569€ suite. Children 11 and under stay free in parent's room. Extra guest 40€/night. Rates include full breakfast. AE, DC, DISC, MC, V. **Amenities:** 2 restaurants; 2 bars; ATM; babysitting; bocce court; children's program w/clubhouse and playground; concierge; fitness center; full-service marina; 2 pools; spa; volleyball; watersports center/dive center; watersports equipment (extensive); water taxi service. *In room:* A/C, flatscreen TV/DVD, minibar, MP3 docking station, Wi-Fi (free).

Moderate

Club Orient Naturist Resort ★   Occupying an isolated spot on Orient Beach, this is the only true nudist resort in the French West Indies, but it's hardly the wild, swinging, party place you might imagine. Celebrating nearly 35 years of business, it's clean, utterly respectable, and even family friendly. Many of the guests are older and fairly conservative, just looking for a tropical beachside spot to walk around unclothed. There's no pool on the premises, but the chalets are right on an excellent beach, with plentiful activities to facilitate hanging out (in every sense). Accommodations, set in red-pine chalets imported from Finland, sport a basic Ikea-meets-scout-cabin look, though the decor has been spruced up. All have outside showers, and most have both front and back porches. At **Papagayo Restaurant,** you can dine alfresco; the popular 5-to-7pm happy hour allows guests to compare, er, notes. However, each unit has a kitchen, and there's a well-stocked general store, **La Boutique,** on-site if you need beach basics, the occasional article of clothing, or provisions to cook your own meals.

1 Baie Orientale, 97150 St. Martin, F.W.I. www.cluborient.com. ℂ **877/456-6833** in the U.S., or 590/87-33-85. Fax 590/87-33-76. 136 units. Winter 225€–240€ studio and suite, 315€–370€ chalet, 750€ villa; off season 140€–210€ studio and suite, 200€–310€ chalet, 470€–600€ villa. Extra person 12 and over 25€. Children 11 and under stay free in parent's room. AE, MC, V. Closed Aug 20–Oct 6. **Amenities:** 2 restaurants; 2 bars; babysitting; fitness center; library; 2 lighted tennis courts; wellness center (w/spa treatments); watersports equipment (extensive). *In room:* A/C and ceiling fan, kitchen, Wi-Fi (free).

Hotel La Plantation ★ ☺ It's the best of both worlds here: You're but a few minutes' walk from the action on Orient Bay's white-sand beach, and you'll sleep in quiet, almost residential resort environs to the sounds of birdsong and rustling palms. Seventeen colonial-style villas are scattered over more than 3 hectares (7 acres) of landscaped tropical gardens that slope down to the sea. Each villa contains a suite and two studios, which can be rented separately or combined. Each spacious unit is furnished in a colorful Creole theme, complete with pitched ceilings and its own terrace or balcony, some with ocean views. The commodious studios have kitchenettes and queen-size beds; the suites have separate bedrooms with king-size beds, big living rooms, full kitchens, and beautifully tiled full bathrooms. **Café Plantation,** next to the hotel pool, is the resort's beating heart, serving French and Creole dinners (Mon is lobster night).

C5 Orient Bay, 97150 St. Martin, F.W.I. www.la-plantation.com. ℂ **590/29-58-00.** Fax 590/29-58-08. 53 units. Winter $340–$360 studio for 2, $410–$475 suite, $640–$1,145 villa; off season $180–$210 studio, $240–$280 suite, $380–$740 villa. Children 12–17 $40–$60/night; children 6–11 $20/night. Children 5 and under stay free in parent's room. Rates include buffet breakfast. DISC, MC, V. Closed Sept 1 to mid-Oct. **Amenities:** Restaurant; beach bar and grill; babysitting; bikes; concierge; health club; horseback riding; outdoor pool; 2 tennis courts; watersports equipment; Wi-Fi (free, in public spaces). *In room:* A/C and ceiling fan, TV, CD player (in some), fridge, kitchen or kitchenette.

Mercure St. Martin & Marina ✍   This is a good-value hotel on the French side of the island. The complex occupies a flat, sandy stretch of land between a saltwater lagoon and the beach, 8km (5 miles) west of Princess Juliana International Airport. Decorated throughout in bold, Creole-inspired hues, its five three-story buildings are each evocative of a large, many-balconied Antillean house. In its center, a pool serves as the focal point for a bar built out over the lagoon, an indoor/outdoor restaurant, and a flagstone terrace that hosts steel bands and evening cocktail parties. Each unit offers, in addition to a kitchenette, a terrace with a view. The most desirable accommodations, on the third (top) floor, contain sloping ceilings sheltering sleeping lofts, and two bathrooms.

Baie Nettlé (B.P. 172), 97150 St. Martin, F.W.I. www.mercure.com. ✆ **800/515-5679** in the U.S., or 590/87-54-54. Fax 590/87-92-11. 169 units. Year-round $115–$205 double. Rates include buffet breakfast. AE, DC, MC, V. **Amenities:** Restaurant; bar; babysitting; billiards; outdoor pool; tennis court; dive center; watersports equipment (extensive). *In room:* A/C, TV, minibar, Wi-Fi (free).

ANGUILLA

For years one of the Caribbean's best-kept secrets, this small, serene island embarked on a careful plan of marketing itself as a top-end resort destination in the 1980s. Anguilla (rhymes with "vanilla") deliberately turned its back on the package tours, casinos, cruise ships, and glitz of neighboring St. Maarten. It's remained a chic but unaffected island destination, with dozens of secluded powdery-soft-sand beaches and sparkling green seas.

Beaches **Shoal Bay East** offers both activity and seclusion: Its western end is lined with beach bars and barbecue shacks, while you can snorkel about undisturbed on its less-crowded eastern side. Sunbathers can relax in 3 miles of curving white sand at **Rendezvous Bay.** Watch fishermen haul a boatload of silver bonito onto the sugary crescent at **Meads Bay.** Disappear for the day on idyllic offshore islands such as **Sandy Island** or **Prickly Pear.**

Things to Do To get an overview of this small island, take a taxi tour, with your driver as local guide. Arawak Indian tools, slave shackles, and household items belonging to 19th-century island settlers are part of the **Heritage Museum Collection** at **Pond Ground.** Watch the fishermen bring up their nets as the sun sets at **Sandy Ground.** Enjoy the laid-back vibe and music at a beach shack like **Smokey's.**

Shopping Serious shoppers head to nearby St. Martin for designer brands, but Anguilla has a thriving arts and crafts scene. The island has a surprising number of art galleries, including that of American painter **Lynne Bernbaum,** in George Hill; Louise Brooks' **Alak Gallery** on Shoal Bay East; and **Devonish Art Gallery** in Long Bay, with work by Anguillan potter and sculptor Courtney Devonish. Hit the **Art Café** for a tasty lunch and an exciting lineup of rotating art exhibits.

Eating & Drinking Fresh, locally caught fish—red snapper, yellowfin tuna, grouper, mahimahi, and red hind—gets plenty of play on restaurant menus, as does

7

Essentials

ANGUILLA

Anguilla: A Love Affair

The first time we went to Anguilla, in 1989, my husband and I were fleeing Puerto Rico after 2 waterless and powerless weeks following Hurricane Hugo. When Anne Edwards of Sydans Villas met us at the airport and asked if we had some bottled water, I thought, *What have I gotten into?! Have I fled an island disaster only to land on an island where you're expected to have your own water?* (Turns out, in those days some people *did* bring bottled water with them to Anguilla. The local water has a sea-tang, and bottled water was still expensive on Anguilla.) When we arrived that first time, there were no lights between the airport and Sandy Ground. Really. I had no idea where we were going or if there was any *there* there. We woke up in the morning to find a small goat staring at us through the screen door of our room and nibbling my towel, which I had left as an unintentional snack on a chair outside the room. And, I admit, this may not sound like a prelude to 20 years of regularly returning to Anguilla (and Anne Edwards' Sydans), but it sure turned out to be.

—*Sherry Marker, Travel Writer*

Anguillian lobster and big, sweet local crawfish. Anguilla has some of the best beach bars and grills in the Caribbean, serving up grilled lobster and saucy barbecued ribs with homemade johnny-cakes on the side. Splurge at award-winning restaurants or kick back at a barefoot beach bar.

ESSENTIALS

For further on-the-ground resources, see "Fast Facts: Anguilla," on p. 192.

Visitor Information

The **Anguilla Tourist Board,** Coronation Avenue, The Valley, Anguilla, B.W.I. (http://ivisitanguilla.com; © **800/553-4939** or 264/497-2759; fax 264/497-2710), is open Monday to Friday from 8am to 5pm.

In the United States, contact Ms. Marie Walker, 246 Central Ave., White Plains, NY 10606 (© **877/426-4845** or 914/287-2400; mturnstyle@aol.com).

In Canada, contact Ms. Dale Pusching, SRM Marketing, 20–225 Dundas St. E., Ste. 411, Waterdown, Ontario, Canada L0R2H6 (© **866-348-7447** or 905/689-7697; dpusching@anguillacanada.ca).

In the United Kingdom, contact Ms. Carolyn Brown, c/o CSB Communications, Ltd., Ste. 11, Parsons Green House, 21–37 Parsons Green Lane, London SW6 4HH (✆ 0207/736-6030; info@anguilla-tourism.com).

USEFUL WEBSITES In addition to the websites above, other helpful Internet sites include www.gov.ai (Anguilla government) and www.ahta.ai (Anguilla Hotel and Tourism Association). The **Anguilla Guide** (www.anguillaguide.com) and the **Anguilla Forum** (www.anguillaforum.com) can be helpful.

RECOMMENDED READING In the Valley, the **Anguilla Arts and Crafts Center** (✆ 264/497-2263) and the **National Trust Office** (www.axanationaltrust.org; ✆ 264/497-5297) stock books on Anguilla, including guides to the local flora and fauna and Brenda Carty and Colville Petty's *Anguilla, an Introduction and Guide,* which is usually also available at Mr. Petty's **Heritage Museum Collection ★** (p. 98), in the island's East End.

Getting There

BY PLANE During high season, Anguilla's Clayton J. Lloyd International Airport is abuzz with private Gulfstreams and

---

A LITTLE history

The northernmost of the British Leeward Islands in the eastern Caribbean, 8km (5 miles) north of St. Maarten, Anguilla is only 26km (16 miles) long, with 91 sq. km (35 sq. miles) in land area—*anguilla* is Spanish for "eel," the shape of which the outline of the island roughly describes. Once part of an awkward federation with St. Kitts and Nevis, Anguilla gained its independence in 1980 and has since been a self-governing British Dependent Territory. The British government is represented by the governor, who is responsible for a good deal, including foreign policy. There is an elected House of Assembly, and the chief Anguillan elected official is the chief minister. Public holidays, including Anguilla Day (May 30), the Queen's Birthday (June 18), and Separation Day (Dec 19), honor both Anguilla's ties to Britain and its independence from St. Kitts and Nevis. Most government offices are in the Valley, Anguilla's capital, where many of the island's banks, groceries, and shops are also located. While you're in the Valley, be sure to drive up Crocus Hill and see some of the island's oldest Creole-style cottages. Today one of the government's major mandates is sustainable use of the island's precious resources. The one thing that hasn't changed? The truth of Anguilla's slogan: "Tranquillity Wrapped in Blue."

Anguilla

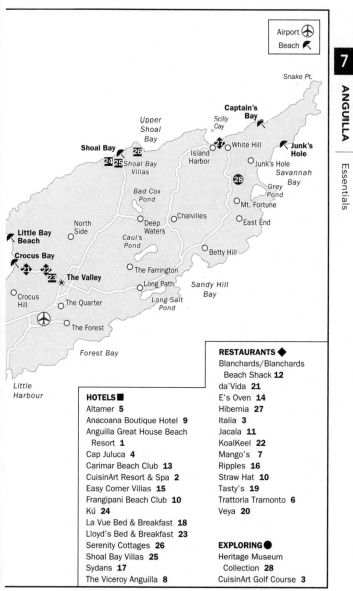

Airport ✈
Beach 🏖

Snake Pt.

Captain's Bay

Scilly Cay

Shoal Bay

Upper Shoal Bay

White Hill

Junk's Hole

24 25 *Shoal Bay Villas*

26

Island Harbor

Junk's Hole

Savannah Bay

Bad Cox Pond

28

Grey Pond

Mt. Fortune

Little Bay Beach

North Side

Deep Waters

Chalvilles

East End

Crocus Bay

Caul's Pond

21 22 23 **The Valley**

Betty Hill

The Farrington

Crocus Hill

The Quarter

Long Path

Sandy Hill Bay

Long Salt Pond

✈

The Forest

Forest Bay

Little Harbour

HOTELS ■
Altamer **5**
Anacoana Boutique Hotel **9**
Anguilla Great House Beach
 Resort **1**
Cap Juluca **4**
Carimar Beach Club **13**
CuisinArt Resort & Spa **2**
Easy Corner Villas **15**
Frangipani Beach Club **10**
Kú **24**
La Vue Bed & Breakfast **18**
Lloyd's Bed & Breakfast **23**
Serenity Cottages **26**
Shoal Bay Villas **25**
Sydans **17**
The Viceroy Anguilla **8**

RESTAURANTS ◆
Blanchards/Blanchards
 Beach Shack **12**
da'Vida **21**
E's Oven **14**
Hibernia **27**
Italia **3**
Jacala **11**
KoalKeel **22**
Mango's **7**
Ripples **16**
Straw Hat **10**
Tasty's **19**
Trattoria Tramonto **6**
Veya **20**

EXPLORING ●
Heritage Museum
 Collection **28**
CuisinArt Golf Course **3**

Fortune 500 executive jets purring on the runway. There are no nonstop flights from mainland North America into Anguilla, so visitors transfer at the Princess Juliana International Airport, the main airport on nearby Dutch St. Maarten; in San Juan, Puerto Rico; Antigua; or on St. Kitts. Alternatively, some fly in by private charter.

Anguilla's airport, located just outside the Valley, is currently equipped to handle small- to medium-size aircraft only. At this time, the only commercial airlines with connecting flights into Clayton J. Lloyd International is **LIAT** (www.liatairline.com; ℭ **888/844-5428** or 268/480-5601), which offers direct and connecting flights from Antigua and St. Thomas.

A fast and convenient option is to hop on one of the handful of regional charter airlines that offer direct flights between Anguilla and St. Maarten/St. Martin or other nearby islands. The official carrier for Winair servicing flights between St. Maarten and Anguilla, **Anguilla Air Services** (www.anguillaairservices.com; ℭ **264/498-5922**) offers three scheduled flights daily between St. Maarten and Anguilla, with one-way flights at rates of $80 for adults ($65 children 2–12). Offering comparable fares is the other Anguillan airline, **Trans Anguilla Airways** (www.transanguilla. com; ℭ **264/497-8690**). **Rainbow International Airlines** (www.rainbowinternationalairlines.com; ℭ **866/966-1881** or 340/690-4202) flies out of San Juan.

BY FERRY   Public ferries run between Marigot Bay, St. Martin, and Blowing Point, Anguilla (ℭ **264/497-6070**) every 30 to 45 minutes. The trip takes 20 to 25 minutes, making day trips a snap. Usually, the first ferry leaves St. Martin at 8am and the last at 7pm; from Blowing Point, the first ferry leaves at 7:30am and the last at 6:15pm. The one-way fare is $15 ($15 children 7 and older, $10 2–6; free 1 and under). A departure tax of $20 ($10 children 5–12) is charged on your return trip to St. Martin; day-trippers and visiting yachts pay a $5 departure tax. No reservations are necessary. Ferries vary in size, and none take passenger vehicles. *Tip:* Keep in mind that if you have a late-arriving flight, you may quite literally miss the (ferry) boat. You can either spend the night in St. Maarten/St. Martin or arrange a charter plane connection into Anguilla.

A 2010 agreement between the St. Maarten and Anguilla governments has worked to facilitate the ease of **private boat transfers** (and passing through immigration) from the airport—which means that ideally, you will be able to get off the plane and jump on a boat straight to Anguilla in under 30 minutes. Anguilla-based charter boats will pick you up at the Princess Juliana airport in St. Maarten and transport you and your luggage to Blowing Point or a hotel on the south side of Anguilla. These boats are more expensive than the public ferries, but they provide an alternative to traveling from the airport to the ferry port in Marigot by taxi (a 10- to 15-min. trip) and are thus a smart option for travelers with a lot of luggage or a lot of kids. Plus, the privately run boats are smaller, have fewer passengers, and can even arrange full-boat charters for groups or families. Keep in mind that these boats don't run as frequently as the government-run ferry, but all provide meet-and-greet service at the airport and direct ground-shuttle transport (3 min.) to the Simpson Bay Immigration Dock for passport clearance. Then you're on the boat and off to Anguilla. Delivering passengers directly to and from the airport are the *GB Express* (www.anguillaferryandcharter.com; $\textcircled{C}$ **264/584-6205** in Anguilla, or 721/581-3568 on St. Maarten; $55 one-way, $105 round-trip; children 1–11 $45 one-way, $90 round-trip); and **Funtime Charters** (www.funtime-charters.com; $\textcircled{C}$ **866/334-0047** or 264/497-6511; $65 per person one-way; half-price for children 11 and under). The **MV *Shauna VI*** ($\textcircled{C}$ **264/476-0975** or 772-2031 in Anguilla; 721/580-6275 on St. Maarten; myshauna6@hotmail.com; $60 adults, $40 children 2–12 round-trip) delivers passengers to the fishing dock at Simpson Bay. Reservations are required.

You might also opt to use one of the private charter boats on your return trip to the airport in St. Maarten. Check each operator's schedule for the time that's most convenient for you. Keep in mind that for international flights you're asked to be at the airport no less than 2 hours before your scheduled departure.

Tip: If you'd like to do some shopping and have lunch in Marigot before taking the ferry to Anguilla, simply store your bags at the ferry landing in the small baggage-storage area ($5 plus tip).

Getting Around

BY RENTAL CAR   To explore the island in any depth, it's essential to rent a car, though be prepared for some poorly paved roads. Four-wheel-drive vehicles are useful for exploring the island's unpaved and pitted back roads but not necessary elsewhere. Car rental agencies on the island can issue the mandatory Anguillan driver's license, which is valid for 3 months. You can also get a license at police headquarters in the island's administrative center, the Valley, and at ports of entry. You'll need to present a valid driver's license from your home country and pay a one-time fee of $20.

Remember: Drive on the left side of the road!

A handful of car rental agencies are conveniently located at the ferry terminal at Blowing Point. Otherwise, the island's car rental agencies will provide free pickup and delivery at the airport and ferry terminal or even drop off a rental car at your hotel when you need it. All rental companies offer unlimited mileage. Rental fees fluctuate according to season (at their highest in high season) and range from around $35 a day (automatic Toyota Corolla, Geo) to $65 (Jeep Wrangler) to $95 (Nisson Armada, Honda Pilot), plus insurance and taxes.

I had a perfectly fine experience renting with **Andy's Car and Beach Rentals** (http://andyrentals.com; ✆ **215/550-7010** in the U.S., or 264/497-0712), located right at the ferry terminal— and Andy's rates are some of the most competitive on the island. Other recommended local firms include **Bryans Car Rental** (www.bryanscarrentals.com; ✆ **203/992-5407** in the U.S., or 264/497-6407); **Connor's Car Rental,** c/o Maurice Connor, South Hill (✆ **264/497-6433**), **Island Car Rentals,** Airport Road (✆ **264/497-2723;** islandcar@anguillanet.com), and **Carib Rent A Car** (✆ **264/497-6020;** caribcarrental@anguillanet. com). **Avis/Apex** in the Valley (www.avis.com; ✆ **800/331-1212** in the U.S. and Canada, or 264/497-2642; avisaxa@anguillanet. com) offers regular cars and some four-wheel-drive vehicles, as does **Hertz**'s representative, **Triple K Car Rental,** Airport Road (www.hertz.com; ✆ **800/654-3131** in the U.S. and Canada, or 264/497-2934; hertzatriplek@anguillanet.com).

BY TAXI Taxi fares are posted at Walblake Airport, at the Blowing Point ferry, and in most taxis. Taxis can be pricey, for numerous reasons—so don't take it out on your driver if you think your fare is, well, unfair. For the lowdown on how taxi fares are determined, see "Taxi Zones: Decoding Anguilla Taxi Fares," above. And if you find a taxi driver you like, ask for his card and cellphone number for future rides. You can also get a cab through the **Airport Taxi Stand** (✆ **264/497-5054**) or **Blowing Point Ferry Taxi Stand** (✆ **264/497-6089**). A $4 surcharge goes into effect between 6pm and 6am.

I highly recommend **Accelyn Connor** (www.premiertaxiand-tour.com; ✆ **264/497-0515** or 235-8931; premiertaxiandtour@ hotmail.com). Connor has an office at the ferry landing, where he also rents bicycles and offers Internet service; bike rentals average $25 per day. I also recommend the taxi service of **Malcolm Hodge** (✆ **264/235-7384** or 235-7381), a gentleman and a stickler for good service (I once saw him ream out the GM of a big resort for dawdling and keeping a guest from making her ferry on time).

Taxi drivers also make great tour guides; check out "Exploring Anguilla," later in this chapter.

taxi zones: **DECODING ANGUILLA TAXI FARES**

If you feel taxi fares are high on Anguilla, you're not alone. But consider this: Not only does each driver have to pay for costly insurance to insure you, the passenger, but gas is astronomically expensive (at press time nearly $5 a gallon), and most drivers have vans, which have poor mileage rates. Plus, Anguilla taxis don't have meters, so if a customer is dragging his feet, drivers are not compensated for the wait. But the main reason a taxi ride costs what it does is that the government has parceled the island into 10 strictly delineated taxi zones, with a set fee schedule based on travel within and out of each zone. So, for example, Zone 1 covers the West End, where many of the top resorts and restaurants are located. Within that zone, a taxi ride will cost $10 (plus an additional $4 after 6pm). But from Zone 1 to Zone 2— another busy resort area 5 minutes away—the fare jumps to $14 (plus $4 after 6pm).

Tipping is at the discretion of the customer. You can check out the latest rate schedules by going to the **Anguilla Hotel & Tourism Association** website (www.ahta.ai/Taxi_Service.html).

Anguilla Calendar of Events

JANUARY

The Big Event Golf Tournament. Celebrating its inaugural tournament in January 2013, the Big Event is a weeklong professional golf challenge featuring 100 golfers from around the globe facing the challenges of the Greg Norman–designed course at CuisinArt Golf Resort & Spa. For details, go to www.cuisinartresort.com. Late January.

MARCH

Moonsplash Music Festival. Founded in 1991 by Anguilla's best-known musician, Bankie Banx, and Sheriff Bob Saidenberg, this 4-day March roving music festival is held at Banx's funky beachside bar, Dune Preserve, on Rendezvous Bay. It's evolved into a big-time beach party with top headliners. For details, go to www.moonsplashmusicfestival.com. Mid-March.

APRIL

Festival del Mar. The sea and the island's colorful fishing traditions are celebrated during this weekend culinary festival in Island Harbor. It features boat races (naturally), model boat races, fishing competitions, live string-band music, and hotly contested culinary competitions. For details, go to www.anguillaregatta.com. Easter Saturday and Sunday.

MAY

Anguilla Regatta. Boat races are Anguilla's national sport, and the Anguilla Regatta features competitive races among the area's racing fraternity over a 3-day weekend, with free entertainment and barbecues every night. For details go to www.anguillafestivaldelmar.com or contact the Anguilla Tourist Board at ☎ **800/553-4939.** Early April.

Anguilla Day. Contact the Anguilla Tourist Board at ☎ **800/553-4939.** Early April.

AUGUST

Anguilla Summer Festival. Anguilla's colorful Carnival lasts 11 days and features parades with floats, costumed dancers, live bands, and beauty competitions. Carnival harks back to Emancipation Day, or "August Monday," in 1834, when African slaves throughout the British colonies were freed. Boat races feature the island's distinctive swift, high-masted, brightly painted open boats. For info go to www.axasummerfestival.com. Thursday before first Monday in August.

NOVEMBER

Tranquility Jazz & Golf Festival. It's golf during the day and jazz at night during this 3-day jazz fest featuring both international and regional artists. For info go to http://anguillajazz.org. Second week in November.

BEACHES

We love Anguilla's limestone and scrub interior, its roaming goats, its salt ponds teeming with birds, and the wildflowers that spring up after rain showers. Still, let's face it, it's the beaches that bring us here. Superb beaches are what put Anguilla on the tourist map. There are some 33 of them, plus another handful of idyllic offshore islets, like **Sandy Island** and **Prickly Pear;** see "A Trip to an Offshore Cay," below. As new roads are built, fewer beaches are reached via the bone-jarring dirt paths that make some of us nostalgic for the old days of, well, 10 or 20 years ago. Most of the best beaches (Barnes, Maundays, Meads, Rendezvous Bay, and Shoal Bay West) are on the island's West End, site of the most expensive hotels. Keep in mind that all beaches—even those of the fanciest resorts—are open to the public. (That said, many locals and old-timers are increasingly unhappy at how many beaches are becoming the *de facto* preserve of new resorts.) The following beaches are listed clockwise from Rendezvous Bay.

Rendezvous Bay ★★ This long, curving ribbon of satiny, pale-gold sand traces the sea for 4km (2½ miles). You can enter the beach from the public access near the Anguilla Great House or

Bankie Banx's Dune Preserve—and pray that future construction does not ruin this beach forever.

Maundays Bay ★★ This 1.5km-long (1-mile) white-sand beach is the site of Cap Juluca and justifiably one of the island's most popular shorelines, with gentle surf for good snorkeling and swimming. Though the waters are luminescent and usually calm, the wind sometimes blows enough to attract windsurfers and sailboats. Most days you see St. Martin across the way; some days you see the pointy peak of Saba in the distance.

Shoal Bay West ★ This beach opens onto the southwest coast, with pristine white sands tinged with pink. Visitors find deluxe accommodations, including Covecastles, and superior snorkeling at its western tip.

Barnes Bay ★ The northwest coast has a number of other beaches worth seeking out, notably the glittering white stretch of Barnes Bay beneath a bullying bluff (and the behemoth Viceroy Resort plunked atop it). You can admire the offshore islands silhouetted against the horizon or join the windsurfers and snorkelers.

Meads Bay ★★★ This picturesque stretch of coast is lined with a number of resorts and beachside restaurants—Frangipani, Carimar, Blanchards, and Jacala—but it never feels crowded. I've been here on May mornings when the only souls on the beach are fishermen in wooden skiffs bringing home boatloads of silver bonito. You'll find good snorkeling off the beach around the rocks of the old Malliouhana resort. You can rent beach chairs and umbrellas for the day from **Blanchards Beach Shack** ($3 for umbrella and two chairs).

Sandy Ground (aka Road Bay) ★ On the northwest coast, Sandy Ground paints an idyllic old-time Caribbean scene, right down to wandering goats, spectacular sunsets, and clear blue waters, often dotted with yachts coming from St. Martin and beyond. You can watch fishermen and lobstermen set out in fishing boats as brightly colored as children's finger paints. **Johnno's** is arguably the archetypal beach bar, serving burgers and grilled fish and rocking at night. Indeed, many of the weathered wooden Antillean houses around here, shaded by turpentine trees and oleander, hold casual beach bars, making Sandy Ground party central on Friday nights.

Crocus Bay ★ Crocus Bay is a mighty fetching swimming spot, with steep limestone cliffs that rise up and good snorkeling along the rocks. The restaurant and beach bar **da'Vida** (p. 108) is set on the beach here. A potential eyesore high above the beach is a sprawling villa development where Anguillian sailors' wives once watched for their husbands' boats on the horizon.

Little Bay Beach ★★ Little Bay lies at the foot of Anguilla's steepest cliffs. The sands are not the characteristic Anguillian white but, well, *sandy*. That said, none of its visitors, who include serious bird-watchers, snorkelers, and scuba divers, seem to mind. You can get here by taking a boat from Crocus Bay most days from about 9am to 4pm for $15 per person round-trip. You can also climb down (and back up) the cliff at Little Bay, holding onto a knotted rope that is bolted into the cliff. The little cove is a terrific spot for snorkeling; thousands of silver jacks have been spotted swirling about the rocks.

Shoal Bay ★★★ In the northeast, this broad, 3km (2-mile) swath of sand is Anguilla's most popular beach. It's a Caribbean classic, with powder-soft sands and a backdrop of sea-grapes. This beach is often called Shoal Bay East to distinguish it from Shoal Bay West (on the western end of the island; see above). The waters are luminous, brilliantly blue, and populated by enough fish to make most casual snorkelers happy (head out to the reef for the best snorkeling). At noon the sands are blindingly white, but at sunrise and sunset they turn a pink to rival any beach in Bermuda. And no trip to Anguilla is really complete without at least one order of ribs (washed down with a Ting or a Red Stripe) at **Uncle Ernie's.** Rental umbrellas and beach chairs ($10 for two chairs and an umbrella) and other equipment are available just behind Uncle Ernie's at the long-established **Skyline Beach Rentals** (② 264/497-8644) from brothers Calvin, Raymond, and Solomon. If you prefer a quieter stretch of beach to sunbathe on, head east to **Elodia's beach bar** (② 264/497-3363), where you can rent even nicer chairs and umbrellas on a beautiful, crowd-free stretch of Shoal Bay.

Island Harbor Still a working fishing port, the harbor is dotted with island-made boats bobbing by the pier. For centuries Anguillians have set out from these shores to haul in spiny lobster, which are still cooked up here at **Smitty's** (② 264/497-4300). It was Smitty who set up generators and started the tradition of live music and grilled lobster at his toes-in-the-water restaurant back in the 1970s, before Anguilla had electricity. Islanders of a certain age remember walking for hours to get to Smitty's on the weekend to hear the music—and then walking back home after dark by the light of the moon.

Captain's Bay ★ Chances are you'll have this beach all to yourself. Here's why: There's no shade and the undertow is very dangerous. The views and rock formations are starkly beautiful, but this is a spot for a stroll, not necessarily a swim.

A TRIP TO AN OFFSHORE CAY ★★★

As beautiful as Anguilla's beaches are, there's something exhilarating and liberating about boating off to a deserted island. (Cruising along in that clear turquoise sea is certainly a big part of it.) Visiting one of Anguilla's tiny offshore gems is a must-do during your visit—and none is more than 20 minutes from shore. Here you can snorkel in gin-clear waters, beachcomb for shells and other treasures, and generally putter about a spit of sand in the castaway spirit. A few cays even have ramshackle beach restaurants, where fresh lobster and fish are always on the grill. Book an offshore excursion with **Shoal Bay Scuba** (www.shoalbayscuba. com; ℂ **264/235-1482**) or **Gotcha! Garfield's Sea Tours** (www. gotcha-garfields-sea-tours-anguilla.com; ℂ **264/235-7902**).

The most westerly cay is the privately owned **Dog Island,** truly a deserted isle, with its 200 hectares (500 acres) of sugary-sand beaches, salt ponds, and limestone cliffs. **Prickly Pear** is perhaps the most popular offshore cay, with good snorkeling and two beach restaurants, an offshoot of **Johnnos** (on Sandy Ground), and the **Prickly Pear Restaurant & Bar** (www.pricklypearanguilla. com; ℂ **264/235-5864**), where the drinks are made in a solar-powered blender. Both Shoal Bay Scuba and Gotcha! Garfield's Sea Tours offer twice-weekly trips to Prickly Pear for $55 to $65 per person (including lunch).

Sandy Island, on the northwest coast, is a tiny islet with a few palms surrounded by a coral reef, with a dilapidated (and seasonally abandoned) beach bar and restaurant. During the high season, a $5 speedboat from **Sandy Ground** takes visitors back and forth to Sandy Island almost hourly from around 9am to 4pm.

Of course, the closest cay lies just 150m (500 ft.) off the pier at Island Harbor. To get to tiny **Scilly Cay** (pronounced "silly key"), just go out on the pier and wave your arms (or dial ℂ **264/497-5123**), and a boatman will pick you up. Five minutes later you're at Eudoxie and Sandra Wallace's glorified tiki hut, **Gorgeous Scilly Cay** (www.scillycayanguilla.com; ℂ **264/497-5123**), picking out a fresh spiny lobster or crawfish (or chicken or veggies). You can snorkel around the reef or just relax over one of Eudoxie's Rhum Punches and watch the pelicans dive for fish. Lunch is daily Tuesday to Sunday from noon to 3pm, with live music most Sundays. This is a place to laze away the day; by the time you leave, you may have spent $100 per person—but what a day.

Savannah Bay (aka Junk's Hole) ★   It's a long drive down a bumpy, unpaved road to reach this uncrowded beach and offshore reefs full of eels, squid, and manta rays. The only attraction here is

Nat Richardson's **Palm Grove Bar & Grill** ★ (seemingly the only building for miles), with its perfectly grilled lobster, crawfish, or shrimp, and barbecued ribs.

EXPLORING ANGUILLA

A great way to get an overview of the island (if you don't have local friends) is on a **taxi tour** ★. In about 2 hours, a local driver (all of them are guides) will show you everything for around $60 (tip expected). The driver will also arrange to let you off at your favorite beach after a look around, and then pick you up and return you to your hotel or the airport. I highly recommend **Accelyn Connor** (www.premiertaxiandtour.com; ✆ **264/497-0515** or 235-8931; premiertaxiandtour@hotmail.com), whose highly personable and informative tours make him a much-sought-after island guide. Three-hour tours may include beaches, historic houses, and the Heritage Museum Collection ($70 single; $100 couple; $140 family of four). Be sure to ask Accelyn about his future **Medicinal Tours.** Before the arrival of modern grocery stores, Anguillans used endemic plants and shrubs for all sorts of medicinal and dietary purposes (the balsam bush was used for scouring pots, for example, and candlebark is a natural insecticide). Accelyn has planted a native garden filled with medicinal and dietary plants, shrubs, and trees that were once used as Anguillian folk medicine.

The **Anguilla National Trust** offers daily **wildlife tours and eco-tours** ★ to places like Big Spring, with 1,000-year-old rock carvings and an underwater spring; and East End Pond, a richly inhabited wildlife conservation site. Call ✆ **264/497-5297** to book a spot ($25 adults; $10 children 2–12). Also ask locally whether former chief minister Sir Emile Gumbs, an Anguilla National Trust volunteer, has resumed his delightful **eco-tours** (✆ **264/497-2711**), spiked with wonderful, often wry historical and political anecdotes.

Heritage Museum Collection ★ MUSEUM The modest look of the museum belies the range of fascinating artifacts inside, which include Arawak Indian tools, slave shackles, and household items belonging to 19th-century settlers. If Mr. Colville Petty, who founded the museum, is here when you visit, you will have an especially memorable visit—the esteemed island historian collected many of these artifacts himself and has even been awarded an OBE from Queen Elizabeth II.

East End, at Pond Ground. ✆ **264/497-4092.** Admission $5, $3 children 11 and under. Mon–Sat 10am–5pm.

OUTDOOR ACTIVITIES

Although sailing, fishing, and watersports are integral parts of the Anguillian culture, some water-borne playthings are not—namely **jet skis,** which are not allowed on the island. Spear fishing is also not allowed on Anguilla.

BICYCLE TOURS   Accelyn Connor's **Premier Taxi & Tours** (www.premiertaxiandtour.com; ✆ **264/497-0515** or 235-8931; premiertaxiandtour@hotmail.com) offers a 1½-hour bike tour that travels the scenic route overlooking the harbor and down to Shoal Bay with a professional cyclist as your guide. Helmets and bikes are provided. Tours start at your hotel ($55/couple). Connor also rents mountain, hybrid, and road bikes ($18–$25/day; $15 delivery); all rentals include helmets and locks.

CRUISES & BOATING   At Sandy Ground, **Shoal Bay Scuba** (www.shoalbayscuba.com; ✆ **264/235-1482**) and **Gotcha! Garfield's Sea Tours** (www.gotcha-garfields-sea-tours-anguilla.com; ✆ **264/235-7902**) arrange excursions and offer boat charters. Private charters run about $125 an hour; sunset cruises cost around $350.

FISHING   **Shoal Bay Scuba** (www.shoalbayscuba.com; ✆ **264/235-1482**) offers offshore fishing charters in a fully equipped Panga Classic; rates are $125 an hour, four person maximum. Your hotel can also arrange for a local fisherman to take you out; bareboating without a local captain is not allowed.

GOLF   Now owned by the CuisinArt Resort, the 18-hole, par-72 Greg Norman–designed **CuisinArt Golf Course** (formerly Temenos Golf Course), between Long and Rendezvous bays (www.cuisinartresort.com; ✆ **264/498-5602**), sits on a sprawling 111-hectare (274-acre) site. Bill Clinton has played here, and so can you, for greens fees of around $180 per person (18 holes). It's closed Mondays in the off season.

HORSEBACK RIDING   First-time and advanced riders can go horseback riding on the beach or "through the bush" with **Seaside Stables,** located at Paradise Drive (next to Paradise Cove in western Anguilla), Cove Bay (www.seaside-stables-anguilla.com; ✆ **264/235-3667**). Per-person rates for scheduled beach rides are $90 to $100; kids' half-hour pony rides to the beach are $35.

SAILING   Sailing is the island's national sport, and local kids learn the ropes from a young age. The **Anguilla Sailing Association** (www.sailanguilla.com; ✆ **264/584-7245**) is the force behind the Anguilla Regatta in early May and offers sailing lessons for kids in Optimist sailing dinghies, Vanguard 420s, and Hobie Cats at its sailing school on Sandy Ground; call for costs.

SCUBA DIVING & SNORKELING   Most of the coastline is fringed by coral reefs, and the crystalline waters are rich in marine life, with coral gardens, brilliantly colored fish, caves, miniwalls, greenback turtles, and stingrays. Conditions for scuba diving and snorkeling are ideal. Over the years, the government of Anguilla has artificially enlarged the existing reef system, a first for the Caribbean. Battered and outmoded ships, deliberately sunk in carefully designated places, act as nurseries for fish and lobster populations and provide new dive sites. At **Stoney Ground Marine Park,** off the northeast coast, you can explore the ruins of a Spanish galleon that sank in 1772. Offshore cays (**Anguillita, Prickly Pear, Sandy Island, and Dog Island**) offer pristine conditions.

Shoal Bay Scuba (www.shoalbayscuba.com; ☎ **264/235-1482**) has a custom-built, state-of-the-art boat. A two-tank dive costs $90, plus $10 for equipment. It also provides snorkeling trips, fishing charters, sunset cruises, and windsurfer rentals and lessons. At Sandy Ground, ask around for PADI-trained **Doug Carty** (☎ **264/235-8438** or 497-4567), who with his company **Special D** takes visitors on scuba excursions, snorkeling trips, and island excursions. At Meads Bay, **Anguillian Divers** (www.anguilliandiver.com; ☎ **264/497-4750**) is a one-stop dive shop that answers most diving needs. PADI instructors are on hand, with a two-tank dive costing $85, plus another $10 for equipment.

Most hotels provide snorkeling gear. Several places, such as long-established **Skyline Beach Rentals** (☎ **264/497-8644**) at Shoal Bay, rent snorkeling gear if your hotel doesn't provide it. The snorkeling's great off the beach at Shoal Bay, Maundays Bay, Barnes Bay, Little Bay, Road Bay, and Mead Bay beneath the rocks at the Malliouhana resort.

TENNIS   Most of the resorts have their own tennis courts (see "Where to Stay," later in this chapter).

SHOPPING

For serious shopping (Gucci, Louis Vuitton, and the like), take the ferry to French St. Martin (see "Getting There," earlier in this chapter) and visit the shops in Marigot. St. Martin is also a good place to stock up on French cheeses and potables if you're planning a long stay on Anguilla. The venerable St. Martin wine store, **Le Goût du Vin,** has opened a shop on Anguilla, in South Hill Plaza (http://french-wines-west-indies.grands-vins-de-france.eu; ☎ **264/497-6498**).

Clothes are not cheap on Anguilla, and most hotel boutiques do not go out of their way to stock bargain brands. Everything you need to be a fashionable Anguillian—flowing kurtas, bejeweled caftans, and slinky bathing suits—is found at **ZaZAA** ★ (© 264/497-0460) in Shoal Bay East at the Ku resort. If you need a bathing suit, T-shirt, stylish sandals, or any beach gear, you'll find it in the colorful cottage at **Irie Life** (© 264/498-6526), on the cliff-side road at South Hill. ("Irie" is Rastafarian for "cool.") Even if you don't buy anything, you'll get a fantastic view down to Sandy Ground.

ENTERTAINMENT & NIGHTLIFE

In high season, hotel resorts host barbecues, West Indian parties, and calypso groups and string bands, both local and imported. But for an immersion in the island's lively music scene and a chance to hang with the easy-going, music-loving locals, ask around—much of the action is down at the bars in Sandy Ground, and things don't really get cooking until after 11pm. Look for such popular soca/reggae/calypso entertainers as the Musical Brothers, Darvin & His DC Band, and the British Dependency. Dancing the night away—well, until around 2am, when things wind down—is absolutely de rigueur.

The island's wonderful beach bars and grills serve great food and drink and feature live music at least 1 day a week. For a rundown on the perpetual favorites, see "Sun, Sand, Music & Barbecue" (p. 108). Keep in mind that Anguilla has no casinos or other gambling spots—the local Church Council, which has its say in matters such as this, ensures that the island stays that way. If you feel the need for some casino action, St. Maarten and its 14 casinos are just a 20-minute ferry ride (and a short cab ride from the ferry port on St. Martin) away.

WHERE TO EAT

To many discerning diners, Anguilla is the Caribbean's premier dining destination, and native Anguillian chefs like Dale Carty (Tasty's and Dune Preserve) and Glendon Carty (Ripple's and Cap Juluca) are essential elements in the island's effervescent food-and-drink scene.

Eating on Anguilla is not cheap, however—a high percentage of what ends up on your plate has been imported. Fortunately, many local chefs are increasingly packing their menus with sustainable choices: **local seafood** and **Anguilla-grown produce and grains.** Fresh, locally caught fish—red snapper, yellowtail snapper, yellowfin tuna, grouper, mahimahi, bass, and bonito—gets plenty of play on restaurant menus, as does Anguillian lobster and local crawfish, big and sweet and at the other end of the size spectrum from

THE ANGUILLA art SCENE

Anguilla has a thriving local arts and crafts scene and a surprising number of small art galleries featuring the works of talented resident artists, both native-born and transplanted from around the world. In the Valley, the **Anguilla Arts and Crafts Shop** (✆ **264/497-2200**) has paintings and ceramics by local artists, as well as embroidery and lovely cloth dolls. If you're looking for collectibles, or just looking for good art, head to the following galleries. Keep in mind that most keep erratic hours even in high season, so call ahead for opening hours.

o **Alak Gallery,** Shoal Bay East Road (✆ **264/497-7270**): Accomplished Anguillian artist Louise Brooks paints genre island scenes and Caribbean flora and fauna in vivid, saturated hues. Roosters hold a particular charm for Brooks. Alak has a new **second location** in South Hill, next to Connor's Car Rental.

o **Art Café,** Coconut Paradise Building, Island Harbor (✆ **264/497-8595**), has intriguing rotating art exhibits and also doubles as a restaurant serving breakfast and lunch (chicken roti, burgers, local fish, and lobster).

o **Bartlett's Collections,** by the roundabout at South Hill (✆ **264/497-6625**), has island crafts (as well as terrific smoothies at its outdoor cafe).

o **Lynne Bernbaum** (http://lynnebernbaum.com; ✆ **264/497-5211**) is an American painter whose George Hill studio

its mudbug cousin, the crawfish. ***Note:*** At many restaurants, prices for fish, lobster, and crawfish rise and fall depending on availability.

A forward-thinking government agricultural initiative to **farm vegetables** on a large swath of land in Central (with a heavy-handed slogan in "Farm Today or Starve Tomorrow") is putting fresh sweet potatoes, peppers, corn, squash, tomatoes, lettuces, and pigeon peas into the marketplace. Former farmers are rediscovering the pleasure of growing food, and new farmers (and future chefs) are being initiated into this agricultural renaissance.

Most, if not all, restaurants tack a **10% to 15% service charge** onto your bill. The menu should state whether service is included, but always confirm whether gratuities are added. In many instances tips are pooled among the staff (including the back of the house), so it never hurts to add a little extra if you feel your server warrants it.

features her bold images of Anguilla, the Caribbean, and France. In addition to paintings, Ms. Bernbaum sells prints of her works, including some very Anguillian cactuses and goats.

o **Cheddie's Carving Studio,** West End Road, the Cove (*②* **264/497-2949**), is the domain of self-taught Cheddie Richardson, who sculpts intricate, whimsical figures from driftwood, stone, and coral.

o **Devonish Art Gallery,** in Long Bay opposite CuisinArt Road (www.devonishai.com; *②* **264/497-2949**), features the work of Courtney Devonish, the well-known Anguillian potter and sculptor, as well as a good collection of paintings from local artists.

o **Savannah Gallery,** Coronation Avenue, Lower Valley (http://savannahgallery.com; *②* **264/497-2263**), on the road to Crocus Bay, has a fine selection of paintings by Anguillian and Caribbean artists.

o **Stone Cellar Art Gallery,** Government Corner, the Valley (www.oldfactory-anguilla.ai; *②* **264/498-0123**): This 1868 former cotton gin has rough-hewn limestone walls and wood-beam ceilings. It's the home of rotating art exhibits (on the second floor) and Sir Roland Richardson's Caribbean Impressionistic paintings on the first.

Expensive

Blanchards ★★★ INTERNATIONAL   In 1994, when Anguilla was just beginning to attract high-spending foodies, Bob and Melinda Blanchard opened a restaurant at the end of a dirt track to the sea. It was elegantly casual and offered a fresh and inventive haute cuisine. Frankly, many wondered how long Blanchard's would survive. Since then this place with indoor-outdoor dining on the beach has become *the* place to eat for many foodies. It's not uncommon to see dinner guests arrive here clutching copies of the Blanchards' book *A Trip to the Beach,* a charming account of how they created their restaurant. Now Blanchards' only problem is how to live up to its reputation. No problem: The crackerjack staff keeps the engine humming night after night. Behind tall teal shutters (open to the sea breezes), diners enjoy sophisticated but unfussy food with a spirited Caribbean flair. Among the perpetual

RESOURCES FOR SELF-CATERING

Vacationing on Anguilla is pricey enough as it is without having to pay marked-up resort prices for basics like milk, soft drinks, snacks, and beer. For groceries, drinks, and kitchen staples (even a wine room), stock up at **Albert's Supermarket** (☎ 264/497-2240), in the Valley, a large, full-service grocery store. In Anguilla's West End, you can purchase a full complement of groceries and other sundries at **Foods Ninety-Five** (☎ 264/497-6196), just after the entrance to Cap Juluca. **Ashley & Sons,** in the South Valley (www. ashleyandsons.com; ☎ 264/497-2641), has a wide selection of beverages, snacks, fruit, and toiletries. Monday through Saturday, don't miss stopping at the **Fat Cat Gourmet** (www.fatcat.ai; ☎ 264/497-2307), by Albert's Supermarket in the Valley; hands down this place has the tastiest takeout goodies (from cakes to entire meals) on Anguilla. This is also a great place to pick up snacks for a picnic on the beach. For fresh vegetables, **Rainbow Farms,** in South Hill, behind the Romcan Grocery (http://rainbow-farms.com; ☎ 264/581-6628), sells fresh tomatoes, sweet peppers, and herbs most days from 8am to noon. For breads, croissants, French pastries, and desserts, head to **Geraud's Patisserie,** South Hill Plaza (www.anguillacakesandcatering.com; ☎ 264/497-5559). A branch of Marigot's venerated wine store, **Le Goût du Vin,** is now open in South Hill Plaza (http://french-wines-west-indies.grands-vins-de-france.eu; ☎ 264/497-6498).

favorites are sublime lobster-and-shrimp cakes—these alone are worth the trip. The Caribbean sampler features oven-crisped mahimahi with coconut, lime, and ginger; roasted Anguilla crawfish; and jerk chicken with cinnamon-rum bananas. You can buy one of the Blanchards' newest tomes on the way out—oh, and those are son Jesse's colorful paintings on the walls. Blanchards serves an affordable three-course prix-fixe meal ($48). Now you can spend the day at the beach and sample the Blanchards' food, too, at **Blanchards' Beach Shack** (see later in this chapter).

Meads Bay. www.blanchardsrestaurant.com. ☎ **264/497-6100.** Reservations required. Main courses $38–$58. AE, MC, V. Mon–Sat 6:30–10pm. Closed Mon in low season and Aug 26–Oct 22.

Hibernia ★★ 👔 FRENCH/INDOCHINESE Anguilla residents since 1987, chef Raoul Rodriguez and his wife, hostess Mary Pat O'Hanlon, have converted a traditional West Indian cottage on Anguilla's East End into an inventive restaurant decorated with French- and Indonesian-inspired objets d'art collected from their annual world travels. The creative food here is equally international, with touches of the West Indies, Indonesia, and France. This is a place where it's tempting to make a meal of starters, perhaps the luscious Caribbean fish soup and a terrine of foie gras with aged rum, cashews, and dates. Main courses include tender duck breast, classic beef tenderloin, and Caribbean seafood prepared Thai style. Good news for wine enthusiasts: Hibernia is now the proud owner of the Malliouhana hotel's splendid wine collection. Hibernia has only 11 tables, so reservations are essential.

Island Harbor. www.hiberniarestaurant.com. ℭ **264/497-4290.** Reservations recommended. Main courses $32–$45. AE, MC, V. Tues–Sat noon–2pm and 7–9pm; Sun 7–9pm. Closed Aug–Sept and Mon–Tues during low season.

Italia ★★ ITALIAN   The signature restaurant in the clubhouse at the CuisinArt Golf Club enjoys a sensational perch overlooking the course and the glittering lights of St. Martin beyond. You dine on a big, breezy terrace that's casually elegant, with an extravagant amount of space between tables. It's truly lovely; happily, the food more than rises to the occasion. Pastas are exemplary, including a homemade lasagna with spinach pasta and Bolognese sauce. The chef is equally adept at cooking fresh fish; the flavorful red snapper is topped with herbs, zucchini, and sweet cherry tomatoes plucked from CuisinArt's hydroponic farm. A nightly courtesy shuttle whisks CuisinArt guests to and from the restaurant.

CuisinArt Golf Course. www.cuisinartresort.com. ℭ **264/498-2000.** Main courses $26–$40; pasta $13–$25. AE, MC, V. Daily noon–3pm and 7–10pm (closed Wed lunch). Closed Aug–Sept.

Jacala ★★★ FRENCH   The new boy on the Meads Bay block feels like it's been around a long time, and that's a very good thing. Jacala was opened by two hospitable veterans of the local restaurant scene, Jacques Borderon and Alain Laurent, who worked at Malliouhana for 24 years. Like its neighbor, Blanchards, Jacala enjoys a bewitching setting on Meads Bay beach, and you can almost reach out and grasp the last rays of sun melting into the sea. It's a romantic spot that feels sexy and laid-back all at once. Candlelight flickers on the pitched white ceiling, and sea breezes waft through the open dining room. The food is uncomplicated and delicious, an apt metaphor for Anguilla itself. It's a fairly simple menu, brilliantly executed, from a modest fettuccine with sautéed fresh tomato, garlic, and basil to a perfectly grilled crawfish. A scarlet-hued conch chowder is scented with fennel; lobster salad comes with jewel-like bites of exotic fruits.

Meads Bay. ℭ **264/498-5888.** Reservations recommended. Main courses $16–$38. AE, MC, V. Tues–Sat noon–2pm and 7–9pm; Sun 7–9pm. Closed Mon–Tues in off season and Aug–Sept.

KoalKeel ★★ CARIBBEAN/ASIAN This handsome restaurant is housed in one of the island's oldest stone houses, a former sugar plantation "Great House" from the 1790s. (The oldest dwelling on the island, originally a building sheltering slaves, is just across the street.) Executive chef Gwendolyn Smith and chef Leonard "Smoke" Sharplis prepare an eclectic menu of local specialties with Asian-inspired flavors and techniques, including island pigeon-pea soup and homemade dumplings, and "rice paper" snapper in a lemon-soya sauce. Meats are slow-cooked in the 200-year-old "Old Rock Oven." Oenophiles will appreciate the 18,000-bottle wine cellar; there's also a lounge for aged rums and cigars. Pastries here are terrific; be sure to stop by the KoalKeel Patisserie one morning between 6 and 9am to get some of the French bread, croissants, or other treats available for takeout. KoalKeel offers complimentary shuttle service to and from a number of Anguilla resorts. With the exception of the delicious pastries, some feel the quality of the food here is inconsistent; that said, the pleasure of dining in this historic house is considerable.

The Valley. www.koalkeel.com. ℂ **264/497-2930.** Reservations required. Main courses $28–$48. AE, MC, V. Mon–Sat 8–10am, 11am–2:30pm, and 6:30–9:30pm.

Mango's ★★ CARIBBEAN This pavilion a few steps from the edge of the sea, on the northwestern part of the island, fulfills anyone's fantasies of a relaxed but classy beachfront eatery; its doors open to the breezes and its walls are brightened by local murals. All the breads and desserts, including ice cream and sorbet, are made fresh daily on the premises. You might start with Barnes Bay lobster cakes and homemade tomato tartar sauce, or creamy conch chowder flavored with smoked bacon and chock-full of onions and potatoes. Grilled local crawfish is splashed with lime, curry, and coconut; chicken is barbecued with rum, and snapper filet is marinated in a soy-sesame-tahini mix, but the simple grilled fish with lemon-and-herb butter shines.

Seaside Grill, Barnes Bay. ℂ **264/497-6479.** Reservations required. Main courses $26–$45. AE, MC, V. Wed–Mon 6:30–9pm. Closed Aug–Oct.

Straw Hat ★ CARIBBEAN/INTERNATIONAL Perched on a deck overlooking the sparkling swells of Meads Bay, the Straw Hat does a brisk business, packing 'em in with consistently good food and that sizzling setting. The indoor dining area is light, bright, and open to the beach and sea, with paintings by local artist Lynn Bernbaum (see "Shopping," earlier in this chapter). The menu shies away from the more contrived touches of some local fusion menus: Sauces may be drizzled, but as of yet, there's no foam. The Straw Hat Seafood Stew (shrimp, crawfish, fresh local fish simmered with ginger, coconut milk, cilantro, and tomatoes, served over coconut rice) is a very reasonable $36. Smart buys include snapper, tuna, chicken, or shrimp "plain grilled" with two sides (fried plantains, Caesar salad, garlic mashed potatoes, and Anguillian rice and peas).

Frangipani Beach Resort, Meads Bay. www.strawhat.com. ℂ **264/497-8300.** Reservations recommended. Main courses $23–$48. AE, DC, MC, V. Daily 7:30–10am, noon–3pm, and 6:30–9pm.

Trattoria Tramonto ☺ NORTHERN ITALIAN   This favorite of many, serving solid Italian food, is on the island's West End. There's even a Bellini, to make Italophiles remember the ones they drank at Harry's Bar in Venice. The chef takes special care with his appetizers, including sautéed shrimp with saffron and a porcini-mushroom sauce, and spicy hot penne with a garlic, tomato, and red-pepper sauce. The house specialty is a sublime lobster-filled ravioli in a heart-stopping cream sauce. Kids are treated like celebrities here.

Shoal Bay West. www.trattoriatramonto.com. ℂ **264/497-8819.** Reservations required. Main courses $24–$38. MC, V. Tues–Sun noon–3pm and 6:30–9pm. Closed Sept–Oct.

Veya ★★★ CARIBBEAN/ASIAN   With the transporting ambience of a warmly lit treehouse, Veya is perched on the hillside above Sandy Ground and enveloped in bamboo, date and coconut palms, and flowering frangipani trees. Veya's fans—and we are among them—love the feeling of looking out into tropical greenery and prize the consistently excellent food and service. Detractors find the setting more memorable than the food. Veya's extensive wine list earned it a 2009 *Wine Spectator* Award of Excellence. The restaurant serves what owners Carrie and Jerry Bogar call the "cuisine of the sun," with ingredients and styles of preparation taken from a wide range of sunny countries straddling the equator. You might start with the grilled watermelon and poached shrimp appetizer, sprinkled with spiced pecans and mint. Favorite entrees include local crawfish with a ginger beurre blanc, vanilla-cured duck breast, and five-spiced pork tenderloin.

Sandy Ground. www.veya-axa.com. ℂ **264/498-8392.** Reservations required. Main courses $28–$46. AE, MC, V. Mon–Sat 6–10pm. Closed Sat in low season and Aug.

Moderate

If you find yourself in the Valley at lunchtime, remember two tasty, good-value spots: Longtime favorite **English Rose** (ℂ 264/497-5353) serves up generous portions of stews and grills, and the **Valley Bistro** (ℂ 264/497-8300) is the place to head if you are

SUN, SAND, MUSIC & BARBECUE

The island's wonderful **beach bars and grills** serve up great food and drink and good-time bonhomie day after day. Most feature live music at least 1 day a week, and you can dine quite well for around $20. These places are about as casual as casual can be, but remember, this is modest Anguilla; if you've been swimming, cover up before you sit down to eat.

At Upper Shoal Bay, check out **Gwen's Reggae Bar & Grill** (🕻 264/497-2120), which features Gwen Webster's barbecue daily into the early evening; on Sunday it showcases live reggae performances. Don't miss Gwen's special slaw. The palm grove here is one of the few naturally shady seaside spots on the island, and it comes with hammocks and picnic tables. At the more populated end of Shoal, island institution **Uncle Ernie's** (www.uncleerniesbeachbar. com; 🕻 264/497-3907) is open from morning 'til at least sunset, serving up generous plates of chicken and ribs, fresh fish, fries, slaw, and cold beer. The beach bar at nearby **Elodia's** (🕻 264/497-3363) is a less-crowded spot to sip a rum punch and rent beach chairs.

At the island's East End, a sign points off the main road down a bumpy road to Nat Richardson's **Palm Grove Bar & Grill** (🕻 264/497-4224) at Junk's Hole. Islanders and visitors flock here for what many think are Anguilla's most succulent grilled lobsters and lightest johnnycakes. Bring swimming gear and snorkel until your lobster comes off the grill.

Down at Sandy Ground, the indoor/outdoor **SandBar** (🕻 264/498-0171; sandbar.anguilla@email.com) is the island hot spot for a sundowner and flavorful tapas (such as grilled shrimp, conch fritters with payaya chutney, and chicken or beef satay with peanut curry), priced from $6 to $12. The SandBar is open from around 4pm to at

longing for pasta, pizza, or delicious French onion soup and a croque-monsieur. Both restaurants have daily specials, and you could eat at either for less than $20 (both closed Sun).

da'Vida ★★ CARIBBEAN   Does it really matter that this place is a little more uptown than other island beach bars? Nah, not with the sunny vibe, the beautiful setting, the delicious food—and the admirable efforts at cooking sustainably with local ingredients. After Roy's casual beachside restaurant moved from Crocus Bay to Sandy Ground a few years ago, Crocus Bay had no restaurant and fell into decline—until the da'Vida complex opened right on the beach in 2009. Anguillian chef Guy Gumbs's restaurant has quickly become one of the island's favorite places for celebratory dinners. Everything is just steps from shimmering Crocus Bay. The least 10pm, and to at least midnight on nights when there is live music. Another island favorite, **Johnno's** (✆ **264/497-2728;** closed Mon) has live music most Wednesday evenings (reggae and soca) and Sunday afternoons (jazz). Burgers and grills are available all day, or you can just order a rum punch, plop down at one of the picnic tables on the beach, and watch the spectacular Sandy Ground sunset. A few minutes' stroll down the beach, **Elvis'** (✆ **264/461-0101**) opened in 2007 and gives Johnno's some sunset competition. Elvis' bar occupies an Anguillian boat beached on the sand, with tables and chairs nearby. There's great rum punch and nibbles (sometimes barbecue) and live music several times a week.

Halfway between Johnno's and Elvis', overlooking the Salt Pond, the **Pumphouse** (www.pumphouse-anguilla.com; ✆ **264/497-5154;** closed Sun) has rafter-shaking live music almost every night, enormous cheeseburgers, and crisp Caesar salads. *Warning:* One Pumphouse rum punch is equivalent to at least two anywhere else! This former rock-salt factory, with some of its original machinery still in place, is the funkiest bar on the island—unless that award should go to Bankie Banx's **Dune Preserve,** at Rendezvous Bay (✆ **264/ 497-2660**), with its own salvaged boats and the island's most seriously relaxed musician. Reggae star Bankie Banx joins in the live music performances here several times a week. Heading west from Bankie's, keep an eye out for the small sign that points from the main road to **Smokey's,** at Cove Bay (www.smokeysatthecove.com; ✆ **264/497-6582**). Delicious crawfish, lobster, ribs, and spicy wings are served up most days—this is one of the island's top spots to chill. Smokey's has live music Saturday afternoons and Sunday evenings.

main restaurant is open to the sea on three sides, but the dark wood tables and crisp linen make the mood more elegant than casual. The menu draws heavily on local seafood (crawfish, snapper, and grouper) and does creative, often Asian-inspired twists on traditional island cuisine. Start with lobster bisque with corn fritters, or try the sweet potato gnocchi with sweet basil and tomato coulis. Mains include pan-roasted island grouper or a garlic-infused lamb loin. One of our favorite lunch spots is da'Vida's casual **Bayside Grill ★**, which shares the same brilliant seaside setting next door. Sample grilled favorites like barbecued ribs or chicken, served up with rice and peas and the best johnnycakes on island. Beach chairs and umbrellas mean that guests can alternate dining with dipping into the sea.

Crocus Bay. www.davidaanguilla.com. ☏ **264/498-5433.** Da'Vida main courses $32–$42; Bayside Grill barbecued ribs or chicken $18–$20. Da'Vida Tues–Sun 11am–3pm and 6–10pm. Bayside Grill Tues–Sun 11am–5pm.

Tasty's ★★ CARIBBEAN/AMERICAN   Set inside a Creole cottage painted in teals, blues, and lavenders is Dale Carty's uplifting hymn to the local cuisine. It's located on the right as you head through South Hill along the main road toward the East End. Colorful island murals by artist Susan Croft line the walls. Trained in international cuisine in the kitchen in Malliouhana, the award-winning chef prepares food that is, well, *tasty.* In Carty's hands, local specialties sing with flavor. Conch Creole is paired with coconut dumplings; grilled snapper is elevated with a savory onion-pepper-tomato herb sauce. Tasty's shrimp come sautéed in coconut curry sauce and served with a sweet potato puree. Try the Caribbean sampler breakfast: fried and salt fish, johnnycakes, fried plantains, and bush tea. Okay, you're not on the sea—you're on a main road with the sounds of passing traffic, in fact—but the interior's bright pastels will raise your spirits nonetheless.

South Hill. www.tastysrestaurant.com. ☏ **264/497-2737.** Dinner reservations recommended. Main courses $18–$30; lobster $36–$40. AE, MC, V. Daily 7:30am–3pm and 7–10pm.

Inexpensive

Delicious, affordable food is served at Anguilla's fabulous beachside bars and barbecue shacks. See "Sun, Sand, Music & Barbecue," above, for details.

Blanchards' Beach Shack ★ INTERNATIONAL   Finally, Meads Bay has some beach-shack love. Even better, it's a labor of love brought to you by Anguilla's powerhouse husband-and-wife

---

📎 Roadside Eats

Especially on the weekends, you'll notice a number of **roadside food stalls** in the Valley near the outdoor People's Market (a great place to get fresh fruit and veggies) and around the roundabout by the school and library. Out on the island, you may see other food stalls, often barbecuing in grills fashioned out of oil drums. This is a great way to sample such local delicacies as bull foot soup, pigtail soup, goat water, roti, and fungi. Keep an eye out for **Hungry's,** the mobile food van that is usually parked near the post office in the Valley. You can eat yourself silly on sandwiches, wraps, curries, or stews, usually for a good deal less than $10.

culinary team, the Blanchards. This has been a hit since the day it opened, a gaily painted Creole shack planted in a shaded spot next to the Blanchards' flagship restaurant on beauteous Meads Bay. This is a beach shack with delicious twists, delicacies such as gazpacho, tacos with homemade corn tortillas, and a succulent shrimp salad roll. Grab a mango colada, rent a beach chair for $3, and dig your toes into the sugary sand. You'll have a wonderful afternoon.

Meads Bay. www.blanchardsrestaurant.com. 📞 **264/498-6100.** Sandwiches/burgers $5–$10. AE, MC, V. Mon–Sat 11:30am–8:30pm. Closed Aug 26–Oct 22.

E's Oven ★ 🏠 CARIBBEAN/INTERNATIONAL   Darting from beach to beach, it's easy to neglect some of Anguilla's inland restaurants. This place at South Hill (by the big curve in the main road) is very popular with locals, and when you eat here, you'll realize why. The coconut-flavored pumpkin soup and garlic-crusted crawfish tails are yummy, and the seafood pasta is one of the main reasons some friends of mine say they keep coming back to Anguilla! The dining room is simple, with tables and chairs—nothing fancy, but perfectly pleasant.

South Hill. 📞 **264/498-8258.** Main courses $10–$20. MC, V. Wed–Mon 11am–midnight.

Ripples 🍴 CARIBBEAN/INTERNATIONAL   Set in a restored clapboard house, Ripples has a raised deck, comfy wicker chairs, a casual West Indian decor, and a nightly crowd of regulars and drop-ins (including Brad Pitt and Jennifer Aniston the night before they announced their separation). No wonder: Caribbean Chef of the Year Glendon Carty is behind the menu. You can get anything from a burger to fresh local fish—mahimahi, snapper, tuna, and grouper—prepared any way you like. The weekly early-bird special offering a choice of three entrees (usually one veggie, one seafood, and one traditional English roast) for $15 is one of the island's best bargains. The bar scene gets increasingly lively as the night wears on.

Sandy Ground. 📞 **264/497-3380.** Dinner reservations recommended. Main courses $15–$25. MC, V. Daily noon–midnight.

WHERE TO STAY

Anguilla has some of the most desirable high-end properties in the Caribbean—no wonder it's a hot honeymoon destination. But it also has a smattering of small hotels, inns, and guesthouses, many just steps from a gorgeous beach. Villas are a popular lodging option, ranging from breathtakingly sumptuous to basic; for guidance in choosing your villa, see "Renting a Villa on Anguilla," below.

If you're looking for ways to cut costs, consider visiting in the shoulder or low seasons, when rates plummet. Look for terrific off-season packages on hotel websites or social media.

Keep in mind that the government imposes a mandatory 10% room tax, and resorts tack on an additional service charge of 10%.

RENTING A VILLA ON ANGUILLA Anguilla has some of the most luxurious villas and beach houses in the Caribbean, but it also offers reasonably priced options. For a list of Anguilla Hotel & Tourism Association–affiliated villas, apartments, and villa rental agents, head to the AHTA website at www.ahta.ai (look under "AHTA Members," then "Villas and Rental Agents"). Keep in mind that "villa" is used on Anguilla to mean either a separate unit *or* a self-contained unit in a building with several other self-contained units. That's a big difference, so check which kind of villa your rental is before you send off your deposit!

Very Expensive

If your idea of a Caribbean getaway includes being waited on by a personal butler and staff of eight, you may want to make one of architect Myron Goldfinger's three beachside villas at **Altamer,** Shoal Bay West, the Valley (www.altamer.com; ✆ **264/498-4000**), your "private palace," as its website suggests. The five- to six-bedroom villas go for prices that nudge upward toward a whopping $50,000 a week in high season, but tumble to a mere $27,500 to $30,000 off season. Creature comforts at all the villas include a private swimming pool, an elaborate game room (with pool table), and an entertainment center (including a home theater).

At press time, the fate of the island's beloved and venerated Malliouhana resort was still up in the air. The hotel was shuttered in 2011.

Cap Juluca ★★★ Recent changes in ownership have not diminished Cap Juluca's status as one of the premier properties on the island, humming along near the top of everyone's list of the Caribbean's best resorts and welcoming a new crop of honeymooners with each passing year. Encircling the lovely white-sand beach on Maundays Bay and nestled in 180 acres of luxuriant grounds, Cap Juluca leads a charmed existence.

Of course, its setting on one of the best beaches on the island doesn't hurt; here beachside pampering is a daylong affair, with custom-made beach loungers turned to face the sparkling blue-green sea. The architectural style throughout is quasi-Moorish, with sun-blasted exteriors, white domes, arched doorways, and walled courtyards. The Main House is capped by a soaring domed ceiling and a palace-size Moroccan chandelier. The 98 spacious rooms and

---

📎 Baby-Equipment Rentals

Many resorts on Anguilla are happy to provide cribs and other baby and toddler essentials. If you're renting a villa or condo, however, a convenient, hassle-free option to dragging everything with you (and paying extra-baggage costs) is to rent the kids' stuff you need. **Travel Lite** (www.travelliteanguilla.com; ℭ **264/476-9990** or 476-0999) delivers premium-brand baby- and toddler-equipment rentals (cribs, strollers, car seats, highchairs, and playpens) to your villa door, as well as swings, safety gates, baby monitors, even DVDs. Travel Lite will also help you plan children's parties, activities, and holiday celebrations.

---

villas have a casbah-meets-British-colonial cinematic flair, with Frette-sheathed beds, ceramic-tile floors, and louvered doors opening onto patios, many with pathways snaking directly to the sea. All are outfitted with the essential mod cons of 21st-century life—flatscreen TVs, iPod docks, and Bose Wave music systems—and a number of villas have private plunge pools. Bathrooms are enormous and sheathed in marble.

Pimm's serves what it calls "Eurobbean" cuisine—a mélange of European and Caribbean cuisines—and **Spice** has a pan-Asian menu. **Blue** is a casual alfresco beachfront spot that's open for breakfast and lunch, and dinner drinks (and the twice-weekly barbecue buffet).

Maundays Bay (P.O. Box 240), Anguilla, B.W.I. www.capjuluca.com. ℭ **888/858-5822** in the U.S., or 264/497-6666. Fax 264/497-6617. 71 units. Winter/spring $995–$1,385 double, $1,785–$3,485 suite, $3,785–$7,985 villa; off season $495–$685 double, $785–$1,585 suite, $1,585–$3,985 villa. Children 11 and under stay free in parent's room. Rates include continental breakfast. Airport private boat/taxi transfers: $450 (up to 4 people; $40 additional person one-way). Shared sea shuttles (semi-private) $85 per person one-way. Meal plans available. AE, MC, V. **Amenities:** 3 restaurants; 2 bars; babysitting; children's programs (in summer only); fitness center; golf course and driving range; outdoor pool; room service; spa; 3 tennis courts; watersports equipment (extensive). *In room:* A/C, TV/DVD, CD player, hair dryer, minibar, MP3 docking station, Wi-Fi (free).

CuisinArt Golf Resort & Spa ★★★ Pillowed in sand dunes on sweeping Rendezvous Bay beach, CuisinArt's whitewashed villas feel transplanted from some sun-streaked Greek isle. This neatly landscaped resort has an infinity pool that flows all the way to the beach, its long stretches of shallow water perfect for toddling kids. CuisinArt has a happy, sunny vibe, with roosters crowing in the morning and lizards skittering in the underbrush and a palm-fringed patio that faces the gleaming pool. And, yes, it is owned by Cuisin-Art (of blender fame), and yes, it takes its food seriously, with Anguilla's first and only hydroponic farm, an herb garden, and weekly **barbecue buffets** ★, laden with grilled lobster, spit-roasted chicken, ribs, homemade desserts, and sides and salads made with farm-fresh produce. Moreover, it appears as if the forlorn but fabulous **Temenos Golf Course** has finally found a good home, merging seamlessly into the sunny mix at CuisinArt. The opening of a road linking the neighbors makes it easier than ever to access the golf course from the resort (and CuisinArt guests enjoy slightly discounted rates).

The newly refreshed rooms are spacious and cheerful, with bright Haitian paintings on the walls and comfy wicker and dark wood furniture. Rooms are refreshed with a 24-hour air-purifying circulation system. Bathrooms are commodious, wrapped in marble and tile. Patios have spectacular ocean views. Six large white-adobe villas on the resort's eastern flank are discreet and utterly luxurious, each with its own gated entry courtyard, shaded by palms and trailing bougainvillea. Choose one with private beach access, a private pool, and a solarium for the utmost in secluded comfort.

The on-site restaurants are excellent indeed; you can tack on full and modified meal plans during your stay. The resort's formal main dining room, **Le Bistro at Santorini,** serves dinner only. The poolside **Mediterraneo** has more casual fare, with stupendous breakfasts that include homemade johnnycakes and fresh fruit smoothies. The resort's newest restaurants are Anguilla's first Japanese restaurant, **Tokyo Bay,** atop the Venus Spa with panoramic beach views; and **Italia,** which enjoys a sensational perch overlooking the golf course (you can drive or take the shuttle to the restaurant). Get head-to-toe pampering in the **Venus Spa,** with 16 treatment rooms, a Thalasso pool of heated seawater, and an oceanfront relaxation room.

Rendezvous Bay (P.O. Box 2000), Anguilla, B.W.I. www.cuisinartresort.com. ⓒ **800/943-3210** in U.S. and Canada, or 264/498-2000. Fax 264/498-2010. 93 units. Winter/spring $875 double, $1,150–$2,600 suite, $3,600–$4,600 villa; off season $450 double, $550–$1,300 suite, $1,200–$2,800 villa. Children 11 and under stay free in parent's room. Rates include full breakfast. Airport boat/taxi transfers available for fee. AE, MC, V. Closed Sept–Oct 12. **Amenities:** 5 restaurants; 3 bars; babysitting; mountain bikes; billiards room; bocce court; croquet; children's playground; fitness center; hydroponic farm; Jacuzzi; outdoor pool; room service; spa; 2 lighted tennis courts; watersports equipment (extensive); Wi-Fi (free). In room: A/C, TV/VCR (DVD in some), CD player, hair dryer, high-speed Internet (free), minibar.

Down on the (Hydroponic) Farm

It's the world's only hydroponic farm in a greenhouse setting, where hundreds of sweet cherry tomatoes, foot-long cucumbers, dewy lettuces, and fragrant herbs ripen spectacularly with little more than water and a sprinkling of plant nutrients. There's no soil, no weeds, no bugs. To help feed guests and staff in a country where much of the soil is non-arable and fresh produce must be imported, CuisinArt hired plant scientist and horticulturist Dr. Howard Resh, Ph.D., to devise a greenhouse that could produce vegetables year-round and withstand strong winds. Today the farm supplies both resort restaurants and the employee cafeteria with an average harvest of 128 heads of lettuce a day. Call ✆ **264/498-2000** to join one of the regularly scheduled free tours with Dr. Resh, who is passionate about every aspect of the farm. You'll even get to sample sweet cherry tomatoes right off the vine.

The Viceroy Anguilla ★★ The crisp white lines and Kelly Wearstler's hyper-designed interiors may not be your cuppa, but you can't deny the property's glittering wow factor. The Viceroy delivers what it promises—and what it promises is an immersion in 21st-century high chic. From afar the 35-acre resort, which opened in December 2009, looks like a small city landed on the promontory between Meads Bay and Barnes Bay. The architecture comes into focus up close, the sleek white structures smartly juxtaposed against the blue Anguillian sea and sky. Rooms and suites are outfitted with every 21st-century toy, furnished in a palette of cream, sand, and brown, and punctuated with golden sunbursts (the Viceroy logo). Every suite (except for the Viceroy King) has its own plunge pool; six "rooftop" suites are duplexes with the plunge pool situated on the second-story terrace, with dizzying sea views. The four- and five-bedroom villas are luxe dialed to 11. Each villa—more like an exquisite minimansion, really—comes with a ridiculously fabulous kitchen, master bathrooms with deep-soaking tubs and outdoor showers, and a pool and outdoor cabana, grill, and hot tub.

Coba, the main restaurant, is encased in glass for seamless sea and sky views. The **Sunset Bar** feels like the heart of the resort, but an entire second, self-contained family-friendly section has at its center a sprawling pool and a restaurant, **Aleta.**

The Viceroy's community spirit is reflected in the fact that its employee base is reportedly 90% Anguillian. The beach around the resort has had some erosion from storms but is building up again; however, the best nearby beach is a short walk (or shuttle) away on Meads Bay.

Barnes Bay (P.O. Box 8028), Anguilla, B.W.I. www.viceroyhotelsandresorts. com/anguilla. © **800/578-0283** in the U.S., or 264/497-7000. Fax 264/497-7100. 166 units. Winter $695–$995 double, $1,095–$1,195 1-bedroom suite, $2,295–$2,695 2-bedroom suite, $4,750–$6,500 3-bedroom suite, $7,500–$9,500 villa; off season $395–$795 double, $895–$995 1-bedroom suite, $1,095–$1,295 2-bedroom suite, $1,795–$2,095 3-bedroom suite, $2,500–$4,500 villa. Airport boat/taxi transfers available for fee. AE, DC, MC, V. Closed Sept–Oct. **Amenities:** 3 restaurants; 2 bars; babysitting; children's programs; concierge; fitness center/gym/spinning room; 3 outdoor pools; room service; spa; watersports equipment (extensive). *In room:* A/C and ceiling fan, TV, kitchen (in 2-bedroom deluxe suites [some kitchenettes], 3-bedroom suites, and villas), hair dryer, minibar, plunge pools (except in Viceroy King rooms), Wi-Fi (free).

Expensive

Frangipani Beach Resort ★ You can't beat the location, directly on a spectacular stretch of Meads Bay beach. This appealing pink-hued resort continues to upgrade its rooms and public spaces to stay competitive in an increasingly competitive market. The Spanish Mediterranean–style buildings feature pleasant doubles and suites in one-, two-, and three-bedroom configurations, many on the smallish side. The one-bedroom suites are the best, with gleaming stainless steel kitchens, ocean views, and spacious living quarters. (All junior, one-bedroom, and two-bedroom suites have full kitchens and washer/dryers.) It has a nice, big infinity pool, and the **Straw Hat** restaurant (p. 106) is an island favorite.

Meads Bay (P.O. Box 1378), ˜Anguilla, B.W.I. www.frangipaniresort.com. © **877/593-8988** in the U.S., or 264/497-6442. Fax 264/497-6440. 18 units. Winter $395–$560 double, $710–$790 junior suite, $885–$1,635 suite, $640–$1,725 penthouse; off season $295–$375 double, $435–$475 junior suite, $625–$940 suite, $395–$910 penthouse. Rates include continental breakfast. AE, MC, V. Closed Sept–Nov. **Amenities:** Restaurant; bar; babysitting; 2 pools; tennis court; watersports equipment. *In room:* A/C and ceiling fans, TV/DVD, CD player, hair dryer, full kitchen (suites only), washer/dryer (suites only), Wi-Fi (free).

Moderate

Anacaona Boutique Hotel ★ 🔥 The small, quiet boutique resort is stupendous value for Anguilla. It's not on the beach but set back in lush greenery and a short walk away along a footpath from one of the island's best stretches of white sand, Meads Bay. Rooms are simply outfitted and bathrooms are smallish, but at these prices, who cares? Touches like cool Frette linens on the beds make things comfy. Plus, all rooms have balconies overlooking tropical gardens. Dine poolside under the canopy at **Firefly** restaurant, which serves a Caribbean/European fusion cuisine with sides of homemade johnnycakes. On Thursday nights the restaurant's island buffet is accompanied by live entertainment from the **Mayoubla Folkloric Theatre,** a native troupe performing traditional Anguillian song and dance. Ask about the resort's informal cultural and nature tours.

Meads Bay (P.O. Box 200), Anguilla, B.W.I. www.anacaonahotel.com. ✆ **877/647-4736** in the U.S., or 264/497-6827. Fax 264/497-6829. 27 units. Winter $265–$325 double, $430 junior suite, $475–$530 suite; off season $160–$190 double, $230 junior suite, $275–$325 suite. Extra person $35/night. Up to 2 children 11 and under stay free in parent's junior suite; one child 11 and under stays free in parent's standard or superior room. Meal plans available. AE, MC, V. Closed Sept–Oct 27. **Amenities:** Restaurant; bar; babysitting; 2 pools; watersports equipment. *In room:* A/C and ceiling fans, TV, hair dryer, kitchen (villa suites only), kitchenette (junior suites only), MP3 docking station, Wi-Fi (free).

Anguilla Great House Beach Resort ✦

This old-time, low-key resort sits on a delicious stretch of beach along Rendezvous Bay. This particular patch of sand has what many do not: a shaded grove of trees, under which you can park yourself in a beach chair for hours of breezy bliss. You may be joined by a handful of guests and a couple of playful dogs—or you may have this paradise to yourself. Unfortunately, that may be because the resort is still not so great, with unkempt lawns and rooms in need of a revamp. On the plus side, the colorfully painted Creole-style cottages are just steps from the beach. Many (especially nos. 111–125) boast water views from their back and front porches—ask for one of these. Rooms in each cottage are cheek by jowl, but guests seem respectful of their neighbors' close proximity. Most rooms have pitched ceilings and bright local artworks, and the shower-only bathrooms are clean and well kept. The alfresco restaurant, **Olde Caribe,** serves food that often is much better than the sad-sack ambience warrants. If you'd like a self-catering unit and don't mind being a few minutes from the beach, ask about the rates for nearby **Kerwin Kottages**—four self-catering one-, two-, and three-bedroom units that enjoy hotel privileges and represent excellent value.

Rendezvous Bay (P.O. Box 157), Anguilla, B.W.I. www.anguillagreathouse.com. ✆ **800/583-9247** or 264/497-6061. Fax 264/497-6019. 35 units. Winter $310–$340 double; off season $210–$240 double. AE, MC, V. **Amenities:** Restaurant; bar; outdoor pool; room service; watersports equipment. *In room:* A/C and ceiling fan, TV, fridge (in some), hair dryer, Wi-Fi (in some, free).

Carimar Beach Club ★ ☺

This 24-apartment resort is sitting pretty on one of the loveliest stretches of beach on the island. It's a small, folksy place, broken into six villas surrounding a flower-filled courtyard. It has no pool or restaurant, but Blanchards and Jacala are just next door, and the restaurants at Frangipani and the Viceroy are within easy walking distance. Villas 1 and 6 are oceanfront, with the priciest rates. The suites are simply but comfortably furnished one- or two-bedroom apartments with fully equipped kitchens; the two-bedroom apartments have two bathrooms, which makes them great for families. Guests get together on their patios or balconies for drinks or else stay glued to their beach lounges for the fabulous sunsets.

Meads Bay (P.O. Box 327), Anguilla, B.W.I. www.carimar.com. © **866/270-3764** or 264/497-6881. Fax 264/497-6071. 24 units. Winter $425–$510 1-bedroom suite, $565–$645 2-bedroom suite; off season $225–$265 1-bedroom suite, $325–$375 2-bedroom suite. Extra person $75. AE, DISC, MC, V. **Amenities:** Babysitting; bikes; concierge; 2 tennis courts; watersports equipment. *In room:* A/C (in bedrooms only) and ceiling fan, TV/VCR, hair dryer, full kitchen, Wi-Fi (free).

Kú 🍴 Many of the most famous of the island's resorts hide themselves away in acres of landscaped privacy. Kú, on the other hand, is happily in the heart of things at Shoal Bay. It's an easy barefoot back-and-forth walk from the island's most popular beach to good-value quarters on stratospherically priced Anguilla. Unfortunately, maintenance of the rooms is long overdue. Maybe that's why Kú's beach bar and pool has become a daylong gathering place for guests, who range in age from 30-somethings to AARP members of long standing. **Uncle Ernie's** (p. 108), one of Anguilla's best-known beach bars and grills, is just next door, as is the Shoal Bay Scuba Center. Other restaurants and bars are strung out for a good mile or so along the beach, which is increasingly chockablock with rental umbrellas, beach chairs, and day-trippers from St. Martin. In short, Shoal Bay is Anguilla's only "crowded" beach, which makes Kú a great place for action and people-watching—but not necessarily for blissed-out Caribbean tranquillity.

Shoal Bay East (P.O. Box 51), Anguilla, B.W.I. © **800/869-5827** or 264/497-2011. Fax 264/497-3355. 27 units. Winter $355–$475 double; off season $180–$220 double. Extra person $35–$55. AE, MC, V. **Amenities:** Restaurant; bar; babysitting; dive shop; gym; outdoor pool; spa. *In room:* A/C and ceiling fan, TV/DVD, CD player, Internet ($8/day), kitchen.

Serenity Cottages ★ 👪 With a great location at the quiet end of Shoal Bay beach, Serenity is one place that lives up to its name. The beach crowds at Uncle Ernie's and Kú (see above) are a brisk 15-minute stroll away. Anguillian owner Kenneth Rogers keeps his eye on the details, and it all runs smoothly. The two cottages are surrounded by lovingly tended flowers and trees (at least one unit's shower has a glass wall brushed by palm fronds). The furnishings have a solid, understated elegance, with a good deal of dark wood furniture offset by cheerful floral fabrics. The views from the rooms and their balconies through the gardens to the sea are marvelous. The bar in the open-air restaurant functions as a meeting place. Serenity also has a beach hut bar and restaurant, and Gwen's Reggae Bar & Grill (p. 108) is just steps away down the beach. One thing to keep in mind: There are coral reefs just off shore at Serenity, and the tides can be rough; a short walk west will take you past the reefs to Shoal's usually calmer waters.

Shoal Bay East (P.O. Box 309), Anguilla, B.W.I. www.serenity.ai. ☏ **264/497-3328.** Fax 264/497-3867. 18 units. Winter $325 $350 studio, $425–$450 1-bedroom suite, $525–$550 2-bedroom suite; off season $195–$225 studio, $295–$325 1-bedroom suite, $395–$425 2-bedroom suite. Extra person $100. AE, MC, V. **Amenities:** 2 restaurants; beach bar; babysitting; limited room service; Wi-Fi (lobby). *In room:* Ceiling fan, TV, fridge, hair dryer (in some), kitchen (suites only).

Shoal Bay Villas 🏖 Swim or snorkel steps from your villa door when you stay at this prime location right on the powdery sands of Shoal Bay. The villas are modest but great value, and fully equipped kitchens make them even more economical. All rooms are sunny and bright, with fairly uninspired wicker furnishings and handsomely renovated bathrooms. All have a patio or balcony overlooking the ocean or the pool. Only the bedroom suites have air-conditioning. The resort is almost doubling in size with the addition of 10 more villas; you might want to ask for one of the brand-new rooms when you book.

Shoal Bay (P.O. Box 81), Anguilla, B.W.I. http://sbvillas.ai. ☏ **264/497-2051.** Fax 264/497-3631. 23 units. Winter $370 studio, $335–$420 1-bedroom suite, $555 2-bedroom suite; off season $250 studio, $210–$290 1-bedroom suite, $370 2-bedroom suite. Extra person $40. AE, MC, V. Closed Sept and 1st 3 weeks of Oct. **Amenities:** Babysitting; pool; watersports equipment. *In room:* A/C (bedroom suites only) and ceiling fan, TV, full kitchen, Wi-Fi (free).

Inexpensive

Easy Corner Villas 🏖 On a bluff overlooking Sandy Ground (aka Road Bay), this place is a good 15-minute drive from the best beaches, so you'll definitely want a car. No problem: The owner is Anguillian Maurice Connor, the same entrepreneur who rents many of the cars on the island. Easy Corner's one-, two-, and three-bedroom apartments (known as villas) are set on modestly landscaped grounds with beach views from some of the private porches. Each comes with kitchen facilities, an airy combination living/dining room, good storage space, and simple furnishings. Some guests have complained about the size of the bathrooms here—but I'm not sure why, especially at these prices. Maid service is available for an extra charge, except on Sunday. Note that new buildings below partially obstruct the views of Sandy Ground and the sea from a number of units—but even with less of a view, this is still an excellent value spot.

South Hill (P.O. Box 65), Anguilla, B.W.I. www.easycornervilla.com. ⓒ **264/497-6433.** Fax 264/497-6410. 12 units. $90 studio; $125 1-bedroom villa; $155 2-bedroom villa; $195 3-bedroom villa. AE, MC, V. *In room:* A/C and ceiling fan, TV/VCR, kitchen.

La Vue Bed & Breakfast 🔖 This nice addition to the low-priced lodging scene in Anguilla is set on a bluff high above Sandy Ground. Its rooms are sprawling and comfortably furnished—all have king-size beds and fully equipped kitchens—and some have patios with splendid views of the harbor below. The upstairs rooms in back are bigger but lack full ocean views, and the units on the first floor are bigger still. Room no. 201 has a nice living-room area and great harbor views; no. 204 has a handsome bed and a bigger patio. A "Caribbean continental" breakfast is included, Wi-Fi is free throughout, and you're minutes from the action at Sandy Ground. La Vue is truly a winner.

Back St., above Sandy Ground (P.O. Box 52), Anguilla, B.W.I. www.lavue anguilla.com. ⓒ **264/497-6623.** Fax 264/498-8804. 17 units. Studio $200; 1-bedroom suite $200; 2-bedroom suite $322. Children 11 and under stay free in parent's room. Extra person $50. Rates include continental breakfast. MC, V. *In room:* A/C and ceiling fan, TV/VCR, hair dryer, kitchen, Wi-Fi (free).

Lloyd's Bed and Breakfast ★ 🔖 The island's oldest inn opened in 1959 on the crest of Crocus Hill in the Valley. This family-owned B&B is the sort of place that makes you feel at home the moment you walk through the door. The butter-yellow exterior, with lime green shutters and a wide, inviting veranda, is exuberantly Caribbean. Inside the neat little rooms are painted in richly saturated tropical hues and comfortably updated with crisp linens. Lloyd's main room—part dining room, part lounge—with its traditional wood and cane furniture, old prints, and small library, is the perfect place for island travelers (many are repeat guests) to trade tall tales. Lloyd's is not on a beach, but just down the hill is an excellent beach at Crocus Bay (the site of **da'Vida,** p. 108, owned by the next generation of Lloyds, David and Vida). A full, family-style breakfast is included in the price, which makes Lloyd's one of the most charming bargains in the Caribbean.

Crocus Hill (P.O. Box 52), Anguilla, B.W.I. http://65.36.226.88. ⓒ **264/497-2351.** Fax 264/497-3028. 10 units. Double $145. Rates include breakfast. MC, V. **Amenities:** Restaurant (breakfast only); bar; Internet. *In room:* A/C and ceiling fan, TV.

Sydans 🏷 Anguillian Anne Edwards is the tirelessly helpful proprietor of Sydans, a hospitable family-run inn that overlooks Sandy Ground's large salt pond and is only steps from the sea. Some guests from the States and Europe have been coming here every year for 20 years; others use this as a long-term home-away-from-home. All rooms have kitchens (some stoves have burners, but not ovens), bathrooms with tub/shower combinations, and homey bed- and sitting rooms. The second-floor units overlooking the salt pond are a birder's delight, providing views of pelicans, cranes, herons, and seasonal birds; ground-floor rooms open into a central courtyard, lack the pond view, and are less quiet. Sydans is very much part of the Sandy Ground neighborhood: You'll hear roosters at sunrise, see the school bus drop off neighborhood children in the afternoon, and know when Johnno's or the Pumphouse has live music until the wee hours. Things are casual here (water outages are not unheard of), but if you ask Ms. Edwards for an extra reading lamp or towels, it will be in your room by the time you're back from the beach.

Sandy Ground, Anguilla, B.W.I. http://inns.ai/sydans. ✆ **264/497-3180** or 235-7740. 10 units. From $185 double. MC, V. *In room:* A/C and ceiling fan, TV, kitchen.

ST. BARTHÉLEMY (ST. BARTS)

I t's been called the French Riviera in the Caribbean. St. Barts is a place where megayachts preen for other megayachts, where the well-heeled come to chase eternal youth under the tropical sun. The island offers pampering without pomp, world-class beaches, and inimitable French flair mixed with a laidback West Indies vibe. In spite of its glitzy reputation, St. Barts maintains a quaintness, a warmth, and an almost old-fashioned storybook quality.

Beaches St. Barts has some 21 white-sand beaches, and while all are public and free, few are crowded, even in high season. The best known is **St-Jean Beach,** a sun-splashed *crescent divided by the Eden Rock promontory. The uncrowded strand at **Gouverneur Beach,** on the southern coast, is gorgeous, ringed by steep cliffs overlooking St. Kitts, Saba, and Statia (St. Eustatius). Equally fine is **Grande Saline Beach,** to the east, where nude sunbathers seem unfazed by the lack of shade.

Things to Do You can snorkel right off beaches such as secluded **Colombier** or in the protected bay at **Petite Anse,** which teems with colorful aquatic life. Kitesurfing is fast becoming one of the most popular sports here—study with former champions to get the hang of it on **Grand Cul-de-Sac. Corossol Beach** offers a typical glimpse of French life with a calm, protected beach and a charming little seashell museum. South of Gustavia, **Shell Beach** is often awash with small, exquisite seashells.

Eating & Drinking Yes, it can be expensive to dine out in St. Barts, but the budget-bound can eat well by opting for the filling and affordable lunchtime *plat du jour* (special of the day) at casual restaurants. Alternatively, do takeout, St. Barts style, from one of the handful of excellent epicurean takeout delis, or *traiteurs,* where plats du jour, from pâtés to *pissaladière* (onion tart), are sold by the gram.

Shopping   Duty-free St. Barts offers liquor and French perfumes at some of the lowest prices in the Caribbean—often cheaper than in France itself. You'll find bargains, albeit in limited selection, in haute couture, crystal, porcelain, watches, and other luxuries from international design brands like Bulgari, Cartier, Dior, and Hermès, especially at Gustavia's **Quai de la République**—nicknamed "rue du Couturier." For island crafts, look for intricately woven straw goods (baskets, bags, and bonnets) and striking art naïf, including models of Creole *cazes* (traditional wooden houses) and fishing boats.

ESSENTIALS

For further on-the-ground resources, see "Fast Facts: St. Barts," in chapter 9.

Visitor Information

Comité du Tourisme de Saint-Barthélemy, St. Barts's official tourism agency, was formed in 2008 when the island became a French Overseas Collectivity in its own right (no longer a French *commune* under the administration of Guadeloupe). Its website is www.saintbarth-tourisme.com. In St. Barts, the tourist office is located in Gustavia, adjacent to La Capitanerie (the Port Authority Headquarters) on the pier, quai du Général de Gaulle, Gustavia (© 590/27-87-27).

Online, the **Insiders' Guide to St. Barthélemy** (www.sbh online.com) offers instructive readers' forums and trip reports.

Island Layout & Neighborhoods

St. Barts lies 24km (15 miles) southeast of St. Martin and 225km (140 miles) north of Guadeloupe. The island's capital and only seaport is enchanting **Gustavia,** named for a Swedish king. This dollhouse-scale port rings a splendid harbor where fishing boats bob alongside sleek yachts. Its narrow streets—lined with 18th-century Swedish and French stone buildings housing gourmet eateries, galleries, chic boutiques, and an excellent **Municipal Museum**—are easily explored on foot. Traveling northwest from Gustavia, you reach the typical villages of **Corossol** and **Colombier,** where a handful of women still weave lantana straw handicrafts from hats to handbags in candy-colored *cazes* garlanded with flowerpots and fishing nets. To the east of Colombier is the island's largest beach, **Flamands.**

St. Barthélemy

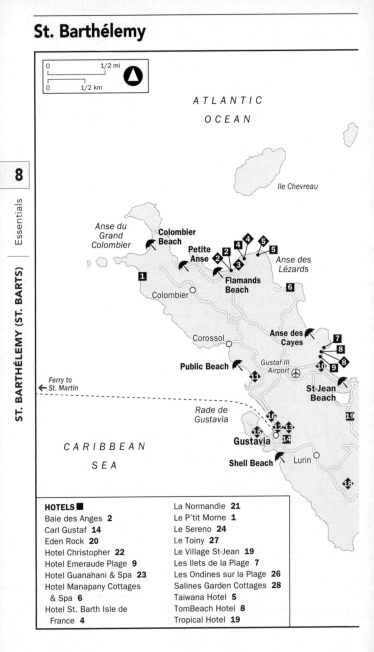

0   1/2 mi
0   1/2 km

ATLANTIC

OCEAN

Ile Chevreau

Anse du Grand Colombier

Colombier Beach

Petite Anse

Anse des Lézards

Flamands Beach

Colombier

Corossol

Anse des Cayes

Gustaf III Airport

Public Beach

← *Ferry to St. Martin*

Rade de Gustavia

St-Jean Beach

CARIBBEAN

SEA

Gustavia

Shell Beach   Lurin

HOTELS ◼
Baie des Anges **2**
Carl Gustaf **14**
Eden Rock **20**
Hotel Christopher **22**
Hotel Emeraude Plage **9**
Hotel Guanahani & Spa **23**
Hotel Manapany Cottages
& Spa **6**
Hotel St. Barth Isle de
France **4**

La Normandie **21**
Le P'tit Morne **1**
Le Sereno **24**
Le Toiny **27**
Le Village St-Jean **19**
Les Ilets de la Plage **7**
Les Ondines sur la Plage **26**
Salines Garden Cottages **28**
Taiwana Hotel **5**
TomBeach Hotel **8**
Tropical Hotel **19**

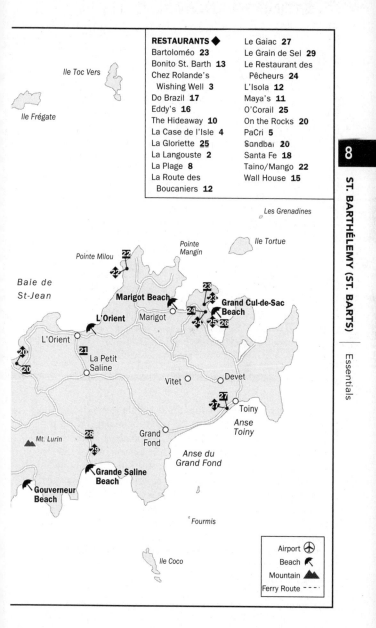

RESTAURANTS ◆

Bartoloméo **23**	Le Gaiac **27**
Bonito St. Barth **13**	Le Grain de Sel **29**
Chez Rolande's	Le Restaurant des
Wishing Well **3**	Pêcheurs **24**
Do Brazil **17**	L'Isola **12**
Eddy's **16**	Maya's **11**
The Hideaway **10**	O'Corail **25**
La Case de l'Isle **4**	On the Rocks **20**
La Gloriette **25**	PaCri **5**
La Langouste **2**	Sandbar **20**
La Plage **8**	Santa Fe **18**
La Route des	Taino/Mango **22**
Boucaniers **12**	Wall House **15**

Ile Toc Vers

Ile Frégate

Les Grenadines

Ile Tortue

Pointe Mangin

Pointe Milou **22**

Baie de St-Jean

Marigot Beach

L'Orient

Grand Cul-de-Sac Beach

Marigot **24**

25 **26**

L'Orient

20 **21**

La Petit Saline

Vitet Devet

27

Toiny

Anse Toiny

▲ *Mt. Lurin*

28

29

Grand Fond

Anse du Grand Fond

Grande Saline Beach

Gouverneur Beach

Fourmis

Ile Coco

Airport	✈
Beach	☚
Mountain	▲
Ferry Route	- - -

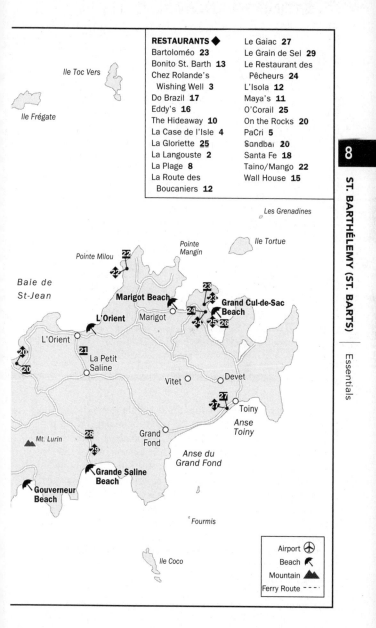

8

ST. BARTHÉLEMY (ST. BARTS) | Essentials

125

GETTING TO KNOW st. barts

New friends call it "St. Barts," while old-time visitors prefer "St. Barth." Either way, it's short for St. Barthélemy (San Bar-te-le-*mee*), named by its discoverer, Christopher Columbus, in 1493. For the most part, St. Bartians are descendants of Breton and Norman fisherfolk; many are of French and Swedish ancestry. The year-round population is small, about 8,000 people living on 41 sq. km (16 sq. miles) of land, just 24km (15 miles) southeast of St. Martin and 225km (140 miles) north of Guadeloupe. In little **Corossol,** you might glimpse wizened *grand-mères* wearing the traditional starched white bonnets known as *quichenottes* (a corruption of "kiss-me-not"), which discouraged the close attentions of men on the island. In the 20th century, the island became a paradise for a handful of millionaires, such as David Rockefeller. It still caters to an ultra-affluent crowd, with European-style discos and flashy yachts elbowing their way into the charming seaport of **Gustavia,** the capital. Old and new money feed a vibrant (and duty-free) luxury-goods market. Yet the island diligently maintains a quaintness and a warm bonhomie. It has an idyllic fairy-tale quality, with gaily painted Creole cottages tucked into hillsides and flower boxes spilling over with colorful blooms. Picturesque cemeteries are dotted with simple white crosses draped in blooms and ringed by picket fences.

Yes, St. Barts can be prohibitively pricey, with its upscale resorts and tony French restaurants. But it doesn't have to cost a fortune to stay here: You can rent a villa (half the visitors who come here do), cook your own meals, and beach-hop with the rest of the

Right by the airport, **St-Jean** is the closest thing to a resort town you'll find here: a West Indies St-Tropez brimming with smart boutiques and beachfront bistros. A few minutes' drive east is serene **Lorient,** site of the first French settlement, with a popular locals' beach; picturesque graveyards; a 19th-century Catholic church, convent, and bell tower; and a reconstructed 17th-century Norman manor. Farther east, **Grand Cul-de-Sac** (Point Milou) is the island's second major resort center, its wide curve of sand surveyed by resorts and eateries. The **Toiny Coast,** on the island's southeast flank, has spectacularly rocky vistas and crashing surf, especially the scenic **Grand Fond** area. To the west, dotting the island's southern midsection, are two of St. Barts's best beaches: **Saline** and **Gouverneur.**

islanders—all the beaches are public and free. And casual dress prevails—sandals, flowing kurtas, tousled hair, bangles, little else—
though the sandals are likely Manolo and the bangles 24-karat gold.

St. Barts has retained its quaint character for a number of reasons. The island has no casinos, and mega cruise ships are discouraged. The little airport has a comically short runway. Local
authorities, keenly sensitive to the perils of overdevelopment, have
placed style and size restrictions on new resorts. For many people,
just getting here can be daunting. Unless you're a passenger on a
zillionaire's yacht, you'll probably be flying in on a tiny plane that
makes a heart-stopping landing on a 661m (2,170-ft.) airstrip lined
up between two mountains. Those who go by boat or high-speed
ferry have the sometimes stomach-churning seas to contend with.

St. Barts's volcanic terrain is vastly different from the flat, sandy
scrubland of its neighbor, Anguilla. On St. Barts, roads carved into
the creases and folds of the landscape have Monte Carlo–style
curves and roller-coaster dips and rises. Driving these roads in a
zippy little European number, hair tousled and kurta flowing, is
almost like flying—one minute you're cruising past pastoral mead-
ows, and the next you're rounding a corkscrew cliff, with nothing
between you and the crashing sea below but a rocky promontory
and that witchy Caribbean air. Add a French-inflected reggae
soundtrack, and that, more than Manolos and 24-karat bling, is
St. Barts.

Getting There

BY PLANE   The flight from St. Maarten is just 10 minutes long,
but for many people, landing on a tiny airstrip between two volcanic hills and braking mere feet from sunbathers on the beach is
10 minutes of terror. The makeshift landing strip at St-Jean airport
on St. Barts is just 661m (2,170 ft.) long and accommodates only
STOL (short takeoff and landing) aircrafts no bigger than 19-seat-
ers. Even on these small planes, landing on St. Barts has often
been compared (and not favorably) to touching down on an aircraft
carrier. The pilot must divebomb between two mountains, then
pull up abruptly—no extra charge for the thrill ride. (In fact, any
pilot who plans to land in St. Barts is required to qualify for a special permit first.) No landings or departures are permitted after
dark.

There are no nonstop flights to St. Barts from North America. From the United States, the principal gateways are St. Maarten, St. Thomas, and Guadeloupe. Most people from the U.S. or Canada first fly into Princess Juliana International Airport in St. Maarten; for details on getting to St. Maarten, see chapter 9. From St. Maarten, **Windward Islands Airways International** (known as **Winair;** www.fly-winair.com; ✆ **866/466-0410** in the U.S. and Canada, or 590/27-61-01) offers around 10 daily flights to St. Barts. One-way passage costs around 65€ to 139€—but that figure excludes taxes and surcharges, which can nearly double the cost (including inflated fees for credit card charges). Flight duration is 10 minutes.

Our favorite carrier is **St. Barth Commuter** (www.stbarth commuter.com; ✆ **590/27-54-54**), which runs four flights Monday through Saturday (two Sun) from little L'Espérance Airport in Grand Case, St. Martin (one-way fares 65€ adults, 45€ children 2–11). It flies several times daily from St. Maarten's Princess Juliana Airport (one-way fares 75€ adults, 50€ children 2–11) on connecting flights only. Prices include taxes and surcharges.

Air Caraïbes (www.aircaraibes.com; ✆ **877/772-1005** in the U.S. and Canada, or 590/29-76-61) flights depart four or five times a day from Pointe-à-Pitre's Pôle Caraïbes Aéroport in Guadeloupe. Round-trip passage to St. Barts starts at 236€; trip time is 45 minutes.

You can bypass St. Maarten altogether by taking a Premium Scheduled Service flight (regularly scheduled first-class charter service) on **Tradewind Aviation** (www.tradewindaviation.com; ✆ **800/376-7922**) to St. Barts from San Juan, St. Thomas, and, most recently, Antigua (added in 2012 to provide easy St. Barts connections to passengers on international flights into Antigua). The flight on the 8-seater aircraft is an hour long, and round-trip cost (including taxes and surcharges) is $420 per person. Pets are welcome aboard the aircraft but must have proper documentation to enter St. Barts.

📎 Airline Advice

Always reconfirm your return flight from St. Barts with your interisland airline. If you don't, your reservation will be canceled. ***Note:*** On rare occasions, a flight will be rescheduled if the booking doesn't meet its fuel quota. Also, to be on the safe side, check your bags to your gateway connecting destination (usually St. Maarten), then take your luggage to your interisland carrier and recheck it to St. Barts.

BY BOAT For those who find the high-wire flight into St. Barts nerve-wracking, the island is easily accessible by boat. If you're transferring from the St. Maarten airport, you will need to take a 20-minute cab ride to reach the ferry ports. The high-speed **Voyager** vessels (www.voy12.com; ✆ **590/87-10-68**) make frequent (usually twice daily) runs between St. Barts and both St. Maarten (Oyster Pond) and St. Martin (Marigot Harbor). The schedule varies according to the season (and the seas). Advance reservations are highly recommended. Round-trip fares (including taxes) run around 85€ for adults and 45€ for children 2 to 12. Each passenger is allowed to carry two pieces of luggage free of charge. It's a 30-minute trip from Oyster Pond and a 1-hour trip from Marigot Harbor. If seas are choppy, the ride can be rough; it's recommended that those with weak tummies take seasickness medication before heading out or buy anti-nausea bracelets aboard the boats. *Voyager 1* is a monohull built to carry 117 passengers; the *Voyager 2* catamaran is outfitted to carry 154 passengers; and the newest Voyager vessel, *Voyager 3 Dreamliner,* is a high-speed hydrofoil catamaran with a 154-passenger capacity and a Business Class cabin on the upper deck.

The high-speed 20m (65-ft.) aluminum monohull ***Great Bay Express*** (www.greatbayferry.com; ✆ **721/542-0032** in St. Maarten) offers two or three daily 45-minute crossings between Gustavia and St. Maarten's Bobby's Marina in Philipsburg. The boat can carry 130 passengers. Reservations are essential; the round-trip fare is 90€ to 95€ adults, 45€ to 65€ children 2 to 11 years (including taxes).

Getting Around

BY TAXI Taxis meet all flights and are not terribly expensive, mostly because destinations aren't far-flung; you can get to most places in under 20 minutes. For service dial the **airport taxi stand** (✆ **590/27-75-81**) or the taxi stand at the **ferry terminal in Gustavia** (✆ **590/27-66-31**). The rates that taxis can charge have been set by the government and range from 10€ to 30€, depending on your destination. The rate from the airport to Grand Cul-de-Sac, for example, is 25€; the fare from the airport to Gustavia is 10€. Fares between 8pm and 6am, and on Sundays and holidays, are 50% higher. Call ahead for taxi service between midnight and 6am. There are taxi stands at the St-Jean airport and in Gustavia. A number of reliable taxi drivers are also listed on the official St. Barts tourism agency website under "Rentals-Taxis" (www.saintbarth-tourisme.com).

The government imposes official fares on tours by taxi as well. The tour rates for one to three passengers are generally 55€ for 30 minutes, 65€ for 60 minutes, and 80€ to 85€ for 90 minutes. For four or more passengers, add 8€ to each of the aforementioned prices.

BY RENTAL CAR   A rental car is essential in St. Barts; it's really the best way to come and go as you please. You can reserve one yourself or have your hotel rent one for you. A number of rental agencies are located at the airport, although all rental agencies offer delivery of cars straight to your hotel or villa (many resorts keep an assortment of rental cars on-site, ready to go; others, like Le Sereno, include a rental car in your resort rates). All valid foreign driver's licenses are honored. Drivers must be 25 years or older.

Cool Rentals (www.cool-rental.com; ☏ 590/27-52-58) has a wide range of rental cars, from four-door automatic-drive Kia Rios to four-wheel-drive Jimnys to snazzy convertible Mustangs and Speedsters. Its cars also come with mobile phones preprogrammed with useful numbers. Rates run from 40€ to 200€ a day, depending on the season. Also at the airport is Gumbs Car Rental (www.gumbs-car-rental.com; ☏ 590/27-75-32), a longtime island car rental company with a fleet of some 65 cars; the reasonable rates start at around 30€ a day in low season. You can pick up your car at the airport or have them drop it off at your hotel or villa.

The big chains with airport locations include Avis (www.avis-stbarth.com; ☏ 800/331-1212 in the U.S. and Canada, or 590/27-71-43); Budget (www.budget.com; ☏ 800/472-3325 in the U.S., or 590/29-62-40); Europcar (www.europcar.com; ☏ 590/27-73-33); and Hertz (www.hertzstbarth.com; ☏ 800/654-3131 in the U.S. and Canada, or 590/27-71-14). The fleet of cars includes sedans, four-wheel-drives, and convertibles; prices run from 30€ a day on up. Keep in mind that booking and paying online with these chains can save you up to 25% on your rental.

DRIVING ST. BARTS   Driving is on the right-hand side, and the island-wide speed limit is 45kmph (30mph); seatbelts are mandatory. Never drive with less than half a tank of gas on St. Barts. The island has only two gas stations: one across from the airport (8am–noon and 2–7pm) and one in Lorient (7:30am–noon and 2–5pm). Both stations are closed on Sunday, holidays, and some Thursday afternoons—and don't forget the 2-hour lunchtime closings from around noon to 2pm. The station near the airport does have a 24-hour automatic pump, but it currently accepts only French credit cards with embedded chips, not U.S. or Canadian credit cards. All of which is to say: If you have a Sunday or early Monday departure, fill 'er up on Saturday or you'll be hit with a hefty refueling charge.

Driving on St. Barts is an invigorating experience, with corkscrewing roller-coaster roads (all two-lane) and blind corners announced by signs displaying no words, just an exclamation point. Fortunately, the maximum speed limit of 45kmph (30mph) encourages drivers to go slow; unfortunately, the French gendarmes hired for 3-month stretches to patrol the island infrequently enforce the speed-limit law. Unless you're comfortable driving up and down steep hills with ease in a standard four-on-the-floor, I say opt for an automatic car. Slow down as you maneuver 90-degree curves, and don't let tailgating motorbikes and scooters push you into speeding up. Also: If you plan to park on the road, say, in St-Jean, amid tight traffic, be sure to pull in your driver's side rearview mirror, or you might find it shorn off when you return. Happy driving!

BY MOTORBIKE & SCOOTER   **Beranger Rental** rents quads and scooters from its central location on 21 rue du Général de Gaulle in Gustavia (www.beranger-rental.com; ✆ **590/27-89-00**). A helmet is provided (helmets are required), and renters must either leave an imprint of a valid credit card or pay a deposit. Rental fees vary from 20€ to 48€ per day, depending on the size of the bike and the season. Presentation of a valid driver's license is required, and renters must be 21 or older.

JOGGING/BY BICYCLE   St. Barts is by no means the ideal place to go for a jog or ride a bike along the roadside. The two-lane roads have few sidewalks and narrow-to-nonexistent shoulders, traffic can be heavy, and the topography consists largely of steep hills and curving roadways with few flat stretches. Serious joggers can use their resort fitness rooms or head to the nicely resurfaced **soccer field track** in St-Jean Carrenage (behind the St-Jean firehouse). Gustavia is also a good place to run when the traffic is light (not during rush hour).

St. Barts Calendar of Events

JANUARY

St. Barts Music Festival. The St. Barts Music Festival features a smorgasbord of musical performances, from jazz to string quartets to orchestral concerts (as well as ballet) held in the island's churches and elsewhere. Tickets are on sale in the tourism office in Gustavia. Performances are free for children 12 and under. For details go to www.stbartsmusicfestival.org. January 6–21.

FEBRUARY

Carnival/Mardi Gras. Celebrated with parties and a splashy Carnival costume parade on the streets of Gustavia, St. Barts's Mardi Gras ends with an Ash Wednesday parade to Shell Beach. February 17–22.

MARCH

St. Barth Bucket Regatta. In its 27th year, this regatta spectacular features 40 of the finest sailboats in the world, both superyachts and classic sailing vessels. For details go to www.bucketregattas.com. March 28–31.

APRIL

St. Barth Film Festival. Since 1996 the St. Barth Film Festival has celebrated "Cinéma Caraïbe"—Caribbean films and filmmakers—with this 5-day fest. For details go to www.stbarthff.org. Late April.

JULY

Summer Festival. Music is in the air on the island's summer cultural calendar, including SB Jam's Caribbean Music Festival from August 16 to 18. July and August.

AUGUST

Fete of St-Barthélemy. The island's patron saint is feted with a day of regattas, music and dancing, and fireworks on the harbor in Gustavia. August 24.

DECEMBER

Christmas Village. Local artists and artisans sell their wares from the stalls at this colorful Christmas market on Gustavia's waterfront docks. December 12–23.

BEACHES

St. Barts has some 21 white-sand beaches. Topless sunbathing is common (nudity is officially permitted on two: Saline and Gouverneur). The following are listed in clockwise order from St-Jean.

St-Jean ★★ The best known beach in St. Barts is actually two beaches cleaved by the Eden Rock promontory. (The beach to the east of the rock is calmer and ideal for small children.) A day at St-Jean is a day spent watching little planes take off from the airport runway, dining in a barefoot beach bar, and strapping on snorkel and mask and spotting turtles around the rock. Watersports and restaurants are right on the beach. A new parking lot across the street has helped alleviate beachgoers' reliance on jammed curbside parking.

Lorient Beach ★ Just to the east of St-Jean is Lorient Beach, on the island's north shore, quiet and calm, with shaded areas. An

ST. BARTHÉLEMY (ST. BARTS) Beaches 8

offshore reef tames breakers, save on the wilder western end, where locals and French surfer dudes hang out.

Marigot Bay ★ Marigot Bay, to the east of Lorient, doesn't have much of a beach, but it's a wonderful spot to snorkel in calm waters (especially around the rocks on either side). You'll see turtles and colorful marine life.

Grand Cul-de-Sac Beach ★★ A curvaceous beach ringed with hotels, restaurants, and watersports, Grand Cul-de-Sac is a shallow lagoon protected by a reef. The lagoon waters aren't great for swimming, but the breezy conditions make it ideal for wind- and kitesurfing, and snorkelers can swim out to the fringing reef for sightings of tropical fish. Coconut palms shade the shoreline.

Grand Fond ★★ Fiercely beautiful, this beach along St. Barts's "untamed" Toiny Coast is strewn with rocks and shells. Seas are rough (and currents unpredictable) and swimming is not recommended, but surfers are drawn to the reef break. On the other side of the two-lane road, a mossy green hill rises sharply; here stone walls embroider pastoral cliff sides.

Grande Saline Beach ★★ Just to the west of the Toiny Coast on the island's southern flank, Saline is one of the island's most scenic stretches of sand. This clothing-optional beach is reached by driving up the road from the commercial center in St-Jean; it's a 10-minute walk from the parking lot up and over a rocky pathway. Lack of shade doesn't deter the nude sunbathers.

Gouverneur Beach ★★ This beautiful southern beach can be reached by driving south from Gustavia to Lurin. Turn at the popular **Santa Fe** restaurant (© **590/27-61-04;** stop for drinks here on the way back to savor sensational sunset views) and head down a narrow road. The (usually) uncrowded strand is ringed by steep cliffs overlooking St. Kitts, Saba, and Statia (St. Eustacius), but there's no shade.

Shell Beach ★ This Gustavia beach is awash in lovely miniature seashells. Rocky outcroppings protect the beach from strong waves, making it a great spot for kids to play. It's also the site of popular **Dõ Brazil,** a favored lunch and dinner spot (see "Where to Eat," later in this chapter).

Public Beach ★ North of Gustavia, the rather unromantic-sounding Public Beach is a combination of sand and pebbles more popular with boaters than swimmers (this is home to the island's sailing school). There is no more beautiful place on the island, however, to watch the boats at sunset while you're having drinks at **Maya's** (see "Where to Eat," later in this chapter).

Corossol Beach ★   In the picturesque fishing village of Corossol, this beach offers a typical glimpse of French life, St. Barts style, facing a bay dotted with bobbing fishing boats. This is a calm, protected beach, with tawny -brown sand and the charming little **Shell Museum** (✆ **590/27-62-97**).

Colombier Beach ★★   A bit of a challenge to get to but well worth the effort, Colombier can be reached only by boat or by hiking a rocky goat path from Petite Anse past Flamands Beach, a 25-minute walk. The lookouts along the way are breathtaking; several adjacent coves are usually patrolled only by peacocks and mules. Shade, seclusion, and good snorkeling in smooth seas are found here—pack a lunch and spend the day. It's also known as Rockefeller's Beach: For many years David Rockefeller owned the surrounding property and blue pyramidal house (now said to belong to Harrison Ford).

Petite Anse ★   This little jewel is a 5- to 10-minute walk past Flamands. Stone steps lead down to a small rocky cove where little children can play in the clear, shallow water. Snorkeling is good in the deeper water along the rocks.

Flamands Beach ★★   The largest beach on the island is truly lovely, dotted with a handful of boutique hotels, and in some areas shaded by lantana palms. Decent-size waves make Flamands a good spot for body-surfing. The crescent of fine white sand fringed by green hills is a fetching sight from the roadway above.

OUTDOOR ACTIVITIES

If you're looking for equipment to rent, **Carib WaterPlay** (✆ **690/61-80-81**), on the sands of St-Jean Beach, rents out kayaks, windsurfers, surfboards, stand-up paddleboards, and even beach chaises (10€/day).

Deep-Sea Fishing   From March to July, deep-sea anglers catch mahimahi; in September, wahoo. Atlantic bonito, barracuda, and marlin also turn up. **Jicky Marine Service,** Gustavia Harbor (www.jickymarine.com; ✆ **590/27-70-34**), operates a 12m (40-ft.) Riviera Offshore Express outfitted for deep-sea sport fishing. A half-day trip for up to eight guests costs 1,200€, which includes fuel, snacks, open bar, and fishing equipment.

Island Excursions/Sunset Cruises   Yannis Marine, Gustavia (www.yannismarine.com; ✆ **590/29-89-12**), offers boat rentals, snorkeling trips, and island excursions. A half-day St. Barts island tour is 800€ (7–11 people; includes captain, open bar, snacks, towels, and snorkeling gear).

Kitesurfing   Kitesurfing is fast becoming one of the most popular sports here, and the best place to do it is Cul-de-Sac. Former champion Enguerrand Espinassou gives expert lessons at **7e Ciel Kitesurf School St. Barth,** at the Ouanalao Dive center (see below) on Grand Cul-de-Sac (www.saintbarthkite.com; *Ⓒ* **690/69-26-90**), open daily from 8am to 5pm. Kitesurfing costs 120€ for a 1-hour lesson, 300€ for a 3-hour lesson, 450€ for a 5-hour lesson, and 800€ for 10 hours. Reservations are recommended, especially in high season.

Sailing   Charter the beautiful *Lone Fox,* a wooden sailing yacht built in 1957, for a day of sailing, swimming, snorkeling, and exploring the St. Barts coastline. You'll have a captain and crew on board to do all the heavy lifting. The maximum number of guests is eight; a full-day charter is $2,000 (www.lonefoxcharters.com; *Ⓒ* **690/33-27-91**). Another outfitter offering cruises and private charters on sailing yachts is **Master Ski Pilou** (www.masterskipilou.com; *Ⓒ* **590/27-91-79**).

Scuba Diving   St. Barts has some 22 different dive sites scattered throughout the protected offshore Réserve Marine de St-Barth (whales are seen on the Atlantic side in winter), none more than 20 minutes from the Gustavia harbor. The most interesting include Pain de Sucre off Gustavia harbor and the remote Grouper, west of St. Barts, close to the uninhabited cay known as Ile de Forchue. **Ouanalao Dive,** Grand Cul-de-Sac (www.ouanalaodive.com; *Ⓒ* **590/27-61-37**), operates from a beach shack next to O'Corail restaurant. Catering to both beginners and advanced divers, the outfit averages three dives a day to both the Atlantic and Caribbean sides of the island. A one-tank dive for certified divers is 65€; a two-tank dive is 120€. PADI dive courses are available for both adults and kids 10 to 14 years of age. Other recommended PADI-certified scuba outfitters are **Plongée Caraïbes** (www.plongee-caraibes.com; *Ⓒ* **590/27-70-34;** five-dive package 280€); and **St. Barth Plongée,** Gustavia (www.st-barth-plongee.com; *Ⓒ* **690/41-96-66;** five-dive package 315€).

Snorkeling   Hundreds of shallow areas right off beaches such as Anse des Cayes teem with colorful aquatic life. You can also test your luck at hundreds of points offshore. **Jicky Marine Service,** Gustavia Harbor (www.jickymarine.com; *Ⓒ* **590/27-70-34**), runs daily snorkeling excursions to places like Colombier Beach or offshore islands like Ile de Forchue. Half- and full-day group excursions aboard a 13m (42-ft.) catamaran, including snacks, open bar, all equipment, and exploration of two separate snorkeling sites, costs from 72€ per person. They also rent snorkeling gear and can direct you to good snorkeling sites.

8

Outdoor Activities

Surfing   Beach clubs rent out equipment for surfing St. Barts's main beaches, including Anse des Cayes, Toiny, Miliou, and Lorient. Contact the **Reefer Surf Club** (✆ **690/76-84-70**).

SHOPPING

St. Barts offers duty-free liquor and French perfumes at some of the lowest prices in the Caribbean—often cheaper than in France itself. You'll find fairly good buys, albeit a limited selection, in haute couture, crystal, porcelain, watches, and other luxuries. Gustavia's **rue de la République** is lined with designer boutiques, including Bulgari, Cartier, Giorgio Armani, Louis Vuitton, and Hermès.

Aside from Gustavia, St-Jean is the island's center of shopping action, with small boutique-y shopping plazas along the main road leading toward Lorient: **Les Galeries du Commerce, La Villa Creole, La Sodexa,** and **L'Espace Neptune,** each filled with small boutiques. Some find St-Jean a more satisfying shopping experience than Gustavia, less of the chillingly pricey luxury brands and more of the St. Barts clothing visitors covet: flirty bohemian-style kurtas and gypsy dresses; sexy, slouchy jersey separates in dusky tones; and gold and silver sandals or bejeweled flip-flops. **La Savane Commercial Center,** across from the airport, has grocery stores, an electronics store, and a handful of boutiques.

As for island crafts, the little old ladies from the fishing village of Corossol have traditionally made intricately braided **straw goods** ★ (baskets, bags, and bonnets) from the dried fronds of the latanier palm. These delicately woven crafts are for sale along the harborside Quai in Gustavia.

Keep in mind that most shopkeepers open around 9 or 10am but close midday for an extended *dejeuner* (lunch) that may last until 2 or 3pm. Closing times are generally 7pm.

Bijoux de la Mer ★   The distinctive, custom-made leather-cord necklaces dripping with Tahitian black pearls sold at this family-owned jewelry store are de rigueur for the cognoscenti on St. Barts. Look also for leather strands strung with seed pearls and colored seaglass. Rue de la République, Gustavia. www.bijouxdelamerstbarths.com. ✆ **590/52-37-68.**

Goldfinger   This is the largest purveyor of luxury goods on St. Barts. The entire second floor is devoted to perfumes and crystal, the street level to jewelry and watches. Prices are usually 15% to 20% less than equivalent retail goods sold stateside. Rue de France, Gustavia. ✆ **590/27-64-66.**

Soldes!

Some folks time their travels to St. Barts to hit **soldes**—the French-decreed **officially designated sales seasons**—twice a year, generally the month of May and from mid-October to mid-November. Much of everything is deeply discounted, including couture, jewelry, and shoes, so expect to find great deals during these times. The fall soldes offers particularly dramatic discounts, as shopkeepers attempt to sweep out the old to stock stores for the upcoming high season.

La Ligne St. Barth ★ The laboratory/shop sells the famed scents and skin-care products still produced on-site by the Brins family, island residents since the 17th century. Brewed from the extracts of native Caribbean fruits and flowers, Ligne St Barth products include sun creams and sunscreens (Solaire) made with oils produced from the tropical roucou tree (a natural insect repellent). *Tip:* The shop offers deep discounts on slightly imperfect lotions, creams, and more during the sales seasons. Rte. de Saline, Lorient. www.lignestbarth.com. ✆ 590/27-82-63.

Le Comptoir du Cigare This place caters to the December-to-April crowd of villa and yacht owners. It's sheathed in exotic hardwood and enhanced with a glass-sided, walk-in humidor storing thousands of cigars from Cuba and the Dominican Republic. Note to Americans: Smoke the Cubans on the island—it's illegal to bring them back to the United States. There's also a collection of silver ornaments, lighters, pens suitable for adorning the desk of a CEO, artisan-quality **Panama hats** from Ecuador, and cigar boxes and humidors. 6 rue du Général de Gaulle, Gustavia. www.comptoirducigare. com. ✆ 590/27-50-62.

Les Artisans This top gallery specializes in fanciful crafts and custom jewelry. It can also arrange visits to ateliers of leading local artists in various media (names to watch include Robert Danet, Jackson Questel, and Hannah Moser). Rue du Général de Gaulle, Gustavia. ✆ 590/27-50-40.

Lili Belle ★ This little shop in St-Jean sells stylish *prêt-à-porter* clothing from such beloved Parisian designers as Isabel Marant and Claudi Pierlot. Look for big discounts during the sales seasons. Le Pélican Plage, St-Jean. ✆ 590/87-46-14.

Linde Gallery ★★ The fabulous collection of must-haves includes vintage Pucci and Alaîa, elegantly stylish *prêt-à-porter* (modern Pucci, Rick Owens, Linde collection), vintage Courrèges and Yves St. Laurent sunglasses from the 1970s and 1980s, Melissa shoes, Steidl artbooks, objets d'art, and more. The rigorously curated clothes, including silk tunics and printed caftans, are beautifully wearable. A smaller second shop is located in the **Hotel Christopher,** in Point Milou. Les Hauts du Carré d'Or, Gustavia. www.lindegallery.com. ℭ **590/29-73-86.**

Lolita Jaca ★   Flirty and ethereal, with more than a nod to "hippie chic" styling and East Indian patterning, Lolita Jaca outfits the quintessentially sexy St. Barts femme in soft, candy-hued satins and silks. Les Hauts du Carré d'Or, Gustavia. www.lolitajaca.com. ℭ **590/27-59-98.**

Made in St-Barth   The MADE IN ST-BARTH logo is everywhere here: on T-shirts, pants, dresses, baby clothes, bags, purses, you name it. Villa Créole, St-Jean. ℭ **590/27-56-57.**

Mademoiselle Hortense   After I expressed my admiration for the effortlessly chic ensembles worn by a stylish St. Barts hostess, she had two words to say: "Mademoiselle Hortense." Look for short dresses in pretty florals and stretchy miniskirts. Rue de la République, Gustavia. ℭ **590/27-13-29.**

Pain de Sucre   Inside this Creole house across from St-Jean Beach is a collection of stylish bikinis and beachwear in eye-catching prints and florals. It also has a small collection of darling matching swimsuits for little girls. Pélican Plage, St-Jean. www.paindesucre.com. ℭ **590/29-30-79.**

Poupette St Barth ★   This little pastel-hued boutique offers hippie-goddess dresses, kurtas, and blouses in meltingly soft fabrics and embroidered designs (floral, Art Nouveau). The Gustavia store also has mini versions of the ladies' frocks for little girls. Poupette now has a second location in the Hotel Taïwana on Flamands. Rue de la République, Gustavia. www.poupette-st-barth.com. ℭ **590/27-94-49.**

Stéphane & Bernard ★★   For nearly 30 years, this has been the couture playground of Stéphane Lanson and Bernard Blancaneau, who have stocked their salon to the rafters with the latest handpicked Leger, Versace, and Missoni creations. Rue de la République, Gustavia. www.stephaneandbernard.com. ℭ **590/27-65-69.**

Un Dimanche à la Mer ★   This charming little toy shop in St-Jean (next door to Andy's Hideaway) is an ode to youthful whimsy, packed with sturdy and imaginative European-made toys and games. Closed Sun. Centre Vaval, St-Jean. ℭ **590/27-56-13.**

ENTERTAINMENT & NIGHTLIFE

Many visitors consider a sunset aperitif followed by dinner under the stars enough of a nocturnal adventure. Beyond that, the lounge and live music scenes are most active in high season.

Dõ Brazil ★ Overlooking Shell Beach, this popular bar and cafe is a great place to hang out after a swim and toast to the day's end with a sunset cocktail. Shell Beach, Gustavia. www.dobrazil.com. ✆ **590/29-06-66.**

Le Bête à Z'Ailes ★ Le Bête à Z'Ailes (also known as the Baz Bar) is a sushi bar and live music club on the Gustavia harbor, where an eclectic assortment of bands play soul, jazz, blues, urban folk, and indie tunes accompanied by excellent fusion food. Gustavia. ✆ **590/92-74-09.**

Le Select ★ This 50-year-old institution is named after its more famous granddaddy in the Montparnasse section of Paris. It's a glorified shanty, though most patrons congregate at tables in the open-air garden (called "Cheeseburgers in Paradise" in homage to honorary St. Barthian Jimmy Buffett), where a game of dominoes might be under way as you walk in. Closed Sunday. Rue de la France, Gustavia. ✆ **590/27-86-87.**

Le Ti St. Barth ★ Draped in red, this charmingly sexy "Caribbean tavern" is set in a pitched-roof Creole-style cottage. The young and nubile model in a fashion show nightly at 11pm in high season (you can buy the clothes modeled in the Le Ti St. Barth shop), and a dinner show, Le Cabaret, takes place on Tuesday, Wednesday, and Thursday. Pointe Milou. www.letistbarth.com. ✆ **590/27-97-71.**

WHERE TO EAT

Fueled by French chefs and hotel dining rooms that keep ratcheting up the excellence quotient, the St. Barts dining scene is among the best in the Caribbean. It's also really, really expensive, and prized tables are often booked along with hotel reservations in high season. But you can eat very well at more casual beachfront, hilltop, and harborside restaurants that aren't quite so heart-stoppingly pricey. Many of the island's most popular spots offer an affordable and filling lunchtime *plat du jour* (daily special) for 10€ to 12€. Restaurants offering plats du jour include the **Wall House** in Gustavia and the **Hideaway** in St-Jean.

Note: Entrée is the French term for appetizer; *plat* means main course.

What was once three local guides to eating, staying, and playing in St. Barts has been consolidated into one hefty paperback
tome—and it's free and available in most hotels and restaurants.
The bilingual *Saint-Barth Collector Guestbook* is an excellent
resource for visitors, largely for its comprehensive restaurant
and *traiteur* (takeout) menus. It also has maps and contact info
for hotels, villas, shopping, tour operators, and services.

I've categorized restaurants on St. Barts by neighborhood rather
than price range, as most fall into the same (unfortunately high)
price category. Virtually all the restaurants on St. Barts include a
15% service charge (*service compris*). Keep in mind that most St.
Barts restaurants close in September and October.

In Gustavia

At press time diners were raving about the delicious and not unrea-
sonably priced brasserie fare at casual, comfortable **Côté Port,** rue
Jeanne d'Arc (📞 **590/87-79-54**), on the Gustavia harborfront.
Look for seafood prepared with French flair, like the *gambas*
(shrimp) with curry sauce and vegetables, and big, fresh salads.

Bonito Saint Barth ★★ FRENCH/LATIN In 2009, La Man-
dala was transformed into the blue-and-white-hued Bonito, with a
saucy ceviche bar and magical harbor views. It's carried on a big
love affair with locals and visitors alike ever since. White is the new
black here, where creamy white tablecloths and painted white
wicker are nicely offset by blue-and-white pillows. A candlelit
lounge with nightly DJs has ramped up the hipness quotient. The
location alone—a house on Gustavia's steepest street with a dining
deck overlooking a swimming pool and the glittering harbor
below—is spellbinding.

Rue Lubin Brin. http://ilovebonito.com. 📞 **590/27-96-96.** Reservations recommended. Main courses 29€–40€. MC, V. Thurs–Tues 7–11pm. Lounge
6pm–1am.

Dõ Brazil ★ FRENCH/BRAZILIAN/ASIAN FUSION This
rambling two-tiered spot overlooking Shell Beach is the place to go
for a sunset cocktail—and in high season a fizzy energy kicks in
during the cocktail hour. The food is creative and quite good, and
the nightly 35€ prix fixe is an excellent value. For an even more
casual experience, dine on the restaurant's beach level at **Dõ Brazil
Snack,** where you can order sandwiches and salads from 10am on.

Shell Beach. www.dobrazil.com. ☎ **590/29-06-66.** Reservations recommended. Main courses 25€–35€. AE, MC, V. Daily noon–10:30pm.

Eddy's ★ 🔥 CREOLE   For some 15 years, charismatic Eddy Stackelborough has satisfied in-the-know locals and regulars with simple but honest island fare (green papaya salad, shrimp curry, barbecued ribs, chicken in coconut sauce, passion-fruit mousse). The setting resembles a Caribbean translation of *The Secret Garden:* a jungle garden hidden behind a rustic stone wall. It's a miracle how Eddy keeps prices affordable by most standards.

Rue du Centenaire (near rue Général de Gaulle). ☎ **590/27-54-17.** Reservations not accepted. Main courses 15€–22€. No credit cards. Mon–Sat 7–10pm.

La Route des Boucaniers ★ FRENCH/CREOLE   Having written a five-volume primer, owner/chef Francis Delage is considered an authority on Creole cuisine. The decor here evokes a rum shack—there's even a boat wreck—and the fare is simple but hearty. The restaurant has a prime perch overlooking Gustavia harbor. The menu offers such tempting dishes as spiny lobster and pumpkin bisque, coq au vin de Bourgogne, sea scallops and shrimp with crispy risotto and passion-fruit sauce, and a traditional West Indian chicken Colombo curry with Creole sauce. The *assiete Creole* (spicy Caribbean platter) is a tasty seafood mélange of codfish fritters, conch gratin, marinated bonito puff pastry of crab, and a *feroce d'avocat* (a codfish and avocado dish).

Rue de Bord de Mer. ☎ **590/27-73-00.** Reservations required in winter. Main courses 20€–28€. AE, MC, V. Tues–Sat 10am–10pm.

L'Isola ★ ITALIAN   Classic Italian food is served up in the elegant environs of this whitewashed Creole cottage in Gustavia. It's a chic and celebratory spot, brought to the tropics by a Santa Monica restaurateur. Look for well-prepared trattoria favorites (at five-star prices): Caprese with fresh buffalo mozzarella, fritto misto, fettucine Bolognese, mushroom risotto, and côte de veau.

Rue de Roi Oscar II. www.lisolastbarth.com. ☎ **590/51-00-05.** Reservations required in winter. Main courses 25€–45€. AE, MC, V. Daily 6–11pm.

Wall House ★★ 🔥 FRENCH/CREOLE   The Wall House continues its traditions of warm ambience and solid bistro fare at reasonable prices. The dazzling harbor views certainly don't hurt. Owners Bernard and Julien Tatin are friendly, gracious hosts. The menu retains a lively mix of ingredients and influences: Look for a new emphasis on steak—USDA-certified prime Angus beef, thank you very much—and a deft touch with seafood, on display in the lemon-grass-skewered, citrus-marinated mahimahi or the

TRAITEURS: GOURMET FOOD
to go

St. Barts can be so expensive that many visitors often go the epicurean takeout route at one of the gourmet traiteurs on the island. These traiteurs go way beyond the classic French picnic fare of bread, cheese, and a bottle of wine: This is highfalutin grub, or at the very least an incredibly tasty takeout repast, perfect for a midday beach picnic or a candlelit dinner on your hotel balcony or villa terrace. **La Rôtisserie,** in St-Jean ((🕿) 590/29-75-69), is a *boulangerie, pâtisserie,* bakery, and more, selling wine, mustard, pâté, herbs, caviar, chocolate, and exotic oils and vinegars, as well as takeout plats du jour from pâtés to *pissaladières* (onion tarts); the store is open daily 6am to 8pm. Also in St-Jean are two other highly recommended traiteurs. **Maya's To Go** (www. mayastogo.com; (🕿) 590/29-83-70), across from the airport, is operated by the famed island restaurateurs behind Maya's (p. 145) and offers such takeout specialties as shrimp and avocado salad, sesame chicken noodles, ceviche, tuna tataki, meatloaf sandwiches, and more. It's open Tuesday to Sunday 7am to 7pm. American-born I. B. Charneau named **Kiki-é Mo** (www. kikiemo.com; (🕿) 590/27-90-65) after sons Keefer and Marlon. It channels the Italian *salumerias* of her Short Hills, New Jersey, childhood with pizzas, pastas, and panini—and great espresso. It's open daily 8am to 9pm.

In Gustavia, order good pizza day or night at **L'Entr'acte,** boulevard Bord du Mer ((🕿) 590/27-70-11). The snack bar **Le Bouchon,** in L'Oasis shopping complex in Lorient ((🕿) 590/27-79-39), serves pizzas, paninis, and sandwiches to go or to dine in at its covered cafe; it's open 9am to 10pm. For basic supplies and groceries, St. Barts has a number of supermarkets with good selections of imported French wine, cheeses, and bread (bring your own recyclable bag to grocery-shop). The largest, the **Marché-U supermarket** (which replaced the old Match), is located directly across from the airport; it's open on Sundays. For quality meats, an excellent butcher shop, **Boucherie St-Jean,** is located across from the Villa Creole shops in St-Jean ((🕿) 590/29-68-42).

Asian-tinged tuna tataki. The lunchtime plats du jours (10€–12€) are excellent values. The Wall House stays open year-round.

La Pointe. www.wallhouserestaurant.com. (🕿) **590/27-71-83.** Reservations recommended. Main courses 18€–28€. AE, MC, V. Daily noon–2:30pm and 7–10pm.

In the Flamands Area

In 2012 the upscale Italian restaurant **PaCri** (📞 590/29-35-63) moved to a sleek beachfront space in the newly revitalized Taïwana Hotel on Flamands Beach. It offers an updated Italian menu that is both flavorful and chillingly overpriced, even for St. Barts.

More reasonably priced lunch and dinner choices in Flamands include **La Langouste** (📞 590/27-63-61; open daily), which offers French/Creole specialties and fresh lobster in a casual, candlelit seaside setting by the pool at the Baie des Anges hotel. More casual still is **Chez Rolande's Wishing Well** (📞 590/27-51-42; closed Sun), which serves traditional Creole cuisine from a roadside shack shaded by almond trees and palms; garden seating is available.

La Case de l'Isle ★★ FRENCH   Set on a breezy oceanfront promenade, the house restaurant at the Isle de France hotel has a setting so lyrical that the food is almost beside the point. Except of course, as with everything else at the Ile de France, the menu has been carefully sourced and the food impeccably prepared. The famous Isle de France pea soup tastes like spring, and fish preparations are works of art. As dreamy as it is to dine here under the stars, La Case de l'Isle is an even better choice for a **beachside lunch ★★**. The lunch selections are ethereally light and flavorful, and you can make a day of it on the blinding white sands of Flamands. Order the state-of-the-art gazpacho and a crab and quinoa tabouleh, and thank your lucky stars.

Hotel St. Barth Isle de France, Flamands Beach. 📞 **590/27-61-81.** Reservations recommended. Main courses 28€–45€. AE, MC, V. Daily 7–10:30am, noon–2:30pm, and 7–9:30pm.

In the Grande Saline Beach Area

Note that the popular French/Creole bistro **Le Tamarin** closed in spring 2012.

Le Grain de Sel ★ FRENCH/CREOLE   Set against a rocky outcropping on a wooden deck overlooking the old salt ponds of Saline, Grain de Sel has a sun-dappled, treehouse appeal. It's a casual place that's popular with locals, but the crowd is mixed, with families, hipsters, and beachgoers tucking into well-priced Creole classics. The seafood is well prepared, and you can't go wrong with the shrimp, here grilled on kabobs with a buttery herb sauce or swimming in a heady beer sauce. Local fish is grilled or cooked in a tomatoey Creole sauce. Entrees come with traditional rice and peas.

Plage de Saline. 📞 **590/52-46-05.** Reservations recommended. Main courses 19€–28€. MC, V. Daily 9am–4pm and 7–10:30pm.

In the Grand Cul-de-Sac Area

A casual beachside favorite, **O'Corail Restaurant** ★ (© 590/29-33-27) serves breakfast and lunch on the sands between Le Sereno and La Gloriette in front of the Ouanalao Dive shop. It has terrific views out over the bay at Grand Cul-de-Sac, and fresh, tasty food, from burgers to lobster salad to Creole classics. It's open for breakfast and lunch Tuesday to Sunday.

Pizza lovers can head to **La Gloriette** (© 590/29-85-71), next door to O'Corail overlooking the lagoon at Grand Cul-de-Sac. It serves a lunchtime menu of thin-crust pizzas, calzones, and salads. Pizzas range from classic margherita to their version of Napoletana (tomato, mozzarella, anchovies, olives, and capers) to a "Far West" version, with tomato, mozzarella, Angus ground beef, egg, onions, and Emmental cheese.

Bartoloméo ★★ FRENCH/MEDITERRANEAN Even though it's located inside one of the island's most exclusive hotels, Guanahani, Bartoloméo manages to feel warm, informally sophisticated, and gracefully upscale. It's a lovely setting, half inside a Creole cottage under a lime wainscoted ceiling and half outside on a gaily lighted wooden deck with tables under big umbrellas beneath the blue-black sky. Cream-colored walls are romantically lit. The food is impeccable. If you want seafood, try marinated and herb-scented escabèche of fish, shellfish, and baby vegetables; for meat-lovers, there's juicy suckling veal filet. Starters include beet-root gnocchi or an inspired quail risotto. If it's on the menu, order the spaghetti with clams: It comes to the table tangled in sprigs of dill and sprays of white foam, as if it had washed up right out of the sea.

Hôtel Guanahani, Grand Cul-de-Sac. © **590/27-66-60.** Reservations recommended, especially for nonguests. Main courses 32€–44€. AE, DC, MC, V. Daily 7–10pm.

Le Restaurant des Pêcheurs ★★ FRENCH/SEAFOOD The house restaurant at Le Sereno resort is a lively spot during the day, but at night it takes on a romantic tenor. The liberally spaced seating is good for privacy-loving diners, and the sea breezes are a briny aphrodisiac. The food doesn't disappoint, and there's a deft hand in the kitchen, but it's pricey for what is essentially a fishhouse—though what a fishhouse! The menu features a catch of the day, both local (29€) and imported Atlantic/Mediterranean (45€). The salt-crusted fish is a revelation, with layers of meaty flavors. The starters include a flavorful gazpacho and braised sea scallops in lemon-grass butter. The restaurant makes a classic bouillabaisse every Friday.

Le Sereno hotel, Grand Cul-de-Sac. ℂ **590/29-83-00.** Reservations recommended, especially for nonguests. Main courses 29€–47€. AE, MC, V. Daily 7am–10:30pm.

In Pointe Milou

The intriguing menus at the two house restaurants in the newly opened **Hotel Christopher** are worth the drive along the daredevil curves in Pointe Milou. The open-to-the-sea **Taino** ★ offers a French-Caribbean "ingredients cuisine," using sustainably sourced local seafood whenever possible. Lunch is served in barefoot style at **Mango** ★, a 60-seat spot in the sand offering an earthy *"cuisine de bonne femme."*

In the Public Beach Area

Maya's ★★ INTERNATIONAL   This beachfront restaurant just northwest of Gustavia remains the island's premier stargazing (in both senses) spot, thanks to its artful simplicity and preferential treatment for regulars. The rebuilt Antillean house attracts crowds of luminaries from the worlds of media, fashion, and entertainment. It's the kind of *pieds dans l'eau* (feet in the water), picnic-table-on-the-beach French Creole place you might find on Guadeloupe, where its chef, Maya Beuzelin-Gurley, grew up. Maya stresses "clean, simple" food with few adornments other than island herbs and lime juice. You might follow cold avocado soup with lobster with grilled fish in a Creole sauce or a chicken satay. Almost no cream is used in any dish, further endearing the place to its sleek and slender clientele. Views face west and south, ensuring glorious sunset watching.

Public Beach. ℂ **590/27-75-73.** Reservations required in winter. Main courses 33€–38€. AE, MC, V. Mon–Sat 6–10pm.

In the St-Jean Beach Area

The Eden Rock Hotel has two excellent dining choices: The breathtakingly expensive **On the Rocks** ★, serving dinner in a splendid spot high above St-Jean Beach; and the **Sand Bar** ★, open for lunch down on the beach. Call ℂ **590/29-79-99** for reservations.

The Hideaway ★ 🍴 INTERNATIONAL   How can you not embrace a place that advertises "corked wine, warm beer, lousy food, view of the car park" with a staff "hand-picked from the sleaziest dives, mental institutions, and top-security prisons?" Savvy locals and celebrity regulars know that the sound system, food, and prices rock at the beloved haunt nicknamed Chez Andy after Brit owner Andrew Hall. Worthy specialties include shrimp Creole, pastas, and respectable thin-crust pizzas from the wood-burning oven. Andy will finish off your evening (and you) with a bottomless carafe of free vanilla or orange rum.

Vaval Center, St-Jean. www.hideaway.tv. ℰ **590/27-63-62.** Reservations recommended. Main courses 15€–24€. AE, MC, V. Tues–Fri noon–2pm and 7–10pm; Sat–Sun 7–10pm.

La Plage ★ SEAFOOD/FRENCH   This feet-in-the-sand beach bar has been an instant island classic since it opened, with rich tropical colors and comfortable lounges. Tables spill out onto the St-Jean sand under the starry sky. Expect a lively, welcoming scene, with DJ-spun music—but also expect a relaxed vibe and solid food. Dine on grilled fish and lobster, and island-inspired flavors.

TomBeach Hotel, St-Jean. ℰ **590/27-53-13.** Reservations recommended. Main courses 18€–40€. AE, MC, V. Daily 7:30–11am, noon–2:30pm, and 7pm–midnight.

At Morne Lurin

Santa Fe ★ FRENCH/CREOLE/HAMBURGERS   This informal restaurant is a local favorite and set inland atop one of the highest points on the island, overlooking Gouverneur Beach, which makes it a prime spot for watching legendary sunsets from wraparound decks. For decades this place was known as a good burger joint. It still serves a great burger, but the rest of the menu has headed upmarket, specializing in French and Creole dishes along with barbecued meats and fresh fish. In addition to the catch of the day, opt for coq au vin or a saucy lobster thermidor.

Morne Lurin. ℰ **590/27-61-04.** Reservations not accepted. Main courses 16€–35€. MC, V. Thurs–Tues 7–11pm.

In the Toiny Coast Area

Le Gaïac ★★★ FRENCH   This swooningly romantic restaurant is for folks who want to dine among the rich and famous at Le Toiny, one of St. Barts's most expensive hotels. Here's the shocker: You don't have to be rich *or* famous to get the restaurant's seamless, pampered service. You dine in an open-air pavilion adjacent to the resort's infinity pool, with a view that sweeps out over the blue-black Toiny Coast. Lunchtime menu items—an elegant red-tuna tart, perhaps, or a curried prawn wrap—are simple yet exquisitely prepared, and the sumptuous "Le Brunch du Toiny" (45€; 11am–2:30pm) is a must. Dinner courses might include a lighter-than-air tuna and salmon tartar with wheatberries. For your main course, try bacon-roasted lobster on artichoke puree or roasted Iberian pork served in a potato bread crust. A Tuesday night Fishmarket Menu lets you pick out a fresh filet—which is then lightly grilled—and your choice of sauce, whether a creamy tomato or an old-fashioned *moutarde*. It's all first-rate, from the food to the setting to the silky-smooth service.

Hôtel Le Toiny, Anse de Toiny. ☏ **590/27-88-80.** Reservations recommended in winter. Main courses 20€–29€ lunch, 30€–40€ dinner. AE, DC, MC, V. Daily noon–2:30pm and 7–10pm.

WHERE TO STAY

St. Barts has some 30 boutique hotels—no megaresorts and no chains. The largest property on the island is the 67-unit Guanahani Resort. Hotels and inns throughout the island, with some exceptions, tend to be expensive, and a service charge of between 10% and 15% is usually added to your bill (a 5% government room tax is tacked onto the final bill or built into the hotel rates). If you're looking for ways to cut costs, consider visiting in the shoulder or

RENTING A VILLA IN ST. BARTS

If you choose to rent a villa in St. Barts instead of going the hotel route, you won't be alone. St. Barts has some 500 **villas, beach houses, and apartments** for rent by the week or month. Villas are dotted in and around the island's hills—very few are on the beach. Instead of an oceanfront bedroom, you get a panoramic view and hillside breezes. Rentals, priced in U.S. dollars, can range from a one-room "studio" villa away from the beach for $980 per week in off season, up to $40,000 per week for a minipalace at Christmas. Most rentals average between $2,500 and $4,000 a week in the high season between mid-December and mid-April, with discounts of 30% to 50% the rest of the year. One of the best agencies to contact for villa, apartment, or condo rentals is **St. Barth Properties,** 12 Washington St., Ste. 201, Franklin, MA 02038 (www.stbarth.com; ☏ **800/421-3396** or 508/528-7727 in the U.S. and Canada). Peg Walsh, a longtime aficionado of St. Barts, and her capable son, Tom Smyth, will let you know what's available. She can also make arrangements for car rentals and air travel to St. Barts and even book babysitters and restaurant reservations. Another good option, with 250 villa properties to rent, is **Wimco** (www.wimco.com; P.O. Box 1481, Newport, RI 02840; ☏ **800/449-1553** in the U.S., or 401/849-8012). With 200 luxury villas to choose from, St. Barts–based **Sibarth Villa Rentals** (www.sibarth.com; La Maison Suedoise, 37 rue Samuel Fahlberg, Gustavia 97133; ☏ **888/334-7609** in the U.S., or 590/29-88-90) has a top-notch concierge offering services from arranging car rentals to grocery deliveries to chef services.

low seasons. Off-season rates plummet and may include a rental car for stays of a week or more. In March it's difficult to find a place to stay on St. Barts unless you've made reservations far in advance, but during May or June you may have the run of the place. (Most properties close altogether around Sept–Oct.) Look for terrific off-season packages on hotel websites.

Very Expensive

Carl Gustaf ★★★   The "Goose," as it's affectionately known, has always been *the* spot for sunset cocktails. Presiding over the town's harbor from a steep hillside, Gustavia's hotel has ratcheted up the 21st-century glam factor, with a modern restaurant and bar, a state-of-the-art spa, and a four-bedroom suite, the 241½-square-meter (2,600-square-foot) Royale Suite. Each of the hotel's 14 suites is in one of a dozen pink or green, red-roofed villas. Access to each building is via a central staircase. The wood-frame units are angled for maximum views of the boats bobbing far below in the bay and panoramic sunsets, best enjoyed from the plunge pool on the private patio bisecting each suite. Bedrooms are exceedingly well furnished: You'll feel like a pasha as you walk across Italian marble floors under a pitched ceiling to reach your luxurious bed. Shell Beach is a 5-minute downhill hike. In the on-site restaurant **Victoria's,** chef Emmanuel Motte has revitalized the classic French kitchen.

Rue des Normands, 97099 Gustavia, St. Barthélemy, F.W.I. www.hotelcarl gustaf.com. © **800/322-2223** in the U.S., or 590/29-79-00. Fax 590/27-82-37. 14 units. Winter 1,010€–3,850€ suite; off season 490€–2,900€ suite. Extra person 100€/night. Rates include continental breakfast and round-trip airport transfers. AE, MC, V. **Amenities:** Restaurant; bar; outdoor pool; room service; sauna; spa; watersports equipment (extensive). *In room:* A/C, TV/DVD, CD player, fridge, hair dryer, kitchen (Royale Suite only), kitchenette (1- and 2-bedroom suites), minibar (Spa Suite only), MP3 docking station, private plunge pools, Wi-Fi (free).

Eden Rock ★★★   Greta Garbo checked in as Suzy Schmidt for a 3-day holiday but ended up staying 3 weeks. That was eons ago, but this legendary hotel still exerts a magnetic pull for the rich and fabulous. Eden Rock occupies the most spectacular site on St. Barts, a quartzite promontory cleaving St-Jean Bay into two white-sand crescents. When the French aviator Remy de Haenen paid an old woman $200 for the land some 60 years ago, she ridiculed him for paying too much.

Owners David and Jane Spencer Matthews continue to reinvent Eden Rock as one of the Caribbean's most glamorous addresses, where even celebrities people-watch. The attention to detail here is unparalleled. The individually decorated accommodations either climb the rock or are perched steps from the water on either side. The original "Rock" rooms are stuffed with antiques, family heirlooms, silver fixtures, steamer trunks, and four-poster beds. Eight suites with decks open onto the beach, and five one- to three-bedroom beach houses have outdoor Jacuzzis and plunge pools (two have full swimming pools). The **Howard Hughes Suite,** atop the Main House on "the rock," features hardwood floors, three verandas offering 360-degree panoramas, and two bathrooms clad in welded copper. The luxury **Villa Nina** has two bedrooms and its very own art gallery, a private pool, and a beachside location. The beachside **Rockstar Suite** is a 1,486-sq.-m (16,000-sq.-ft.) stunner with four master suites, a screening room, a fully equipped recording studio, a pool table, and a private pool.

Eden Rock's two restaurants have developed menus in a culinary partnership with internationally acclaimed chef Jean-Georges Vongerichten. For lunch head to the casual beachfront **Sand Bar.** Dinner (and people-watching) is served up at the swanky **On the Rocks,** where you can dine overlooking the glittering curve of St-Jean Beach. The **Eden Rock Gallery,** located right off the beach, usually has a barefoot artist-in-residence noodling around on a canvas in the studio or on the beach.

Baie de St-Jean, 97133 St. Barthélemy, F.W.I. www.edenrockhotel.com. ℰ **855/333-6762** in the U.S. and Canada, or 590/29-79-99. Fax 590/27-88-37. 33 units. Winter 715€–1,125€ double, 1,365€–2,575€ suite, 2,235€ and up beach houses and beach villas; off season 505€–665€ double, 805€–1,715€ suite, 1,450€ and up beach houses and beach villas. Extra person: 125€ (free 5 and under). Rates include VIP airport transfers and buffet breakfast. AE, MC, V. Closed Aug 29–Oct 17. **Amenities:** 2 restaurants; bar; babysitting; fitness center; room service; watersports activities. *In room:* A/C, TV/DVD, hair dryer, kitchen (in some), MP3 docking station, minibar (in some), private plunge pools (in some), Wi-Fi (free).

Hôtel Guanahani and Spa ★★★ ☺ St. Barts's largest hotel would be a gem of a small boutique hotel anywhere else. Don't let its casual good nature fool you: Guanahani defines excellence. This resort enjoys a spectacular setting on its own peninsula with two palm-fringed beaches, one fronting the protected shallows of Grand Cul-de-Sac lagoon, and a smaller one girding the frothy Atlantic. The property is bracketed to the west by Marigot Bay; you can dive off a hotel dock for good snorkeling. The low-rise, intimately scaled resort of gaily painted Creole cottages spills down a lush hillside to Grand Cul-de-Sac Beach, where the daily action is. You can settle in on a lounger beneath a straw *palapa*, have a barefoot lunch beneath a grove of coconut palms, or noodle around on a stand-up paddleboard.

The decor throughout is fresh, modern, and colorful—sunny, pastel-hued tropical interiors that manage to avoid tropical resort clichés. The lobby alone is a rich mélange of teal walls, pink and orange furniture, and blue trim—a pleasing Creole palette grounded in earthy wood. Of the resort's 67 rooms, 35 are suites—and 14 of these have private pools. Eight suites and villas have butler service. Among the free-standing villas, the **Garden House** villa is spacious and utterly private, with three bedrooms and a private pool. The two restaurants, airy, alfresco **Indigo** and **Bartoloméo** (p. 144), offer creative Continental cuisine. Guanahani is a children's playground, with a staffed **Kids' Club** (daily 9am–5pm) and that green lagoon to play in—pedal boats stand ready for watery adventures. Sharing the grounds are lounging cats, lizards, and red-footed tortoises. The celebrated **Clarins Spa ★** is simply first-rate, with its own good-size swimming pool. Up above the spa is the Caribbean equivalent of a Parisian garret: The **Wellness Suite** has nearly 360-degree views of Grand Cul-de-Sac, an outdoor shower with a beautiful pebbled floor, and a stone sink that's practically primal—you step on a button on the floor and water spills out as if from a hillside cataract.

Note: The resort's terraced layout may not be ideal for those with mobility problems.

Grand Cul-de-Sac, 97133 St. Barthélemy, F.W.I. www.leguanahani.com. *☏* **800/216-3774** in the U.S., or 590/27-66-60. Fax 590/27-70-70. 67 units. Winter 646€–1,050€ double, 1,200€–4,360€ suite/villa; off season 390€–656€ double, 786€–2,860€ suite/villa. Extra person 100€/night. Rates include full American breakfast and round-trip airport transfers. AE, MC, V. Closed Aug 27–Nov 15. **Amenities:** 2 restaurants; 3 bars; babysitting; butler services (villas only); children's programs; concierge; fitness center; horseback riding; Jacuzzi; 2 outdoor pools; room service; spa; 2 tennis courts; watersports equipment; Wi-Fi (free). *In room:* A/C and ceiling fan, butler service (villas only), TV/DVD, hair dryer, minibar, MP3 docking station, private terrace.

Hôtel St. Barth Isle de France ★★★ Effortless elegance and a welcoming warmth make this family-run hotel a jewel. Year after year, the Isle de France racks up awards for its luxurious lodging and unpretentious but exemplary service—its charms linger long after you leave. The hotel opens right onto glorious Flamands Beach, its architecture a pleasing blend of whitewashed colonial and sunny Caribbean. Guest rooms are unusually spacious for St. Barts. Each of the newly refurbished beach suites in the main building has a private patio or terrace overlooking the pool or beach. But the garden rooms have their own magic. Tucked in lush garden plantings are 12 bungalows and a sprinkling of free-standing cottages. Honeymooners climb stairs to reach the **Hillside Bungalow,** a treetop aerie above the gardens with a private pool.

The two, two-bedroom garden villas (**Eden** and **Garden**) have an enchanting cottage-in-the-woods charm, with spacious bedrooms, patio kitchens, and private splash pools all tucked in plantings of banana trees and bougainvillea. Each of the four massive one-bedroom beach suites is the size of a small barn—complete with antiqued wood beams and parquet floors—and opens onto the beach, with fully equipped kitchens; commodious, marble-clad bathrooms; and private infinity plunge pools that overlook the beach. The newest additions, two, three-bedroom **Flamands suites,** are utterly spectacular, with rooms done by London designer Penny Morrison in eggshell pastels and soft linens, with artwork throughout, private fitness rooms, home cinema rooms, private pools, and direct access to the beach.

The quintessential beachfront brasserie, **La Case de l'Isle** serves island-tinged French fare in breezy alfresco style. On-site is the **Spa at Isle de France,** created by Molton Brown, where you can get a pampering massage or a game-changing "intraceutical" facial. Come sip a cocktail on the seaside pool deck for the **Tuesday night fashion show,** featuring frothy St. Barts wear from the hotel boutique.

Baie des Flamands (B.P. 612), 97098 St. Barthélemy, F.W.I. www.isle-de-france. com. ✆ **800/810-4691** in the U.S., or 590/27-61-81. Fax 590/27-86-83. 37 units. Winter 695€–1,465€ double, 1,760€–2,675€ junior suite/1-bedroom suite, 2,110€–2,745€ 2-bedroom suite, 4,190€ 3-bedroom Flamands villa, 1,255€–2,110€ bungalow/cottage; off season 470€–860€ double, 1,140€–1,500€ junior suite/1-bedroom suite, 1,240€–1,605€ 2-bedroom suite, 2,755€ 3-bedroom Flamands villa, 725€–1,240€ bungalow/cottage. Extra person 115€/night. Rates include continental breakfast and round-trip airport transfers. AE, MC, V. Closed Sept–Oct 15. Note that rooms in the main building do not accept children. **Amenities:** Restaurant; bar; babysitting; exercise room; 2 outdoor pools; room service; spa. *In room:* A/C and ceiling fan, TV, fridge, hair dryer, minibar, MP3 docking station, Wi-Fi (free).

Le Sereno ★★ Opening onto Grand Cul-de-Sac Beach, this intimate, all-suites hotel is a chic and sleek retreat. It was designed by the fabled Parisian designer Christian Liaigre (who also did NYC's Mercer Hotel) and is the latest reincarnation of a much older (and much-beloved) hotel that many felt had grown stale. Le Sereno's star may be on the ascent; it is now in the capable hands of general manager Christian Langlade, an Orient-Express pro who played a key role in the Hotel Christopher's remarkable recent transformation. The suites here are both relaxingly understated and exquisitely a la mode, with all those dreamy touches and mod cons that make for luxe living (linens from Porthault, plasma TVs, personal iPods)—but some are better than others. Definitely ask for the Grand Suite Plage room nos. 20 to 35; they are the same category as the other Grand Suite Plage rooms (and a step up from the simple Garden Rooms) but much, much roomier. The pool and **Le Restaurant des Pêcheurs** (p. 144) are the resort's social hubs. The three, **three-bedroom villas ★★★** above the hotel are spectacular, each with a private pool, personal butler, and views of Grand Cul-de-Sac (so high up you can even see whales passing by). Inside are designer kitchens stocked with Le Creuset pots and pans, and underwater music in each villa's pool.

Grand Cul-de-Sac, 97099 Barthélemy, F.W.I. www.lesereno.com. ✆ **888/ LESERENO** (537-3736) in the U.S., or 590/29-83-00. Fax 590/27-75-47. 37 units. Winter 690€–1,210€ suite, 1,330€–2,390€ one-bedroom villa, 6,500€ three-bedroom villa; off season 490€–790€ suite, 990€–1,990€ one-bedroom villa, 3,750€ three-bedroom villa. Rates include full breakfast and airport transfers. AE, DC, MC, V. **Amenities:** Restaurant; 2 bars; gym and spa; outdoor pool; room service; watersports equipment. *In room:* A/C, TV, bar, fridge, hair dryer, MP3 docking station, Wi-Fi (free).

Le Toiny ★★★   One of the Caribbean's most glamorous resorts, this Relais & Châteaux enclave has but 15 villas, scattered among a half-dozen buildings clinging to a gently sloping hillside overlooking the windswept Toiny Coast. Flowering shrubs protect privacy-seekers from prying eyes, though Brad Pitt, on vacation with his then-girlfriend Gwyneth Paltrow, was supposedly so relaxed that he dropped inhibitions and more for the paparazzi. Each sumptuous suite features its own private plunge pool, tropical-wood floors, teak and mahogany furnishings, espresso machines, Villeroy & Boch tubs, and beds swaddled in silky linens. Outside, the patio's plunge pool overlooks hills and sea, with bougainvillea spilling out of big blue pots. The charming bathrooms have impeccable hand-painted moldings and colorful tiles. **La Villa** is the hotel's three-bedroom villa, with French Colonial four-posters and a secluded private pool. Le Toiny now has direct beach access—a pleasant 5-minute path through a coconut grove—but the waters at Toiny Beach can be rough. Spa treatments are offered in the **Serenity Spa Cottage,** where therapists use spa products from Le Ligne of St. Barts. The outstanding restaurant, **Le Gaïac** (p. 146), remains the island's gold standard. At Le Toiny, you don't have to see or be seen by anyone—even breakfast arrives in a hush, set out on a patio table sheathed in crisp linens and silver cutlery. From every vantage point—even reflected in your bathroom mirror—the vista of sea, sky, and mountain is utterly soul-stirring.

Anse de Toiny, 97133 St. Barthélemy, F.W.I. www.hotelletoiny.com. ✆ **800/ 680-0832** in the U.S. and Canada, or 590/27-88-88. Fax 590/27-89-30. 15 units. Winter 1,310€–1,710€ suite, 2,810€ villa; off season 580€–960€ suite, 1,350€–1,960€ villa. Extra person 100€/night. Rates include continental breakfast, round-trip airport transfers, and service charges. One child 11 and under stays free in parent's room. AE, DC, MC, V. Closed Aug 20–Oct 25. **Amenities:** Restaurant; bar; babysitting; bikes; concierge; fitness center; outdoor pool; room service; spa; watersports equipment. *In room*: A/C, TV/ DVD, hair dryer, kitchenette, minibar, MP3 docking station, private plunge pool, Wi-Fi (free).

Expensive

Hotel Christopher ★★ 🔥   Set on a dramatic, sun-splashed promontory above the sea, this Pointe Milou hotel has undergone a spectacular renovation. With sensational views over the blue Atlantic and two very good restaurants, the Christopher is a life-style hotel that's "contemporary but not intimidating," serving up a supremely relaxed atmosphere against a background of precise service. The hotel is not adjacent to the beach (guests must drive about 10 minutes to reach Plage de Lorient), but it has the biggest pool on the island, a sprawling, low-slung pair of interconnected ovals facing the sea. Doubles are on the smallish side (around 30 sq. m/322 sq. ft.) but are loaded with everything you need for pampering comfort. The one-bedroom ocean suites are spacious, with rainforest showers, bleached louvered ceilings, and granite designer tubs. The Panoramic Suite has a big private terrace with breathtaking ocean views. Everything is impeccably sourced: Floors are a cool concrete composite laid with a trowel; tables and benches were made from recycled timber from Indonesia; and beds are swathed in organic Belgian coverlets. Turin-based Laura Tonatto created the soaps and shampoos.

Of the two on-site restaurants, **Taino** ★ (open for breakfast and dinner) hangs over the lip of the sea and serves a French-Caribbean "ingredients cuisine," using sustainably sourced local seafood whenever possible; croissants are homemade and the fish is smoked in-house. **Mango** ★ is a 60-seat barefoot lunch spot where the tables are literally set down in the sand; it serves a homey *"cuisine de bonne femme,"* where fresh local fish are sprinkled with fresh herbs and fire-roasted. The resort is largely a couples' retreat in the high season, but families are welcome the rest of the year. Spend the day around the hotel pool and enjoy lunch at Mango with a **Christopher Day Pass** (80€; with spa treatment 120€).

Pointe Milou (B.P. 571), 97133 St. Barthélemy, F.W.I. www.hotelchristopher. com. ℂ **590/27-63-63.** Fax 590/27-92-92. 42 units. Winter 450€–495€ double, 600€–900€ suite; off season 370€–410€ double, 450€–600€ suite. Rates include full American breakfast. Extra person/bed 100€. Children 3 and under stay free in parent's room. Airport transfers 20€ per trip. AE, MC, V. Closed Sept–Nov 14. **Amenities:** 2 restaurants; 2 bars; babysitting; gym; outdoor pool; room service; spa; watersports equipment. *In room*: A/C and ceiling fan, TV, hair dryer, minibar, MP3 docking station, Wi-Fi (free).

Hotel Emeraude Plage ★ Location, location, location: It doesn't get more central than this hotel, planted right on the golden sands of St-Jean. The hotel has one villa, two cottages, four suites, and 21 bungalows, all connected by a maze of walkways. The nicely renovated rooms (Porthault linens, rainforest showers) are drenched in white, with accents in cappuccino and tan, and all have fully equipped kitchens for maximum self-catering options. Rooms that can accommodate up to four people are the Stone House, Bungalow F, and Villa Emeraude. The only real public space is a book-filled reception and **Club Eau de Mer,** a small outdoor bar/restaurant on a deck facing the beach (open for breakfast, light lunch, snacks, and sunset cocktails)—oh, and that glorious beach, with Eden Rock to the right and planes zooming in on the left.

Baie de St-Jean, 97133 St. Barthélemy, F.W.I. www.emeraudeplage.com. ℂ **590/27-64-78.** Fax 590/27-83-08. 11 units. Winter 390€–1,020€ bungalow, 600€ cottage, 1,450€ villa; off season 290€–920€ bungalow, 485€–550€ cottage, 1,170€–1,300€ villa. Extra person 100€–150€ (depending on season). AE, MC, V. **Amenities:** Babysitting; concierge; watersports equipment; Wi-Fi (free; in lobby). *In room:* A/C and ceiling fan, TV, CD player, hair dryer.

Hôtel Manapany Cottages & Spa ★ This stylish resort climbs a steep, landscaped hillside tucked into the curve of the Anse de Cayes. Manapany is intimate and accommodating; the name, translated from Malagese, means "small paradise." The gingerbread-trimmed Antillean cottages are set on the sloping hillside or directly on the beach. The rambling verandas and open-sided living rooms let in the cooling trade winds. The decor is a mix of white rattan and Caribbean colonial pieces carved from mahogany. Mosquito netting covers most of the four-poster beds for a romantic touch.

Anse des Cayes, 97098 St. Barthélemy, F.W.I. www.lemanapany.com. ℂ **590/27-66-55.** Fax 590/27-75-28. 42 units. 321€–365€ double; 437€–798€ junior suite; 632€–1,218€ suite. AE, MC, V. **Amenities:** Restaurant; bar; fitness room; outdoor pool; room service; spa; tennis court. *In room:* A/C, TV/DVD, CD player, hair dryer, minibar, Wi-Fi (free).

Taïwana Hotel ★★ This newly renovated boutique hotel on beautiful Flamands Beach has had an interesting trajectory: It began 30 years ago as a restaurant, which then added the island's first swimming pool (drawing the island kids, plus their parents). The eccentric owner began buying up land around the restaurant and building charming villas on the steep hillside overlooking Flamands. On an entirely informal and under-the-radar basis, he began renting out rooms to interested patrons—reservations not necessary, you just showed up to see if the hotel had availability— all by word of mouth. In 2011 the hotel was bought by former guests and given a smart refurbishment, and made a splashy debut on the hotel scene—Taïwana is under the radar no more. Each of the 20 uniquely outfitted suites has unobstructed views of the sea; four suites have private pools—one even has a kid-pleasing red tepee! All have separate living rooms and are done in either a traditional Caribbean style or all-white modern, with adobe tile floors. Two suites open directly onto the beach; the rest are scattered along the lush hillside. Those with mobility issues might request a room on the third level, which is accessible from ample hillside parking. The popular local restaurant **PaCri** (p. 143) has moved to the hotel's beachfront restaurant space and is open for dinner; **La Taïwana** serves breakfast and lunch.

Flamands, 97133 St. Barthélemy, F.W.I. www.hoteltaiwana.com. ℰ **590/29-80-08.** Fax 590/27-94-07. 20 units. Winter 500€–3,500€ suite; off season 350€–2,300€ suite. Extra bed 120€–200€/night. Rates include round-trip airport transfers. AE, MC, V. **Amenities:** 2 restaurants; bar; fitness room; outdoor pool; room service; salon; spa. *In room:* A/C, TV/DVD, hair dryer, minibar (complimentary), MP3 docking station, Wi-Fi (free).

Moderate

Note that **Le Banane,** the charming little Lorient hotel, is no longer a hotel but rents rooms or the entire property as a villa.

Baie des Anges ★ 🍴   Opening right onto the gorgeous white sands of Flamands Beach, this cheerful retreat is cooled by trade winds. The two-story, ocean-fronting property is relatively simple but good value for St. Barts—if your sinks must be clad in cool marble and your beds in Porthault, this is not the place for you. But a major renovation in 2013 will add a spa, a breakfast area, and several multibedroom suites, almost doubling the size of the hotel. The existing 10 studio apartments are attractive and comfortable, decorated in sea colors of blue and green, with king-size beds (some four-poster), sofa beds, kitchenettes, and private terraces—and all with ocean views. The inn has a popular on-site restaurant, **La Langouste** (p. 143), where guests and nonguests alike dine poolside on Creole and French classics and the house specialty, local lobster. Multistay room packages come with rental cars and continental breakfast.

Baie des Anges, Flamands, 97133 St. Barthélemy, FWI. www.hotelbaiedes anges.fr. ℰ **590/27-63-61.** Fax 590/27-83-44. 17 units. Winter $395–$550 single, $465–$630 double, $515–$695 triple; off season $210–$340 single, $265–$420 double, $295–$472 triple. MC, V. **Amenities:** Restaurant; bar; babysitting; pool; room service. *In room:* A/C and ceiling fan, TV, hair dryer, kitchenette, Wi-Fi (in some).

Les Îlets de la Plage ★ 😊   Homey and warm, set on a serene, secluded stretch of St-Jean Beach (even with planes arriving and departing next door), Les Ilets is a charming departure from resort sleek and chic. In the lexicon of typical beach resort landscaping, Les Ilets is a sweet anomaly. Each cottage faces out toward curving beach and intensely blue sea, but the tropical terrain is more like the sun-dappled and slightly overgrown summer backyards of a bygone past. Les Ilets has 11 cottage-style bungalows, with one-, two-, and three-bedroom units available (four are directly on the beach), all with room to spare and fully equipped kitchens. The villas are smartly outfitted and very private—and in that location you're just minutes away from St-Jean restaurants and shopping.

Baie de St-Jean, 97133 St. Barthélemy, F.W.I. www.lesilets.com. (C) **590/27-88-57.** Fax 590/27-88-58. 11 units. Winter 450€–560€ 1-bedroom villa, 690€ 2-bedroom villa, 710€ 3-bedroom villa; off season 200€–410€ 1-bedroom villa, 300€–350€ 2-bedroom villa, 325€–400€ 3-bedroom villa. Rates include morning pastries. Rollaway beds 50€/night. AE, MC, V. **Amenities:** Babysitting; concierge; outdoor pool; watersports equipment. *In room:* A/C and ceiling fan, TV/DVD/VCR (available on request), CD player, hair dryer, kitchen, Wi-Fi (free).

Les Ondines Sur la Plage ★   This postmodern all-suites hotel, set on the beauteous sands of the Grand Cul-de-Sac lagoon, has six spacious one-bedroom and two, two-bedroom suites ranging from 60 to 139 sq. m (646–1,496 sq. ft.)—enormous by St. Barts standards. Most suites have glorious ocean views—you almost feel as if you're floating on the lagoon from the upper-level beachfront suites. All feature such necessities as fully equipped kitchens, high-speed Internet access, and fax (two-bedroom units even have a washer/dryer and dishwasher). Creative touches extend to mod-ish kitchens and track-lit bathrooms (stunning bas-relief moldings and mosaics). The hotel also has a fish-shaped freshwater pool.

Grand Cul-de-Sac, 97133 St. Barthélemy, F.W.I. www.stbarth-lesondineshotel.com. (C) **590/27-69-64.** Fax 590/52-24-41. 6 units. Winter 350€–690€ double; off season 215€–450€ double. Rates include continental breakfast and round-trip airport transfers. AE, MC, V. Closed Sept–Oct. **Amenities:** Outdoor pool; room service; watersports equipment. *In room:* A/C and ceiling fan, TV/DVD, hair dryer, kitchen, Wi-Fi (free).

Le Village St-Jean ★   This family-owned cottage colony hide-away, 2km (1¼ miles) from the airport toward St-Jean, is a gem of comfort and charm. Lying in the center of St. Barts, it's a 5-minute drive (or walk) uphill from St-Jean Beach. A collection of stone-and-redwood buildings scattered about the flower-filled garden and hillside holds five handsomely furnished hotel rooms (fridge only) and 20 cottages and three villas—all of which are being refurbished with large marble bathrooms and local artworks. Add well-equipped kitchens, sun decks or gardens, tiered living rooms, and balconies with soothing breezes and spectacular ocean views, and it's a winner. The Family Cottage can accommodate up to six people. A lovely infinity pool comes with killer views of the sea. The **Well-Being Cottage** holds a gym and a relaxation room for massages and other treatments.

Colline de St-Jean (B.P. 623), 97133 St. Barthélemy, F.W.I. www.villagestjean hotel.com. ⓒ **590/27-61-39.** Fax 590/27-77-96. 30 units. Winter 235€–350€ double, 260€–580€ cottage, 680€ suite, 850€ and up villa; off season 140€–350€ double, 250€–400€ cottage, 400€–480€ suite, 590€ and up villa. Extra person 50€–70€. Children 7 and under 30€–35€. Rates include continental breakfast. AE, MC, V **Amenities:** Restaurant; bar; babysitting; gym; Jacuzzi; outdoor pool; room service; Wi-Fi (free). *In room:* A/C and ceiling fan, fridge, hair dryer, kitchen (except hotel rooms), MP3 docking station.

TomBeach Hotel ★ This bustling boutique hotel has a prime location on St-Jean Beach; next door are windsurfing and water-sports rentals, not to mention the island's airport runway—watching little planes lift off practically at the beach's edge makes for great fun. The flamboyantly painted villas have been handsomely renovated and are enveloped in a Caribbean garden. Bedrooms are spacious and stylish, each adorned with draped four-poster beds, opening onto terraces complete with wet bars. The hotel's popular "feet-in-the-sand" **La Plage** restaurant is open for breakfast, lunch, and dinner.

Baie de St-Jean, 97133 St. Barthélemy, F.W.I. www.tombeach.com. ⓒ **590/ 52-81-20** from the U.S., or 590/27-53-15. 12 units. Winter 450€–690€ double; off season 290€–450€ double. Extra bed 140€ adult, 70€ children 2–12. AE, MC, V. **Amenities:** Restaurant; bar; Internet; outdoor pool. *In room:* A/C, TV/ DVD, hair dryer, minibar, MP3 docking station.

Tropical Hôtel 🛏 The facade of this small, unpretentious hotel looks like a picture-postcard Caribbean colonial inn. It's set in a lush garden on a hillside about 40m (131 ft.) above St-Jean Beach. Each sun-filled room contains a shower-only bathroom, a king-size bed, tile floors, and a fridge. Nine units have sea views and balco-nies; no. 11 has a porch that opens onto a garden that's so lush it looks like a miniature jungle. The hotel has an antiques-filled hospitality room where guests can read, listen to music, or order drinks and snacks at a paneled cocktail bar. The pool is small, but watersports are available down on St-Jean Beach.

Baie de St-Jean (B.P. 147), 97133 St. Barthélemy, F.W.I. ⓒ **800/223-9815** in the U.S., or 590/27-64-87. Fax 590/27-81-74. 22 units. Winter 225€–230€ double, 280€–305€ triple; off season 155€–180€ double, 195€–220€ triple. Rates include continental breakfast. AE, MC, V. Closed Sept 1–Oct 20. **Ame-nities:** Babysitting; outdoor pool; watersports equipment. *In room:* A/C and ceiling fan, TV, fridge, hair dryer, Wi-Fi (Superior rooms only; free).

Inexpensive

La Normandie ✎ This modest, unassuming, family-owned Antillean inn has undergone a transformation: No longer a plain Jane, the Normandie has become a smart boutique inn with completely updated rooms. The owners, however, are committed to keeping the rates down, and lucky for you—this is a very good value. A Brazilian-wood deck connects the two buildings that hold the guest rooms. The Normandie is located near the intersection of two major roads, about 200m (656 ft.) from Lorient Beach. Ask about the hotel's "Stay Longer/Pay Less" option.

Rte. de Saline, Lorient, 97133 St. Barthélemy, F.W.I. www.normandiehotelst barts.com. ✆ **590/27-61-66.** Fax 590/27-98-83. 8 units. Winter 198€ double; off season 130€ double. Rates include continental breakfast and evening wine (weekdays). AE, DC, MC, V. **Amenities:** Outdoor pool. *In room:* A/C, TV (in some), fridge, Wi-Fi (free).

Le P'tit Morne ★ ✎ This is hardly the most luxurious or stylish lodging on an island that's legendary for its glamorous five-star hotels. But the hotel's moderate rates, fully equipped kitchens (in every apartment), and the warm welcome extended by its island-born owners make it a worthy vacation site. It's a 10-minute drive from the beach, but every apartment has terraces or balconies with stupendous sea views of Colombier and beyond. The colonial-style guest rooms are filled with completely unpretentious furniture and comfortable king-size beds. There's plenty of elbow room, and units were built to catch the trade winds.

Colombier (B.P. 14), 97095 St. Barthélemy, F.W.I. www.timorne.com. ✆ **590/52-95-50.** Fax 590/27-84-63. 15 units. Winter 185€–230€ double; off season 95€–150€ double. AE, MC, V. Closed Sept. **Amenities:** Babysitting; pool; room service. *In room:* A/C, TV, fridge, kitchen, Wi-Fi (free).

Salines Garden Cottages ★ ✎ This is a crazy-good value on pricey St. Barts. Guests stay in stylish gingerbread *cazes* (traditional Creole houses), three with kitchenettes, nestled amid flowering trees and birdsong just steps from one of the island's loveliest beaches. Each has a private tiled terrace shaded by bougainvillea. Interiors have brilliant batik fabrics, island crafts in various mediums, and four-poster or cast-iron beds. Asian and African antiques, collected by the peripatetic owners, enliven public spaces and grounds. Romantics and independent types can cherish utter seclusion—and Grande Saline Beach is just minutes away.

Anse de Saline, 97133 St. Barthélemy, F.W.I. www.salinesgarden.com. ✆ **590/ 51-04-44.** Fax 590/27-64-65. 5 units. Winter 140€–190€ double; off season 100€–130€ double. Extra person 50€. Continental breakfast, airport transfers, taxes, and service charges included. AE, MC, V. **Amenities:** Babysitting; outdoor pool. *In room:* A/C and ceiling fan, hair dryer, kitchen (in some).

PLANNING YOUR TRIP TO ST. MAARTEN/ ST. MARTIN, ANGUILLA & ST. BARTS

T his chapter tackles the how-tos of a trip to St. Maarten/St. Martin, Anguilla, and St. Barts, including everything from finding airfares to deciding whether to rent a car. But first, let's start with some background information about these increasingly popular destinations.

9

For additional assistance in planning your trip and for further on-the-ground resources, see "Fast Facts," beginning on p. 188.

THE ISLANDS IN BRIEF
St. Maarten/St. Martin

For an island with a big reputation for restaurants, hotels, and energetic nightlife, St. Maarten/St. Martin is small—only 96 sq. km (37 sq. miles), about half the area of Washington, D.C. It's the smallest territory in the world shared by two sovereign states: the Netherlands and France. St. Maarten (Sint Maarten) is the Dutch half, and St. Martin is the French half.

The island was officially split in 1648, but the two nations have coexisted so peacefully since then that if you're not paying attention, you won't even know you've crossed over from one side to the next. Still, the differences are there. Development is on the march in Dutch St. Maarten, and the Dutch capital, Philipsburg, is often bustling with cruise-ship hordes: Some

St. Maarten: Cruisin'

Some 20 cruise lines and 1.7 million cruise passengers arrive in St. Maarten annually. St. Maarten has a total of six dedicated cruise berths—making it one of the Caribbean's largest cruise-ship ports—and the big ones do pull in here, including a recent visit by *Oasis of the Seas*, the 2,700-cabin behemoth that has enjoyed record-breaking passenger numbers (over 6,000). For more about the port, go to www.portofstmaarten.com.

1.7 million cruise-ship passengers arrive here annually, swarming the oceanfront boardwalk on Segways, on bikes, and on foot. Traffic congestion in Simpson Bay, caused in large part by the six-times-daily drawbridge openings and closings, has become a major irritant.

Despite these issues, St. Maarten continues to attract visitors who want to kick back on a sunny Caribbean island that also offers a splash of Vegas nightlife. All of the island's casinos are on the Dutch side, as are most of the flashy nightclubs and discos. This is where you'll find the island's handful of multistory megahotels. Still, the old girl has charm to spare: The landscape of undulating green hills is magical, and it's easy to find a secluded patch of pristine white sand among the island's 39 sun-splashed beaches.

St. Maarten also has what many other Caribbean nations do not: a real cosmopolitanism. The island isn't known as the "crossroads of the Caribbean" for nothing. As one thriving expat from Suriname said: "St. Maarten is much more accepting of outsiders than some other Caribbean destinations. Here nearly everyone is from somewhere else."

The Dutch capital, **Philipsburg,** curves like a toy village along Great Bay. The town lies on a narrow sand isthmus separating Great Bay and the Great Salt Pond. Commander John Philips, a Scot in Dutch employ, founded the capital in 1763. To protect Great Bay, Fort Amsterdam was built in 1737. Philipsburg is one of the Caribbean's busiest duty-free stopping shops (especially when cruise ships are in port), although a handsome beachside boardwalk has made strolling the waterfront a real pleasure.

The French side of the island has a quieter, less frenetic pace. It's sleepier than the Dutch side and much less Americanized. Most hotels in French St. Martin are small and boutique-y, and cruise ships don't dock here. People come to French St. Martin to relax on its lovely (clothing-optional) beaches and experience "France in the Tropics." Indeed, St. Martin has a distinctly French air. The towns have names like Colombier and Orléans, the streets are *rues,* and the French flag flies over the *gendarmerie* in **Marigot,** the French capital. A good number of atmospheric restaurants serve authentic French cuisine with saucy Creole inflections.

About 15 minutes by car beyond Marigot is **Grand Case,** a tiny outpost of French civilization, with a number of excellent restaurants and a couple of top-notch boutique hotels. Grand Case is a French/Creole small town with dogs roaming the streets, kids doing wheelies on bikes, and bougainvillea spilling over picket fences. Top that off with a soulful beachside setting, a narrow main street crammed with one fine restaurant after another, and an airport where commuter-size airplanes buzz the town at regular intervals daily. It's like a French Mayberry, except here Aunt Bea is a five-star chef.

In 2010 both Dutch St. Maarten and French St. Martin underwent major administrative changes. No longer governed from Guadeloupe, French St. Martin is now an overseas collectivity (COM) of France. And St. Maarten has become a self-governing country within the Netherlands for the first time since 1815.

Anguilla

Just 20 minutes by ferry from Marigot, flat, arid, scrubby Anguilla has become one of the Caribbean's choicest destinations, despite its unprepossessing landscape and utter lack of colonial grandeur. The reasons are obvious: The island is more or less one big

A LITTLE history

Excavations suggest that the island was settled around 2,500 years ago by American Indian Arawaks. Christopher Columbus sighted the island during his second voyage in November 1493, naming it without setting foot on land. The Spaniards couldn't spare the expense of military maintenance after several devastating European wars, so they literally abandoned it in 1648, enabling opportunistic French and Dutch settlers from St. Kitts and St. Eustatius, respectively, to claim the island. After initial skirmishes, mostly political, the two nations officially settled their differences later that year. Even so, St. Maarten changed hands 16 times before it became permanently Dutch, while the French side endured the usual colonial tugs of war throughout the Napoleonic era. Alas, there appears to be no truth to the colorful legend of a wine-drinking Frenchman and gin-guzzling Dutchman walking the island to determine the border.

VISITOR information

For the latest information on **Dutch St. Maarten** and **French St Martin,** go to www.vacationstmaarten.com and www.st-martin. org, respectively. On St. Maarten, go to the **Tourist Information Bureau,** Vineyard Office Park, 33 W. G. Buncamper Rd., Philipsburg, St. Maarten, N.A. (℃ **721/542-2337**), open Monday to Friday from 9am to 5pm.

The tourist board on French St. Martin, called the **Office du Tourisme,** is at Route de Sandy Ground, Marigot, 97150 St. Martin (℃ **590/87-57-21**), open Monday to Friday from 8am to 1pm and 2:30 to 5:30pm.

Please note that Dutch St. Maarten has a new area telephone code: **721.**

For details on Anguilla and St. Barts, see chapters 7 and 8, respectively.

sugary-sand beach enveloped by luminous turquoise seas. The leading resorts and villa complexes define luxury, and the food is among the finest in the Caribbean. And yet the vibe is pleasingly laid-back in even the toniest resorts; it's barefoot luxury at its least pretentious.

St. Barts

A quick flight or 45-minute ferry ride 24km (15 miles) east of St. Maarten/St. Martin, this rugged, hilly, 21-sq.-km (8-sq.-mile) island ("St. Barths," to the locals) is practically synonymous with international glamour and glorious beaches. The cost for effortless chic is high, but the jet set has never minded. Despite its reputation for celebrity glitz—and its sometimes ostentatious display of wealth—St. Barts has retained its French soul and sunny, easy-going West Indian heart. The 8,000 locals—many descended from the original hardy Norman and Breton settlers—are matter-of-fact about the jet-setting crowd. And why not? Their cultural traditions are firmly entrenched in a fairy-tale capital, **Gustavia;** the Caribbean equivalent of the Riviera, **St-Jean;** exceptionally pretty fishing villages in **Colombier** and **Corossol;** and, along a gnarled coastline, some of the world's most stunning beaches.

THE THREE-ISLAND ITINERARY

It's become incredibly easy to get to these islands from North America. A number of major carriers fly direct routes from North

American hubs into Dutch St. Maarten's Princess Juliana International Airport, just minutes from several of the Dutch side's top beaches. If you're heading on to another island, you won't even have to bother with a taxi. You can leave straight from the airport on a 10-minute puddle-jumper to St. Barts, or hop on a private shuttle boat (30 min.) to Anguilla. If your time is limited, St. Maarten/St. Martin is a great long-weekend getaway, ideal for a quick break from the winter doldrums: You can take a direct flight out of New York City, for example, and be at the St. Maarten airport in under 4 hours. The islands are also perfect for longer stays, where you really get under the skin of the place and as close as these islands are to one another (so near that from certain vantage points the lights of another island twinkle across the waters), there's a world of difference among them, both culturally and physically. I say you should experience them all: These are three of the Caribbean's gems.

Seeing all three islands in one trip is easy to do and highly recommended, especially if you have the time to spend at least 3 nights on each. The following itinerary does just that.

Days 1–2: St. Maarten/St. Martin

Fly into **Princess Juliana International Airport** in Dutch St. Maarten. You can pick up a rental car at the airport, but I suggest a 2-night stay at the **Radisson Blu,** in **Anse Marcel** (see p. 82), French St. Martin. It's a beautiful spot and the perfect place to ease into a tropical holiday—but it also has something most other resorts don't: a **water taxi ride** straight from the airport. Talk about instant immersion! It's a lovely 30-minute trip tracing the curves of the island's northwest coast on the catamaran *Scoobi-Too.* Once you're at the resort, relax by the huge infinity pool or on the half-moon beach of this picturesque cove. On Day 2, plan a day trip to nearby **Îlet Pinel** or head to **Orient Beach** or **Happy Bay.**

Days 3–5: St. Barts

Take a taxi to tiny **L'Esperance Airport** in nearby **Grand Case** and fly a little six-seater on **St. Barth Commuter** for a 3-night stay on St. Barts. The flight is just under 10 minutes, but it's a doozy, with sweeping views of the volcanic rocks that pepper the sea and a daredevil landing on an abbreviated strip of asphalt that ends within a hair of St-Jean Beach. Whew! If you're staying at a resort, most provide airport pickup, but if you're staying at a villa, you'll likely want to rent a car at the airport. *Tip:* Drive carefully on the island's twisting roller-coaster roads. You can get supplies at the **Marché-U supermarket** (see p. 142) across from the airport or hit **Maya's To Go** (see p. 142)**,** next door, which sells delicious takeout specialties. (And keep in mind that even though everyone accepts dollars, the **euro** is the main currency on St. Barts and French St. Martin—and at press time, paying in euros gave better bang for the buck.)

If you arrive early enough, this is a good day to hit a couple of the island's famous beaches. Head to **Grand Salines Beach** and have lunch at Grain de Sel, or go to **Flamands Beach** and lunch at breezy **Case de l'Isle** at **Hôtel St.-Barth Isle de France** (see p. 143). Or just make a day of it on St-Jean, with a beachside repast at Eden Roc's **Sand Bar** (see p. 149) or **La Plage** at the TomBeach Hotel (see p. 146). On the second day, head to the charming little port of Gustavia for a morning of shopping (shops close for lunch); have the daily *plat du jour* at the **Wall House** (see p. 141), and if it's high season, stroll the **waterfront quay** for an eye-popping primer in Yachts, Mega.

You can spend your third day taking a snorkeling trip with **Marine Service** to gorgeous **Colombier Beach** (which is reached only by boat or by climbing one of two hillside goat paths) or windsurfing/shopping along **St-Jean Beach.**

Day 6: Marigot, St. Martin

Fly back into Grand Case on St. Barth Commuter and take a 15-minute taxi to the **Port de Saint-Martin** in Marigot, the waterfront ferry depot where the Anguilla public ferry arrives and departs on a regular basis. The small ferry terminal has a luggage storage area, where you can secure your bags ($5 plus tip) while you spend a few hours sightseeing and shopping in Marigot. The village of Marigot is a colorful slice of France in the Caribbean. It has a rich cache of duty-free shops and tony international brands (Chanel, Cartier, Hermès) as well as French and Creole restaurants clustered around the waterfront and marina. It's a charming place to poke about—and the spot to do your shopping (Anguilla has few shops, and goods are often sold at inflated prices). Marigot has a number of excellent wine shops, including **Le Goût du Vin** (see p. 56), where you can find fine French wines at decent prices. Along Marigot's harbor side, a lively **morning market** on Wednesday and Saturday hosts vendors selling clothing, spices, and handicrafts. Have a late lunch at one of the **lolos** alongside the waterfront; I like **Enoch's Place** (see p. 45) for its reasonably priced platter of garlicky shrimp, rice and peas, and salad.

Days 6–8: Anguilla

After your exploration of Marigot, pick up your luggage at the ferry terminal and buy your ticket for a ride on the **public ferry** to

The Three-Island Itinerary

PLANNING YOUR TRIP

Anguilla. It's a 30-minute trip to this long, sandy, relatively flat island, a radical topographical departure from the mossy volcanic hills of St. Martin and St. Barts. (The last ferry leaves around 6:15pm.) It's a departure of a cultural kind, too; you're no longer in France but on English-speaking turf, and the dollar is the currency of choice on this self-governing British overseas territory. Once you've arrived at **Blowing Point** and passed through immigration, either your resort will pick you up or you can take a taxi to your hotel or villa. (Most car rental agencies are happy to drop off rental cars wherever you're staying.) If you arrive before the sun sets, head to one of the resorts or restaurants along **Mead's Bay** on the **West End** to drink in the sunset, such as **Jacala** (see p. 105), **Straw Hat** (see p. 106), or **Blanchards' Beach Shack** (see p. 110).

Anguilla is all about breathtaking beaches: On your second day on the island, do a little beach-hopping. Head to Meads Bay or Shoal Bay East and enjoy some of the barbecue grub at beach shacks like **Gwen's** (see p. 108). Or grab your snorkeling equipment and drive the winding, bumpy road to the beach at **Junk's Hole,** where you can dine in barefoot splendor on grilled lobster, local crawfish, or ribs at Nat Richardson's **Palm Grove Bar & Grill** (see p. 108) on the beach.

On your third day in Anguilla, plan a snorkeling trip to an idyllic **offshore island** such as **Prickly Pear** or **Sandy Island.** Here you can snorkel, look for shells, and generally putter about on a spit of sand in the castaway spirit. A couple of these uninhabited islands have ramshackle beach shacks where fresh lobster and fish are always on the grill and a stiff rum drink is de rigueur.

Day 9: Grand Case, St. Martin

Head back on an afternoon ferry to Marigot. Take a taxi to the little French village of **Grand Case.** I highly recommend a stay at the **Hôtel L'Esplanade** (see p. 80), which is nestled into a cliff overlooking Grand Case beach. Grand Case is the culinary heart of St. Martin (some say it has the best assemblage of top restaurants in the Caribbean). This sleepy little town comes alive in the evening, when folks head to the **Calmos Café** (see p. 64) or neighbor **Zen It** (see p. 64) to watch the sunset. It's a favored culinary destination for visitors from all over the island, who arrive in waves of shuttle vans to descend on the narrow two-lane **Boulevard de Grand Case** to pick a place to dine. The food is largely French/Creole, with most places offering local lobster and fish. The restaurants overlooking the beach are hard to resist, but the ones without a seaside setting may try harder. *Bon appétit!*

Day 10: Princess Juliana International Airport, St. Maarten

Fly home out of Princess Juliana International Airport—but before you leave, have the taxi driver take you to **Hilma's Windsor Castle** (see p. 39), a trailer-turned-roadside-cafe on Airport Road in Simpson Bay that serves some of the best johnnycakes on the island. Two dollars will get you a johnnycake filled with saltfish simmered with onions, peppers, and seasonings. It's greasy and great.

WHEN TO GO
The High & Low Seasons

Hotels on all three islands charge their highest rates during the peak winter season, from mid-December to mid-April. Christmas week rates may double those tariffs. You should make reservations months in advance for Christmas and February, especially over Presidents' Day weekend. School spring breaks are also busy family times.

The off season on all three islands runs roughly mid-April to mid-December (though exact dates vary according to the property). Even though August can be a popular month for vacationing Europeans, it's one big summer sale: Most hotels, inns, condos, and villas slash their prices 20% to 50%. The beaches are less crowded, and many top lodgings and restaurants shutter for 1 or 2 months as the owners take their own vacation or perform necessary renovations. Be sure to request a room away from noise if the hotel remains open during construction. I provide closing dates wherever possible, but visitors should double-check before booking.

Weather

High season on all three islands features a temperate climate, rarely exceeding 90°F (32°C), with lower humidity and the famed cooling trade winds blowing in from the northeast. It's ideal beach weather, with the occasional cloudy day. Usually rain showers are brief: Islanders call them "liquid sunshine."

Rainy season runs from late May to mid-November. This doesn't mean it rains for days at a time or even every day. But this also roughly corresponds to the official Atlantic hurricane season, June 1 to November 30. Fortunately, satellite surveillance provides enough advance warning to allow people to take precautions and, rarely, evacuate.

St. Maarten/St. Martin Average Daily Temperature & Rainfall

	JAN	FEB	MAR	APR	MAY	JUNE	JULY	AUG	SEPT	OCT	NOV	DEC
TEMP. (°F)	77	77	77	79	81	81	83	83	83	81	80	79
TEMP. (°C)	25	25	25	26	27	27	28	28	28	27	27	26
RAINFALL (IN.)	2.5	1.3	1.6	2.3	2.3	3.8	3.8	3.5	3.7	4.4	3.8	3.7

St. Maarten/St. Martin Calendar of Events

For Anguilla and St. Barts, see chapters 7 and 8, respectively.

JANUARY & FEBRUARY

Harmony Nights: Tuesdays in Grand Case. Starting on January 10 and running until early April, Tuesdays in Grand Case is a nightly food, music, and shopping festival in the village of Grand Case. From 6 to 10pm, the town's main street is closed to traffic, shops stay open late, and live Caribbean music provides a lilting soundtrack for the festivities.

Carnival. Festivities on French St. Martin last for nearly 2 months, starting the second Sunday in January with parade rehearsals and band tryouts. Carnival reaches its frenzied peak on the French side in February, with jump-ups, barbecues, and pageants. It all leads to J'ouvert, the weekend before Mardi Gras, and lasts until Ash Wednesday. The dancing-in-the-streets parades represent the culmination of an entire year's preparation, from creating the feathered, sequined costumes to writing unique musical themes. The streets are crowded with young and old following trucks with enormous sound systems in Marigot until everyone congregates at "Carnival Village" come nightfall for concerts and events, including the crowning of the Carnival King and Queen.

MARCH

Heineken Regatta. Celebrating its 33rd year in 2013, this annual series of major boat races features more than 200 vessels, from converted family fishing dinghies to race prototypes, competing in several categories. It's a prime excuse for partying, particularly on the Dutch side. Post-race performances have included the Black Eyed Peas, Wyclef Jean, and Jimmy Cliff. For details, call © **721/544-2079** or visit www.heineken regatta.com. First weekend of March.

APRIL

Carnival. The Dutch side chimes in with its own, even more extravagant version of Carnival, beginning the Wednesday after Easter Sunday and continuing for 18 riotous days of beauty pageants, costume and calypso competitions, Mas bands, parades, shows, and assorted revelry.

The Carnival Village features stands dishing out spicy local fare and an enormous stage where local and international musicians perform nightly. J'ouvert, the opening jump-up, showcases local and international bands, and thousands of revelers line the streets and follow the performers until they arrive at Carnival Village.

More parades are held the next morning, and the grandest of all takes place on the Queen's Birthday. Crowds pack the streets of Philipsburg vying for a spot to see the musicians, the outrageous costumes, and the colorful floats. The Last Lap, the grand finale of the Carnival, includes a symbolic burning of King Momo, a straw figure who embodies the spirit of Carnival. Island legend claims that burning the king in effigy will purge the village of its sins and consequent bad luck. Visit www.stmaarten carnival.net for more information.

St. Maarten Open Golf Tournament. Residents and visitors alike are invited to participate in this 3-day, 54-hole event at Mullet Bay Golf Resort. For details, go to www.stmaartengolf.com. Second weekend in April.

MAY

Fish Day at French Cul-de-Sac. Fish is the focus at this popular festival in the traditional fishing village of Cul-de-Sac, where you can sample local fish dishes, enjoy boat races, and move to the rhythms of live bands. Some 80 stands offer culinary delights, local crafts, and fruits and vegetables. May 6.

Fête du Nautisme. This watersports festival organized by METIMER, the St. Martin Sea Trades Association, focuses on (re)discovering the rich marine environment just off St. Martin's shores. Free activities include yacht and motorboat excursions and regattas, jet-skiing, kayaking, and windsurfing, with lessons available. Usually second or third weekend of May.

JUNE

Billfish Tournament. One of the Caribbean's most prestigious fishing competitions is a 5-day extravaganza out of the Fort Louis Marina on the Marigot waterfront, attracting anglers from Europe and the Caribbean. About 30 fishing boats battle at the "Marlin Boulevard" area, rich fishing grounds about 48km (30 miles) east of St. Maarten. Call ✆ **690/61-81-61** or visit www.billfish-tournament.com for details. First week of June.

JULY

Bastille Day. The French holiday is celebrated island-wide with fanfare and fireworks, races and revelry. July 14.

Grand Case Fete. A family day featuring boat races and traditional games is held in honor of Victor Schoelcher, a Frenchman who fought against slavery. July 21.

NOVEMBER

St. Maarten's Day. Christopher Columbus named the island St. Maarten/St. Martin because he discovered it in 1493 on November 11, the feast day of St. Martin of Tours. Island residents on both sides still celebrate it as an official holiday, organizing various sporting events, parades, and jump-ups over 2 to 3 days. November 11.

ENTRY REQUIREMENTS
Passports

U.S. and Canadian citizens must have a passport or a combination of a birth certificate and photo ID, plus a return or ongoing ticket, to enter St. Maarten/St. Martin. Citizens of the United Kingdom, Commonwealth countries of the Caribbean, the Republic of Ireland, and E.U. countries must also have a current passport. See p. 192 and 194 for information on Anguilla and St. Barts.

All travelers coming from the Caribbean, including Americans, are now required to have a passport to enter or re-enter the United States. Those returning to Canada are also required to show passports. Cruise-ship passengers must also meet the requirement. You'll certainly need identification at some point, and a passport is the best form of ID for speeding through Customs and Immigration. Driver's licenses are not acceptable as a sole form of ID.

Customs

Generally, you're permitted to bring in items intended for your personal use, including tobacco, cameras, film, and a limited supply of liquor—usually 40 ounces.

Just before you leave home, check with the St. Maarten/St. Martin (as well as St. Barts and Anguilla) Customs or Foreign Affairs department for the latest guidelines—including information on items that are not allowed to be brought into your home country—because the rules are subject to change and often contain some surprising oddities.

Visitors to St. Maarten/St. Martin (as well as St. Barts and Anguilla) may not carry any form of firearm, spear guns, pole spears, illegal drugs, live plants or cuttings, and raw fruits and vegetables. Visitors 18 and over may bring in—duty-free—items intended for personal use (generally up to 4 liters of alcohol, a carton of cigarettes, or 25 cigars), as well as laptops, cellphones, and cameras.

You should collect receipts for all purchases made abroad. You must also declare on your Customs form the nature and value of all gifts received during your stay abroad.

If you use any medication that contains controlled substances or requires injection, carry an original prescription or note from your doctor.

For specifics on what **U.S.** citizens can bring back home, contact **U.S. Customs and Border Protection (CBP),** 1300 Pennsylvania Ave. NW, Washington, DC 20229 (www.cbp.gov; ✆ **877/ 227-5511**).

RECOMMENDED reading

For flavorful novelizations and true-life tales of St. Maarten/St. Martin, Anguilla, and St. Barts, check out the following books. **The Captain's Fund** by Raina Wissing Harris, a "romance suspense" novel of murder, heiresses-in-distress, and black market diamonds, is notable for its St. Maarten/St. Martin setting, with such familiar landmarks as Friar's Beach Café, the Horny Toad Guesthouse, and Joe's Jewelry International. Much of celebrity chef/author Anthony Bourdain's comedic crime novel **Gone Bamboo** takes place in St. Martin. Melinda and Bob Blanchard's **A Trip to the Beach: Living on Island Time in the Caribbean** is the true-life restaurateurs' hilarious yet sympathetic, ungarnished version of Herman Wouk's riotous fictional account of an American hotelier in the Antilles, *Don't Stop the Carnival*. The Blanchards' cookbook, **At Blanchard's Table,** features 160 island recipes. **Murder in St. Barts** is a fast-paced Gendarme Trenet novel by J. R. Ripley, better known for the Tony Kozol whodunits. Jimmy Buffet's **Tales from Margaritaville** offers fictional short stories of West Indian life, many based on his years of St. Barts residency.

U.K. citizens should contact **HM Revenue & Customs** at © **0845/010-9000** (020/8929-0152 from outside the U.K.) or visit www.hmrc.gov.uk.

For a clear summary of **Canadian** rules, contact the **Canada Border Services Agency** (www.cbsa-asfc.gc.ca; © **800/461-9999** in Canada, or 204/983-3500).

Citizens of **Australia** should call the **Australian Customs Service** (© **1300/363-263**) or visit www.customs.gov.au.

For **New Zealand** Customs information, contact **New Zealand Customs** (© **0800/428-786** in New Zealand, or 09/927-8019) or visit www.customs.govt.nz.

GETTING THERE & GETTING AROUND
Getting to St. Maarten/St. Martin

The island has two airports. Your likely arrival point will be St. Maarten's **Princess Juliana International Airport (PJIA)** (www.pjiae.com; © **721/546-7542**), which has grown from a military airfield built by the United States in 1943 into the second-busiest airport in the eastern Caribbean, topped only by San Juan,

Puerto Rico. Princess Juliana is a thoroughly modern facility, with restaurants, snack bars, ATMs, and car rental kiosks. The much smaller **Grand Case Airport,** also known as **L'Espérance Airport,** in Grand Case on French St. Martin (© 590/59-04-47), caters largely to inter-island commuter airlines and small private aircraft.

American Airlines (www.aa.com; © 800/433-7300 in the U.S. and Canada) offers more options and more frequent service into St. Maarten than any other airline—currently one daily nonstop flight from New York's JFK and one from Miami. Additional nonstop daily flights into St. Maarten are offered by American and its local affiliate, **American Eagle** (© 800/433-7300), from San Juan.

Delta Airlines (www.delta.com; © 800/221-1212 in the U.S. and Canada) flies into St. Maarten from Atlanta.

United (www.united.com; © 800/864-8331 in the U.S. and Canada) also offers flights from New York and Newark, New Jersey (flight times vary in off season).

US Airways (www.usairways.com; © 800/428-4322 in the U.S. and Canada) offers nonstop daily service between St. Maarten and both Philadelphia and Charlotte, North Carolina.

JetBlue Airways (www.jetblue.com; © 800-JETBLUE [538-2583] in the U.S.) has a daily nonstop flight from New York's JFK into St. Maarten. It also offers service from San Juan, Puerto Rico.

Spirit Airlines (www.spiritair.com; © 800/772-7117 in the U.S. and Canada) has nonstop service from Fort Lauderdale to St. Maarten.

KLM (www.klm.com; © 721/546-7747 in St. Maarten) offers direct flights from Amsterdam to St. Maarten.

Air Caraïbes (www.aircaraibes.com; © 590/52-05-10) offers flights from Paris's Orly airport into both the Princess Juliana International Airport in St. Maarten and the Grand Case Regional Airport in St. Martin.

Caribbean Airlines (www.caribbean-airlines.com; © 800/920-4225 in the U.S. and Canada, or 800/744-2225 on St. Maarten), the national airline of Trinidad and Tobago (replacing the now-defunct BWIA), has flights from New York, Miami, Toronto, and London with connections to St. Maarten.

The regional airline **LIAT** (www.liatairline.com; © 888/844-5428 in the U.S. and Canada) has direct daily 40-minute flights and connecting flights into St. Maarten from its hub in Antigua. From St. Maarten, LIAT offers ongoing service to and from a number of other islands, including Antigua, St. Croix, Puerto Rico, St. Kitts, and Dominica.

Winair (www.fly-winair.com; © **888/255-6889** in the U.S. and Canada, or 721/545-4237) specializes in flying the short routes of the northeastern Caribbean islands, from Tortola to Montserrat. Winair offers island trips from its main gateway at the Princess Juliana International Airport.

Getting Around St. Maarten/ St. Martin

TAXIS

Most visitors use taxis at some point to get around the island. Taxis are plentiful at Princess Juliana International Airport; taxi stands are conveniently located just outside the airport Arrivals section. Taxi rates are fixed and determined by zone, and drivers are required to carry government-issued rate sheets based on two-person occupancy.

Taxis have minimum fares for two passengers, and each additional passenger pays $5 extra. One piece of luggage per person is allowed free; each additional piece is $1 extra (boxes or bundles $2). Typical fares around the island for up to two passengers and all their luggage are as follows: Princess Juliana airport to Grand Case, $25; Princess Juliana airport to anywhere in Marigot, $15 to $20; Marigot to Grand Case, $15; Princess Juliana airport to La Samanna, $15; Princess Juliana airport to Philipsburg, $15; and Princess Juliana airport to the Maho Beach Hotel, $6. *Note:* Fares are 25% higher between 10pm and midnight, and 50% higher between midnight and 6am.

Set rates for 3-hour **taxi sightseeing tours** are $90 for one or two persons (each additional person $25).

A couple of recommended taxi drivers are **Gerard Taxi Service** (© **721/553-4727** [Dutch side] or 0690/76-73-13 [French side]), and **Renaldo,** who runs **Taxi 257** (© **0690/87-09-97** or 718/355-8166 in the U.S.).

For late-night cab service on St. Maarten, call © **147.** To reach the **Taxi Dispatch offices** in St. Maarten, call © **721/546-7759** (airport) or 542-2359 (Philipsburg). On the French side of the island, **Taxi Service & Information Center** operates at the port of Marigot (© **590/87-56-54**).

RENTAL CARS

A car is the best way to experience and explore St. Maarten/St. Martin. And renting a car here couldn't be easier; car rental agencies are a dime a dozen, with locations at the airports and throughout the island. It's also a cost-efficient way to see the island, with short distances between towns and rates starting around $30 or

21€ a day, with unlimited mileage. You will need to show a valid driver's license from your country of origin to rent a car in St. Maarten/St. Martin.

Many visitors rent cars upon arrival at Princess Juliana International Airport. If you haven't already made a car rental reservation, you can choose from one of the many agencies that have kiosks at the airport, both international chains (like Budget, Avis, and Hertz) and local. To get around the law (strictly enforced by St. Maarten taxi drivers' union) that forbids anyone from picking up a car at the airport, every rental agency parks its cars at a location nearby. When you rent a car at one of the agency kiosks on the Arrivals floor of the Princess Juliana airport, you will be taken by free shuttle 5 to 10 minutes away to pick up your car. *Note:* Always ask how far away from the airport rental cars are located; some of the smaller agencies are a couple of miles away—which can turn into a long trip when traffic is heavy around the airport.

Rental agencies will also deliver cars directly to your hotel, where an employee will complete the paperwork. Some hotels, like La Samanna, actually have a fleet of cars to rent on the premises, but try to reserve well in advance because supply is limited.

Car rental agencies at the Princess Juliana International Airport include **Budget** (http://budgetsxm.com; ✆ 800/260-9856 in the U.S. and Canada, or 721/545-4030 on the Dutch side), **Avis** (www.avis-sxm.com; ✆ 800/331-1084 in the U.S., 800/321-3652 in Canada, 721/542-2847 on the Dutch side, or 590/87-50-60 on the French side), **Hertz** (http://hertz.sxmrentacar.com; ✆ 866/978-5625 in the U.S., 721/545-4541 on the Dutch side, or 590/77-77-77 on the French side), and **Alamo/National** (www.nationalcar.com; ✆ 877/222-9058 in the U.S. and Canada, or 721/545-5546 on the Dutch side). Also at the Princess Juliana airport are **Best Deal Car Rental** (www.bestdealscarrental.com; ✆ 305/735-2024 or 721/545-3061) and **Safari Car Rentals** (www.safaricarrentals.com; ✆ 800/736-6917 or 721/545-3185).

Car rental agencies with locations in Grand Case or at the Grand Case Airport include **Justice Car Rental** (http://justicecarrental.com; ✆ 590/87-80-91); **Grand Case Car Rental** (www.grandcasecarrental.com; ✆ 690/77-80-37 or 721/587-3131); **Avis** (www.avis-sxm.com; ✆ 590/87-50-60); and **Thrifty** (www.thrifty.com; **721/545-2393**).

Both **Budget** and **Avis** have locations at or near the cruise-ship terminal in Philipsburg.

All these companies charge roughly equivalent rates. The major car rental agencies require that renters be a minimum age of anywhere from 21 to 25 years old.

Driving is on the **right side of the road.** (Only in Anguilla is it on the left.) Seat belts and child car seats are mandatory. International road signs are observed, and there are no Customs formalities at the border between the French and Dutch sides—in fact, you might not even realize you crossed the border.

Gas stations are plentiful. Prices listed are per liter, not per gallon. *Tip:* Most gas stations accept only cash.

Expect **traffic jams** in and around Philipsburg during rush hours (8am and 5pm)—particularly in the Simpson Bay area and when the Simpson Bay drawbridge is raised to let boat traffic through (six times daily Dec–May; three times daily May–Nov). Tune your car radio to **Island 92** (91.9 FM) for traffic updates.

PUBLIC BUS

Traveling by public bus (more like a minivan) is a reasonable means of transport on St. Maarten/St. Martin if you don't mind a bit of inconvenience and overcrowding. Buses run daily from 5am to midnight and serve most major locations on both sides of the island. The most popular run is from Philipsburg on the Dutch side to Marigot on the French side. Privately owned and operated, minibuses tend to follow specific routes; the fare is $2 ($2.50 8pm–midnight). Buses accept both dollars and euros.

Getting to Anguilla & St. Barts

For more information on getting to and around Anguilla and St. Barts, see "Getting There" in chapters 7 and 8, respectively, as well as "Getting to St. Maarten/St. Martin," earlier in this chapter.

ANGUILLA   Public ferries run between Marigot Bay, St. Martin, and Blowing Point, Anguilla (© **264/497-6070**) every 30 to 45 minutes. The trip takes 20 to 25 minutes, making day trips easy. Usually, the first ferry leaves St. Martin at 8am and the last at 7pm; from Blowing Point, the first ferry leaves at 7:30am and the last at 6:15pm. The one-way fare is $15 ($15 children 7 and older, $10 children 2–6; free 1 and under). A departure tax of $20 ($10 children 5–12) is charged on your return trip to St. Martin; day-trippers and visiting yachts pay a $5 departure tax. No reservations are necessary. Ferries vary in size, and none take passenger vehicles. *Tip:* Keep in mind that if you have a late-arriving flight, you may quite literally miss the boat. You can either spend the night in St. Maarten/St. Martin or arrange a charter plane connection into Anguilla.

A 2010 agreement between the St. Maarten/Anguilla governments has worked to greatly facilitate the ease of **private boat transfers** (and passing through immigration) from the airport—which means that, ideally, you will be able to get off the plane and jump on a boat straight to Anguilla in under 30 minutes. Anguilla-based charter boats will pick you up at the Princess Juliana airport in St. Maarten and transport you and your luggage to Blowing Point or a hotel on the south side of Anguilla. These boats are more expensive than the public ferries but let you avoid having to travel from the airport to the ferry port in Marigot by taxi (a 10- to 15-min. trip)—a smart option for travelers with a lot of luggage or a lot of kids. Plus, the privately run boats are smaller and have fewer passengers, and can even arrange full-boat charters for groups or families. Keep in mind that these boats don't run as frequently as the government-run ferry, but all provide meet-and-greet service at the airport and direct ground-shuttle transport (3 min.) to the Simpson Bay Immigration Dock for passport clearance. Then you're on the boat and off to Anguilla. Delivering passengers directly to and from the airport are the **GB Express** (www.anguillaferryandcharter.com; © **264/235-6205** in Anguilla, or 721/581-3568 on St. Maarten; $55 one-way, $105 round-trip; children 1–11 $45 one-way, $90 round-trip) and **Funtime Charters** (www.funtime-charters.com; © **866/334-0047** or 264/497-6511; $65 per person one-way, half-price for children 11 and under). The **MV _Shauna VI_** (© **264/476-0975** or 772-2031 in Anguilla, 721/580-6275 on St. Maarten; myshauna6@hotmail.com; round-trip fare $60 adults, $40 children 2–12) delivers passengers to the fishing dock at Simpson Bay. Reservations are required.

You might also opt to use one of the private charter boats on your return trip to the airport in St. Maarten. Check each operator's schedule for the time that's most convenient for you. Keep in mind that for international flights you're asked to be at the airport no less than 2 hours before your scheduled departure.

Tip: If you'd like to do some shopping and have lunch in Marigot before you take your ferry to Anguilla, simply store your bags at the ferry landing in the small baggage-storage area ($5, plus tip).

ST. BARTS   For those who find the high-wire flight into St. Barts nerve-wracking, the island is easily accessible by boat. If you're transferring from the St. Maarten airport, you will need to take a 20-minute cab ride to reach the ferry ports. The high-speed **Voyager** vessels (www.voy12.com; © **590/87-10-68**) make frequent (usually twice daily, sometimes more) runs between St. Barts and both St. Maarten (Oyster Pond) and St. Martin (Marigot harbor). The schedule varies according to the season (and the seas). Advance reservations are highly recommended; fares run around 85€ adults, 45€ children 2 to 12 round-trip (including taxes). Each

TIPS ON dining

Some folks—myself included—consider the food on the three islands in this book to be the best in the Caribbean. For St. Maarten/St. Martin specifics, see chapter 3; consult chapters 7 and 8 for respective details on Anguilla and St. Barts. The restaurant listings have been separated into four categories in this book based on the average cost per person per meal, service charge included, but keep in mind that each island has slightly different relative costs—and many, if not most, restaurants in St. Martin and St. Barts price their menu in euros. Roughly, the categories are **Very Expensive** ($35 and up); **Expensive** ($25–$40); **Moderate** ($15–$30); and **Inexpensive** ($15 and under).

Due to the high costs of importing food, dining out can be costly. To save money on meals, stock up on basics (snacks, soft drinks, milk, and beer) at local grocery stores. St. Maarten/St. Martin has a number of big, well-stocked supermarkets; to locate them, see "Resources for Self-Catering," in chapter 3. Several restaurants on St. Martin and St. Barts offer 1€=$1 exchange rates for customers paying cash (this rarely applies to credit card users). For eating out, lunch is generally less expensive, when you can fill up on gently priced midday *plats du jour.* Keep in mind that many restaurants tack on a service charge to the bill (virtually all the restaurants in French St. Martin and St. Barts have a 15% *service compris*—service included—in the final bill). The menu should state whether service is included, but always confirm whether gratuities are added. In many instances tips are pooled among the staff (including the back of the house), so it never hurts to add a little extra if you feel your server warrants it.

Note: *Entrée* is the French term for appetizer; *plat* means main course.

passenger is allowed to carry two pieces of luggage free of charge. It's a 30-minute trip from Oyster Pond and a 1-hour trip from Marigot harbor. If seas are choppy, the ride can be rough; it's recommended that those with weak tummies take seasickness medication before heading out or buy anti-nausea bracelets aboard the boats. *Voyager 1* is a monohull built to carry 117 passengers; the *Voyager 2* catamaran is outfitted to carry 154 passengers; and the newest Voyager vessel, *Voyager 3 Dreamliner,* is a high-speed hydrofoil catamaran with a 154-passenger capacity and a Business Class cabin on the upper deck. The high-speed 20m (65-ft.) aluminum monohull **Great Bay Express** (www.greatbayferry.com; © 721/542-0032 in St. Maarten) offers two or three daily 45-minute crossings between St. Maarten's Bobby's Marina in Philipsburg and Gustavia. The boat can carry 130 passengers. Reservations are essential; the round-trip fare is 90€ to 95€ adults, 45€ to 65€ children 2 to 11 (including taxes).

MONEY & COSTS

THE VALUE OF THE U.S. DOLLAR VS. OTHER POPULAR CURRENCIES

US$	Can$	UK£	Euro (€)	Aus$	NZ$
$1	C$1.00	£0.64	€0.81	A$0.95	NZ$1.23

Frommer's lists exact prices in the local currency. The currency conversions quoted above were correct at press time. However, rates fluctuate, so before you depart, consult a currency exchange website such as www.oanda.com/convert/classic to check up-to-the-minute rates.

Despite the dominance of the euro since January 2002 within the mother country, the Netherlands, the legal tender on the Dutch side of St. Maarten is still the **Netherlands Antilles florin (NAf), or the Antillean guilder;** the official exchange rate is NAf 1.78 for each $1. **U.S. dollars** are really the coin of the realm here, and prices in hotels and most restaurants and shops are designated in dollars. On the French side (as well as on St. Barts), the official monetary unit is the **euro,** with most establishments widely quoting and accepting either dollars or NAf guilders as well. Anguilla's official currency is the **East Caribbean Dollar,** though U.S. dollars are accepted everywhere; the exchange rate is set permanently at roughly 2.70EC to $1.

Prices throughout this book are given in U.S. dollars for establishments on the Dutch side and Anguilla, and in either euros or U.S. dollars for establishments on the French side and St. Barts, according to whether establishments quoted their prices in euros or dollars at press time.

Some establishments on St. Barts and French St. Martin advertise a 1-to-1 exchange rate if you use cash. Always confirm before you get the bill.

ATMs The easiest and best way to get cash away from home is from an ATM. Be sure you know your daily withdrawal limit before you leave home. Also keep in mind that many banks impose a fee every time a card is used at a different bank's ATM, and that fee can be higher for international transactions than for domestic ones. Check with your bank about withdrawal and

WHAT THINGS COST ON ST. MAARTEN/ST. MARTIN

	$
Taxi from Princess Juliana to Marigot	15.00–**21.00**
Double room, moderate	200.00–**250.00**
Double room, inexpensive	100.00–**140.00**
Three-course dinner for one without wine, moderate	15.00–**25.00**
Bottle of Carib beer	1.00–**1.50**
Bottle of Coca-Cola	1.00
Cup of coffee	1.00–**1.50**
1 gallon of premium gas	5.00

WHAT THINGS COST ON ANGUILLA

	$
Taxi from the ferry to Cap Juluca	26.00
Double room, moderate	250.00–**350.00**
Double room, inexpensive	120.00–**160.00**
Three-course dinner for one without wine, moderate	25.00–**30.00**
Bottle of Carib beer	1.50–**2.00**
Bottle of Coca-Cola	1.50
Cup of coffee	1.50–**2.00**
1 gallon of premium gas	5.00

WHAT THINGS COST ON ST. BARTS

	€
Taxi from the airport to Cul-de-Sac	10.00–**30.00**
Double room, moderate	250.00–**300.00**
Double room, inexpensive	150.00–**200.00**
Three-course dinner for one without wine, moderate	25.00
Bottle of Carib beer	1.50–**2.00**
Bottle of Coca-Cola	1.50
Cup of coffee	1.50
1 gallon of premium gas	5.00

international transaction fees before you leave home. On top of this, the bank from which you withdraw cash may charge its own fee.

Note: Keep in mind that ATMs in St. Maarten give you a choice of dollars or euros, while ATMs on St. Martin dispense only euros.

For bank and ATM information on St. Maarten/St. Martin, St. Barts, and Anguilla, see their respective "Fast Facts" sections, later in this chapter.

TRAVELER'S CHECKS   Traveler's checks are widely accepted on all three islands. You can get traveler's checks at almost any bank. They are offered in denominations of $20, $50, $100, $500, and, sometimes, $1,000. Generally, you'll pay a service charge ranging from 1% to 4%. The most popular traveler's checks are offered by American Express (© **800/807-6233** or 800/221-7282 for cardholders—this number accepts collect calls, offers service in several foreign languages, and exempts Amex gold and platinum cardholders from the 1% fee); **Visa** (© **800/732-1322**—AAA members can obtain Visa checks for a $9.95 fee [for checks up to $1,500] at most AAA offices or by calling © **866/339-3378**); and **MasterCard** (© **800/223-9920**).

If you carry traveler's checks, be sure to keep a record of their serial numbers separate from your checks in the event that they are stolen or lost. You'll get a refund faster if you know the numbers.

CREDIT CARDS   Major credit cards are widely accepted on all three islands.

Almost every credit card company has an emergency toll-free number that you can call if your wallet or purse is stolen. Credit card companies may be able to wire cash advances immediately, and in many places they can deliver an emergency credit card in a day or two. **Citicorp Visa**'s U.S. emergency number is © **800/336-8472. American Express** cardholders and traveler's check holders should call © **800/221-7282** for all money emergencies. **MasterCard** holders should call © **800/307-7309.**

HEALTH
Availability of Healthcare

The best medical facilities are on St. Maarten/St. Martin, with good clinics on Anguilla and St. Barts. Emergency airlift to Puerto Rico is available from all three destinations.

It's fairly easy to obtain major over-the-counter medication, with most major North American brands available, as well as brands manufactured in Europe under unfamiliar names. Some leading prescription drugs for such common ailments as allergies, asthma, and acid reflux are also available over the counter, albeit by European pharmaceutical companies.

Common Ailments

There are no major health concerns for travels to St. Maarten/St. Martin, Anguilla, or St. Barts. The most common issues are insects and overexposure to the tropical sun.

BUGS, BITES & OTHER WILDLIFE CONCERNS   The biggest menaces on all three islands are mosquitoes (none are disease vectors) and no-see-ums, which appear mainly in the early evening. Window screens aren't always sufficient, so carry insect repellent. In St. Barts, it appears that the old Belou line of essential oils (including a great insect repellent) is no more; however, many of the products in the **Ligne St. Barth** (www.lignestbarth.com) line of creams and sunscreens contain roucou, considered to be a natural insect repellent. The shop/laboratory for Ligne St. Barth is on the Route de Salines in Lorient.

SUN EXPOSURE   The tropical sun can be brutal. Wear sunglasses and a hat, and apply sunscreen liberally. Increase your time on the beach gradually. If you do overexpose yourself, stay out of the sun until you recover. Sun and heatstroke are possibilities, especially if you engage in strenuous physical activity. See a doctor immediately if fever, chills, dizziness, nausea, or headaches follow overexposure.

What to Do if You Get Sick Away From Home

It's easy to find good English-speaking doctors on all three islands. You can find **hospitals** and **emergency numbers** in the respective "Fast Facts" sections, later in this chapter.

If you suffer from a chronic illness, consult your doctor before your departure. You may have to pay all medical costs upfront and be reimbursed later. If you are especially worried about getting sick away from home, you might want to consider buying medical travel insurance.

CRIME & SAFETY

Petty crime has become an issue of concern on Dutch St. Maarten, with thefts and break-ins increasingly prevalent. Travelers are urged to lock their cars and lodging doors and windows at all times. Visitors should exercise common sense and take basic precautions everywhere on the island, including being aware of their surroundings, avoiding walking alone after dark or in remote areas, and locking all valuables in a rental or hotel safe.

Anguilla is one of the safest destinations in the Caribbean, but you should still take standard precautions. Although crime is rare here, secure your valuables. Crime is also extremely rare on St. Barts; it's one of the safest islands in the Caribbean. But never leave valuables unguarded on the beach or in parked cars, even if locked in the trunk.

SPECIALIZED TRAVEL RESOURCES

In addition to the destination-specific resources listed below, visit Frommers.com for other specialized travel resources.

hurricanes

The northeastern Caribbean has seen its share of destructive hurricanes. Fortunately, modern technology and satellite surveillance provide plenty of advance warning of impending storms. Hurricane season officially begins in June and ends in late November, but high hurricane season in this neck of the woods is the month of September. A number of resorts use this time (early fall) to close for renovations, especially on St. Barts. If you are caught in a hurricane or tropical storm during your stay, follow the instructions of officials (especially in the event of an evacuation to higher ground). Keep in mind that low-lying areas may be prone to flooding, and that the seas may have dangerous rip currents even after a hurricane has passed. For the latest satellite imagery and hurricane information, go to the National Oceanic and Atmospheric Administration's **National Hurricane Center** (www.nhc.noaa.gov).

Travelers with Disabilities

Be aware that most flights arriving in St. Maarten do not deplane through gates but down movable steps on the tarmac. Many of the newer hotels and resorts on the islands are equipped with handicapped-accessible bathrooms. Beaches can be difficult to access for those in wheelchairs, however. One exception: The nudist resort, **Club Orient** (www.cluborient.com), on Orient Beach in French St. Martin, has not only wheelchair-accessible bathrooms but also provides some of the island's few beach wheelchairs. The **oceanfront boardwalk** in Philipsburg is wide and flat, making it ideal for wheelchair travel.

LGBT Travelers

St. Barts may be the most gay-friendly island in the Caribbean. With its sunny cosmopolitanism, St. Maarten/St. Martin is also a popular destination for gay travelers. Anguilla, like many a British colony, is more conservative in attitude, but individual deluxe resorts welcome gay and lesbian travelers.

The **International Gay and Lesbian Travel Association** (**IGLTA;** www.iglta.org; ✆ **954/630-1637**) is the trade association for the gay and lesbian travel industry and offers an online directory of gay- and lesbian-friendly travel businesses; go to its website and click on "Plan Your Trip."

Senior Travel

Though the major U.S. airlines flying to St. Maarten no longer offer senior discounts or coupon books, some hotels extend deals, especially during slower periods. Members of **AARP,** 601 E St. NW, Washington, DC 20049 (www.aarp.org; ✆ **888/687-2277**), get discounts on hotels, airfares, and car rentals. AARP offers members a wide range of benefits, including *AARP The Magazine* and a monthly newsletter. Anyone 50 and over can join.

Family Travel

All three islands are great family destinations. St. Maarten/St. Martin has a number of family-friendly resorts and restaurants featuring kids' menus. Anguilla is very family-friendly, particularly during spring break, the shoulder seasons, and summer; the calm, clear waters are perfect for beginning swimmers. Although some St. Barts resorts discourage children during high season, the island is a heavenly kid-friendly playground the rest of the year.

Even those hotels and resorts with specific adults-only aspects offer some sort of kid-friendly amenities or programs. Older kids will have plenty of nonmotorized watersports activities (snorkeling, sailing, parasailing) to keep them happy.

To locate accommodations, restaurants, and attractions that are particularly kid-friendly, refer to the "Kids" icon throughout this guide.

RESPONSIBLE TOURISM
St. Maarten/St. Martin

Rampant development on the Dutch side of the island has been cause for concern for environmentalists for some time. The local environmental nonprofit **Sint Maarten Pride Foundation** claims that the island's natural biodiversity is threatened because inadequate government controls have allowed developers to over-run the environment and destroy delicate ecosystems. Equally concerning to environmentalists are the lack of a modernized waste-management infrastructure (and recycling capabilities) and the presence of an ever-expanding landfill situated in a wetlands estuary. Also active in conservation awareness is the **Nature Foundation St. Maarten** (www.naturefoundationsxm.org), established by the government in 1997.

Anguilla

Sustainability and "going green" are hot topics of discussion on Anguilla these days. When development came to a virtual standstill during the global recession, the island's movers and shakers decided to take the long view in protecting and preserving Anguilla's natural resources. A **Sustainable Energy Committee** has been looking at ways (wind power, solar power) to make the country less dependent on traditional energy sources. In other developments, a forward-thinking government agricultural initiative to **farm vegetables** on a large swath of land is putting fresh sweet potatoes, peppers, corn, squash, tomatoes, lettuces, and pigeon peas into the marketplace. Former farmers are rediscovering the pleasure of growing food, and new farmers (and future chefs) are being initiated in this agricultural renaissance. Local chefs are also getting in on the act, designing menus around **local seafood** instead of expensive imported fish. Eco-tourism is on the rise, with increasingly popular eco-tours offered by the Anguilla National Trust. The Trust also makes monthly species counts on the local ponds and wetlands.

St. Barts

Perhaps the most environmentally enlightened of the three islands, St. Barts has long been doing its bit to protect the environment—even though getting food and goods onto the island is a massive daily (and carbon-footprint-heavy) enterprise. Islanders are **natural recyclers**—they've had to be, as the island has little arable land and no fresh water. Many of the old-timers still collect rainwater in cisterns; some even drink it! Most people bring recycled or cloth bags to grocery stores, and eco-conscious chefs are building menus around local and sustainable food sources. Trash is rarely seen on beaches; visitors are asked to take out whatever they bring in.

STAYING CONNECTED

Telephones

CALLING ST. MAARTEN/ST. MARTIN FROM ABROAD

Note: As of 2012, Dutch St. Maarten has a new area code, **721.**

1. To call the French side, dial the international access code: **011** from the U.S. and Canada; **00** from the U.K., Ireland, or New Zealand; or **0011** from Australia. To call the Dutch side, dial the country code **1**.
2. Dial the country code **590** for St. Martin or the dialing code **721** for St. Maarten.
3. For St. Martin, dial the city code **590** (a second time) and then the six-digit number. Dial the St. Maarten city code **(54)** and then the five-digit number.

CALLING WITHIN ST. MAARTEN/ST. MARTIN

From the Dutch to the French side (and St. Barts), dial **00,** then **590590** (590690 for cellphones) and the six-digit number. From the French to Dutch side, dial **00-721**, followed by **54** and the five-digit number.

INTERNATIONAL CALLS FROM ST. MAARTEN/ ST. MARTIN

From St. Maarten/St. Martin, first dial **00** and then the country code (U.S. or Canada 1, U.K. 44, Ireland 353, Australia 61, New Zealand 64). Next, dial the area code and number. For example, if you wanted to call the British Embassy in Washington, D.C., you would dial 00-1-202-588-7800.

Both the Dutch side and the French side have public phones from which you can make overseas calls using prepaid phone cards. On the Dutch side there are phones from which you can also make overseas credit-card and collect calls. The public phones on the French side accept only prepaid phone cards. You can buy phone cards in $5, $10, and $20 increments throughout the island at gas stations, newsstands, phone stores, and post offices. At the Marigot post office, you can purchase a prepaid phone card called a télécarte, giving you 40 units. A typical 5-minute call to the States takes up to 120 units. There are two public phones at the Marigot tourist office from which it's possible to make credit card calls. There are six public phones at the post office.

If you need operator assistance in making a call, dial **0** if you're trying to make an international call (include the St. Maarten/St. Martin number if you're calling between the two countries). For directory assistance, dial **150** if you're looking for a number inside St. Maarten/St. Martin, and dial **0** for numbers to all other countries.

ST. BARTS   St. Barts is linked to the Guadeloupe telephone system. To call St. Barts from home, dial your country's international access code, then **590** (the country code for Guadeloupe), and then the city code and number. To call home from St. Barts, first dial **00** and then the country code (U.S. or Canada 1, U.K. 44, Ireland 353, Australia 61, New Zealand 64), followed by the area code and number.

The island has a handful of public telephones for making local and international calls that use télécartes; these prepaid phone cards are sold at the gas station across from the airport and at post offices in Gustavia and St-Jean. To reach an AT&T operator from anywhere on St. Barts, dial *©* **0800-99-00-11;** to reach **Verizon,** dial *©* **0800-99-00-19;** and to reach **Sprint,** dial *©* **0800-99-00-87.**

ANGUILLA   To call Anguilla from the U.S. and Canada, dial **1** and then **the 10-digit number;** to call the U.K. and New Zealand from Anguilla, dial **00** plus **1** and then the area code and number; to call Australia from Anguilla, dial **0011** plus **1** and then the area code and number.

To call the U.S. and Canada from Anguilla, dial **1** (the country code), the area code, and the seven-digit number. To call the U.K. from Anguilla, dial **011,** then **44,** then the telephone number. To call Australia from Anguilla, dial **011,** then **61,** then the area code and number. To call New Zealand from Anguilla, dial **011,** then **64,** then the area code and number.

Telephone, cable, and Telex services are offered by **LIME** (formerly Cable & Wireless Ltd.), Wallblake Road, the Valley (*©* **264/497-3100**), open Monday to Friday from 8am to 5pm. **Digicel** (*©* **264/498-3444**), with its main office by the public library in the Valley, usually has better rates for renting or buying a cellphone than LIME does.

TOLL-FREE NUMBERS   There are no toll-free numbers on St. Maarten/St. Martin, Anguilla, or St. Barts, and calling an 800 number in the States from them is not toll-free. In fact, it costs the same as an overseas call.

Cellphones

The three letters that define the islands' wireless capabilities are **GSM** (Global System for Mobile Communications), a big, seamless network that makes for easy cross-border cellphone use. If your cellphone is on a GSM system and you have a world-capable multiband phone such as many Sony Ericsson, Motorola, or Samsung models, you can make and receive calls across the islands covered in this book. Just call your wireless operator and ask for "international roaming" to be activated on your account. (Note that depending on your cellphone plan, this might be extremely expensive.)

For many, **renting** a phone on one of the islands is a good idea. You can rent a phone from any number of island sites, including kiosks at airports and at car rental agencies. Mobile phone rentals are available from **Friendly Island Cellphone Rentals** (✆ 721/553-7368), in Simpson Bay, St. Maarten; they'll even deliver the phone to your resort or villa. On Anguilla you can arrange a phone rental through your hotel or resort or directly from **LIME** (formerly Cable & Wireless Ltd.), Wallblake Road, the Valley (✆ 264/497-3100), or **Digicel** (✆ 264/498-3444), with its main office by the public library in the Valley. On St. Barts, **Centre @lizés,** rue de la République, Gustavia (✆ 590/29-89-89), is a full-service Internet cafe that also offers cellphone and laptop rentals.

Voice-over Internet Protocol (VOIP)

If you have Web access while traveling, you might consider a broadband-based telephone service (in technical terms, **Voice-over Internet protocol,** or **VoIP**) such as Skype (www.skype.com) or Vonage (www.vonage.com), which allows you to make free international calls if you use their services from your laptop or in a cybercafe. For all the details on restrictions and availability, check the websites above for details.

Internet/E-Mail
WITHOUT YOUR OWN COMPUTER

Most resorts have small business centers with a computer or two for guests. For more information on Internet access on the islands, see "Internet Access" in their respective "Fast Facts" sections, later in this chapter.

WITH YOUR OWN COMPUTER

Most hotels, resorts, airports, cafes, and retailers offer high-speed **Wi-Fi** (wireless fidelity), either free or for a small fee. Most laptops sold today have built-in wireless capability.

For dial-up access, most business-class hotels offer dataports for laptop modems.

TIPS ON ACCOMMODATIONS

The rates given in this book are only "rack rates"—that is, the officially posted rate that you'd be given if you just walked in off the street. Almost everyone ends up paying less than the rack rate through packages, discounts, and strategic planning. Think of the rates in this book as guidelines to help you comparison-shop. Check online for great deals and multiday packages on hotel websites. Roughly, the price categories in this book are **Very Expensive** ($650 and up); **Expensive** ($375–$650); **Moderate** ($215–$375); and **Inexpensive** ($215 and under).

You can save big on your lodging bill simply by traveling in the off season. The high season on all three islands is the winter season, roughly from the middle of December through the middle of April. Hotels charge their peak rates during the winter, rates that spike stratospherically during the 2 weeks around the Christmas holidays. The off season is the rest of the year—although the so-called "shoulder seasons," roughly late spring and late fall (after hurricane season is over)—are increasingly popular. Expect rates to fall outside the traditional high season, however, particularly in the summer. You'll find that during the off season, many resorts offer deals on multinight stays or sweeten the deal with meals or activities included in the rates.

Keep in mind that each island government imposes an occupancy or room tax (called a "tourism tax" on St. Barts), applicable to all hotels, inns, and guesthouses. On St. Maarten a government tax of 5% is added to your hotel bill. Hotels on French St. Martin tack on a local room tax *(taxe de séjour)* of 4% to 5%. On Anguilla the government collects a 10% tax on rooms. The St. Barts tourism tax is 5%. Ask whether taxes are included in the original rates you're quoted. Furthermore, many hotels routinely tack on 10% to 12% for "service." That means that with tax and service, some bills are 15% or even 25% higher than the price originally quoted to you!

And, of course, some hotels are particularly adept at tacking on extra charges that can add up quickly. The minibar is one money trap you won't want to fall into; look for a grocery or convenience store to stock up on sodas, snacks, water, and beer. Another big extra is phone charges. Making direct international calls from your hotel phone can be exorbitant, and many hotels also charge fees for local calls. If you have a GSM cellphone with international roaming capabilities, you're in business; otherwise, you may want to consider renting a cellphone or buying a prepaid cellphone when you're on one of the islands. See "Cellphones," above.

Types of Accommodations

HOTELS & RESORTS All three islands have a broad range of accommodations, from five-star luxe to guesthouse modest. Deals are out there, however, even at the priciest resorts. Be sure to get on a resort's e-mail list or Twitter feed: Many offer terrific money-saving packages (*especially* during low season) advertised via e-mail or Twitter. Look into air/hotel packages offered by online travel agencies such as Orbitz, Travelocity, and Priceline for big savings.

CONDOS & VILLAS If you're traveling with your family or a group of friends, a "housekeeping holiday" can be one of the least expensive ways to vacation in St. Maarten/St. Martin, Anguilla, and St. Barts. It's a good way to go if you value your privacy and independence. The savings, especially for a large group or family, can be substantial, particularly for the self-catering capabilities—it's a lot cheaper than eating all your meals at restaurants. St. Maarten offers a number of condominium rooms and suites—many of which are timeshare units (timeshares account for some 60% of the lodging rental market on the island). Timeshare members of **RCI** (www.rci.com; ☎ **317/805-9000**) or **Interval International** (www.intervalworld.com; ☎ **888/784-3447**) can look into the feasibility of exchanges on St. Maarten. Villas are extremely popular on St. Barts and Anguilla, and, to a lesser degree, on St. Maarten/St. Martin. **Wimco** (www.wimco.com; ☎ **800/932-3222**) is a reputable company handling properties on all three islands. For villas in St. Barts, **St. Barth Properties** (www.stbarth.com; ☎ **800-421-3396**) is affiliated with Sotheby's. (For other suggestions for Anguilla and St. Barts, see chapters 7 and 8, respectively.)

[FastFACTS] ST. MAARTEN/ ST. MARTIN

Area Codes The country and area code for St. Martin is 590. The new country and area code for St. Maarten is 1-721.

Banks Banks affiliated with the **Cirrus** (www.mastercard.com; ☎ **800/424-7787**) and **PLUS** (www.visa.com; ☎ **800/843-7587**)

ATM networks are located on St. Maarten/St. Martin. **Note:** Keep in mind that ATMs in St. Maarten give you a choice of dollars or euros, while ATMs on St. Martin dispense only euros. **On the Dutch side:** A number of banks are clustered along Front and Back streets in Philipsburg. **Windward Island Bank (WIB)** (http://wib-bank.net) has 22 ATM locations on island, including at the Princess Juliana International Airport arrival hall, the A.C. Wathey Cruise Facility, the Oyster Bay Resort, and the Greenhouse Restaurant. **Scotiabank** (www.scotiabank.com) has ATMs on Back Street in Philipsburg, at the cruise terminal facility, at Simpson Bay Yacht Club, and at the Atlantis Casino. **FirstCaribbean Bank** (www.cibcfcib.com) has ATMs on Back Street in Philipsburg and at the Laguna View Professional Center in Cole Bay. **RBTT N.V.** (www.rbtt.com) has six ATM locations on island, including in Marigot, at 24 Cannegieter St. in Philipsburg, and at the La Terrasse building on Rhine Road in Maho. **On the French side:** Most banks are located along rue de la République in Marigot, including the **Banque des Antilles Francaises** (www.bdaf.fr), **Banque Populaire Bred** (www.bred.fr), and **Crédit Mutuel** (www.creditmutuel.fr), which also has an ATM location in Hope Estate near Grand Case.

Business Hours Banks: On the Dutch side, most banks are open Monday to Friday from 8:30am to 3:30pm, Saturday from 9am to noon. On the French side, they are usually open Monday to Friday from 8:30am to 1:30pm. **Stores/shops:** Although French St. Martin stores open around 9am and close around 7pm, most shopkeepers close to take an extended lunch break from around 12:30 to 2pm, or even longer. Dutch side shops stay open continuously from 9am to 6pm (and later).

Currency On the Dutch side, the official currency is the Netherlands Antilles florin (NAf) guilder, although U.S. dollars are widely accepted, and prices in hotels and most restaurants and shops are most often designated in dollars as well. On the French side, the official monetary unit is the **euro** (€), with most establishments widely quoting and accepting either dollars or NAf guilders as well. *Prices throughout this book are given in U.S. dollars for establishments on the Dutch side, and in euros or dollars for establishments on the French side.*

Driving Rules See "Getting Around St. Maarten/St. Martin," p. 172.

Drinking Laws Eighteen is the legal drinking age on St. Maarten/St. Martin. Alcohol is sold in grocery stores and restaurants.

Drugstores Both sides have several pharmacies, though none are open 24 hours. On the **French** side, try **Pharmacie du Port,** rue de la Liberté, Marigot (*©* **590/87-50-79;** Mon–Sat 8am–7:30pm, Sun hours vary). On the **Dutch** side, try **Philipsburg Pharmacy,** 4 E. Voges St., Philipsburg (www.philipsburgpharmacy.com; *©* **721/542-3001;**

Mon–Fri 7:30am–7pm, Sat 9am–1pm, Sun 10am–noon); **Simpson Bay Pharmacy,** Simpson Bay Yacht Club, 163 Welfare Rd. (℃ **721/544-3653;** Mon–Fri 8:15am–7pm, Sat 9am–1pm, Sun 5–7pm); and the **Druggist,** Airport Road, Simpson Bay (℃ **721/545-2777;** Mon–Fri 8:30am–7:30pm, Sat noon–7pm, Sun 1–3pm).

Electricity   Dutch St. Maarten and Anguilla use the same voltage (110-volt AC, 60 cycles) with the same electrical configurations as North America, so adapters and transformers are not necessary for Americans or Canadians. However, on French St. Martin and St. Barts, 220-volt AC, 60 cycles prevails; North Americans will usually need transformers and adapters. To simplify things, many hotels on both sides of the island have installed sockets suitable for both European and North American appliances.

Embassies & Consulates   For St. Maarten/St. Martin, **citizens of the U.S.** are represented by its consulate at 1 Gorsiraweg, Willemstad, Curaçao (℃ **599/461-3066**). There is a Canadian consulate at Dawn Beach Estate, Green Starshell Rd. #18, St. Maarten (℃ **721/543-6261**). **Citizens of the U.K.** can register with the consulate at 6 Werfstraat in Willemstad, Curaçao (℃ **599/461-3900**).

Emergencies   For emergencies, dial ℃ **919** on the Dutch side or ℃ **18** on the French side. On the **Dutch** side, call the **police** at ℃ **542-2222** or an **ambulance** at ℃ **542-2111;** to report a **fire,** call ℃ **919.** On the **French** side, you can reach the **police** by dialing ℃ **87-88-33** or an **ambulance** by dialing ℃ **29-04-04.** In case of fire, dial ℃ **18.**

Holidays   National holidays are New Year's Day (Jan 1); Epiphany (Jan 6, French side); Carnival (early Feb); Good Friday and Easter Monday (usually Apr); Labor Day (May 1); Ascension Day (early May); Bastille Day (July 14, French side); Schoelcher Day (July 21, French side); Assumption Day (Aug 15); All Saints' Day (Nov 1); Concordia Day and St. Martin Day (Nov 11); Christmas Day (Dec 25); and Boxing Day (Dec 26). For more information, see "St. Maarten/St. Martin Calendar of Events," on p. 167.

Hospitals   On the Dutch side, go to the **St. Maarten Medical Center,** Welegen Road, Cay Hill (www.sintmaartenmedicalcenter.com; ℃ **721/543-1111**). On the French side, the local hospital is **Hospital Louis-Constant Fleming,** near Marigot in Concordia (www.chsaintmartin.org; ℃ **590/52-25-25**).

Internet Access   Cybercafes can be found in both Marigot and Philipsburg, and most hotels have high-speed Internet access and/or a computer center.

Mail   On St. Maarten, the **main post office** (℃ **721/542-2298**) is located on Walter Nisbeth Road. The **main post office** (Bureau Principal; ℃ **590/51-07-64**) on the French side is in Marigot, on rue de la Liberté.

Fast Facts: St. Maarten/St. Martin

PLANNING YOUR TRIP

Newspapers & Magazines In addition to several local newspapers (*The Daily Herald* is the leading English-language publication), visitors can pick up (from hotels, grocery stores, and so on) one of several free and useful tourist magazines, including *St. Maarten Nature, St. Maarten Events, Discover St. Martin/St. Maarten, St. Maarten Nights, Ti Gourmet,* and *Vacation St. Maarten.*

Passports See "Embassies & Consulates," above, for whom to contact if you lose your passport while traveling. For other information, contact the following agencies:

For Residents of Australia Contact the **Australian Passport Information Service** at (℃) **131-232,** or visit www.passports.gov.au.

For Residents of Canada Contact the central **Passport Office,** Department of Foreign Affairs and International Trade, Ottawa, ON K1A 0G3 (www.ppt.gc.ca; (℃) **800/567-6868**).

For Residents of Ireland Contact the **Passport Office,** Setanta Centre, Molesworth Street, Dublin 2 ((℃) **01/671-1633;** www. foreignaffairs.gov.ie).

For Residents of New Zealand Contact the **Passports Office,** Department of Internal Affairs, Level 3, 109 Featherstone St., Wellington 6140 ((℃) **0800/225-050** in New Zealand or 04/463-9360; www.passports.govt.nz).

For Residents of the United Kingdom Visit your nearest passport office, major post office, or travel agency, or contact the **Identity and Passport Service (IPS),** 89 Eccleston Sq., London SW1V 1PN (www.homeoffice.gov.uk; (℃) **0300/222-0000**).

For Residents of the United States To find your regional passport office, check the U.S. State Department website (http:// travel.state.gov/passport) or call the **National Passport Information Center** ((℃) **877/487-2778**) for automated information.

Police See "Emergencies," above.

Safety See "Crime & Safety" (p. 181).

Smoking While many larger properties offer nonsmoking rooms, there are no regulations against smoking—for now. Legislation has recently been proposed to ban smoking in all St. Maarten restaurants, bars, and casinos; check before your trip to see if the law has been passed.

Taxes For departures to international destinations from Princess Juliana airport on the Dutch side, there's a departure tax of $30 ($10 if you're leaving the island for St. Eustatius or Saba; if you're leaving by ferry from Marigot Pier to Anguilla, the departure tax is $4). There is a 3€ ($4.50) departure tax for departures from L'Espérance Airport on the French side. *Note:* The departure tax is often included in the airfare.

In St. Maarten, a government tax of 5% is added to your hotel bill. On top of that, many hotels tack on a service charge of 10% to

15%. Hotels in French St. Martin add a 10% service charge and a *taxe de séjour*, a local room tax of 4% to 5%.

Telephones   See "Staying Connected" (p. 184).

Time   St. Maarten/St. Martin operate on Atlantic Standard Time year-round. Thus in winter, if it's 6pm in Philipsburg, it's 5pm in New York. During daylight saving time in the United States, the island and the U.S. East Coast are on the same time.

Tipping   See "Tips on Dining" (p. 176) for restaurant guidelines. Porters and bellmen expect $1 per bag. Taxi drivers should receive 10% of the fare, more if they offer touring or other suggestions.

Toilets   Public facilities are few and far between, other than a couple of options in Marigot, Philipsburg, and Orient Beach. Hotel lobbies and restaurants are the best options, though technically you should be a guest or customer.

Water   The water on St. Maarten/St. Martin is safe to drink. In fact, most hotels serve desalinated water.

[FastFACTS] ANGUILLA

Area Codes   The country and area code for Anguilla is 264.

Banks/ATMs   Banks with ATMs are open Monday to Thursday 8am to 3pm, Friday 8am to 5pm. The **National Bank of Anguilla** (www.nba.ai; ℭ **264/497-2101**) has ATMs at eight locations, including the bank's main branch in the Valley; in Palm Plaza, right across from the CuisinArt Resort turnoff; at Wallblake Airport; and at Syd-Ann's in Sandy Ground. The main branches of both **Scotiabank,** the Valley, Fairplay Commercial Complex (www.scotiabank.com; ℭ **264/497-3333**), and **FirstCaribbean,** the Valley (www.cibcfcib.com; ℭ **264/497-2301**), have ATMs that are usually accessible after hours. The **Caribbean Commercial Bank** (http://ccb.ai; ℭ **246/497-2571**) has ATMs at its main branch in the Valley and at Ashley's & Sons Supermarket.

Business Hours   Banks are open from 8am until 3pm Monday through Thursday and Friday until 5pm. Businesses keep widely varying schedules (some boutiques and art galleries close for lunch), although grocery stores are generally open Monday to Saturday from 8am to 9pm (until noon Sun).

Drinking Laws   The legal drinking age is 18. Wine, beer, and liquor are sold in grocery stores and restaurants 7 days a week during regular hours.

Driving Rules   See "Getting Around," in chapter 7.

Electricity   See "Fast Facts: St. Maarten/St. Martin," above.

Embassies & Consulates   There is no U.S. diplomatic representation on Anguilla. **U.S. citizens** are advised to register with the consulates at Bluff House, English Harbour, on Antigua (© **268/463-6531;** ryderj@candw.ag), or Bridgetown, Barbados (http://bridgetown.usembassy.gov or https://step.state.gov/step). Likewise, **Canadian citizens** should register with the Canadian High Commission on Barbados. **Australian citizens** can register with the Australian High Commission in Port-of-Spain, Trinidad and Tobago (© **868/628-4732**).

Emergencies You can reach the police at their headquarters in the Valley (© **264/497-2333**) or the substation at Sandy Ground (© **264/497-2354**). In an emergency, dial © **911.**

Holidays New Year's Day (Jan 1), Good Friday, Easter Monday, Monday after Pentecost (Whit Monday), May 30–31 (Anguilla Day), June 18 (Queen's Birthday), first Monday in August (August Monday), first Thursday in August (August Thursday), August 6 (Constitution Day), December 17 (Separation Day), Christmas Day (Dec 25), December 28 (Boxing Day).

Hospitals For medical services, consult the **Princess Alexandra Hospital,** Stoney Ground, the Valley (© **264/497-2551**). Many of the larger hotels have a physician on call.

Internet Access Most hotels, large and small, offer free Wi-Fi.

Language English is the main language on Anguilla.

Mail The main post office is on Wallblake Road, the Valley (www.aps.ai; © **264/497-2528**). Collectors consider Anguilla's stamps valuable, and the post office also operates a philatelic bureau, open Monday to Friday 8am to 4:45pm. Airmail postcards and letters cost EC$1.50 (55¢) to the U.S., Canada, and the United Kingdom. *Note:* Anguilla got its first postal code (**AI-2640**) in January 2009. If you're sending a letter to Anguilla from another country, place the new postal code after "Anguilla" and before "British West Indies" (or "B.W.I.").

Passports All visitors must have an onward or return ticket. U.S., British, and Canadian citizens must have a valid passport. See "Entry Requirements" earlier in this chapter, for information on how to obtain a passport.

Pharmacies The **Princess Alexandra Hospital Pharmacy,** Stoney Ground (© **264/497-2551**), is open weekdays 8am to 5pm and Saturday 10am to noon. The **Paramount Pharmacy** has branches at Water Swamp and South Hill (© **264/497-2366**).

Police See "Emergencies," above.

Smoking There are no regulations against smoking in Anguilla.

Taxes The government collects a 10% tax on rooms, and hotels tack on a 10% service charge. Effective January 2008, all visitors traveling through the seaports are required to pay an embarkation tax of $20 per adult, and $10 for children 12 to 18 (free for children 11 and under).

Telephones   See "Staying Connected," p. 184.

Time   Anguilla is on Atlantic Standard Time year-round, which means it's usually 1 hour ahead of the U.S. East Coast—except when the U.S. is on daylight saving time, when clocks are the same.

Tipping   Many restaurants include some sort of service charge in the menu pricing. The menu should state whether service is included, but always confirm whether gratuities are added. In many instances, tips are pooled among the staff (including the back of the house), so it's always a good idea to leave something extra if you feel your server warrants it. Give a 10% to 20% tip to boat captains. Bellhops should get $1 to $2 per bag. Be sure to tip beach attendants and leave something for housekeeping (approximately $1 for every night you spend). Tip taxi drivers an extra 10%.

Toilets   As on St. Maarten/St. Martin, there are few public facilities, although the ferry terminal at Blowing Point has bathrooms. Hotel lobbies and restaurants are your best options.

Water   Water is a precious commodity on Anguilla, and even though the water is potable, it is in short supply. Bottled water is easily available.

Weather   The hottest months in Anguilla are July to October, the coolest, December to February. The mean monthly temperature is about 80°F (27°C). Rain is most heavy in the winter, but few days are without sunshine.

[FastFACTS] ST. BARTHÉLEMY

Area Codes   The country and area code for St. Barts is 590.

Banks   The two main banks, both of which have **ATMs,** are **Banque Française Commerciale,** rue du Général de Gaulle, Gustavia (℃ **590/27-62-62,** or 27-65-88 in St-Jean); and the **Banque Nationale de Paris,** rue du Bord de Mer (℃ **590/27-63-70**).

Business Hours   Keep in mind that most shopkeepers open around 9 or 10am but close midday for an extended *dejeuner* (lunch) that may last until 2 or 3pm. Generally, the closing time is 7pm. Banks are open Monday to Friday 8am to noon and 2 to 3:30pm.

Drinking Laws   The legal drinking age is 18. Wine, beer, and liquor are sold in grocery stores and restaurants 7 days a week during regular hours.

Driving Rules   See "Getting Around," in chapter 8.

Electricity   See "Fast Facts: St. Maarten/St. Martin," above.

Embassies & Consulates U.S. citizens can contact the Consulate General of France in New York, 934 Fifth Ave., New York, NY (© **212/606-3600**). Canadian citizens can contact Canada's Embassy of France, 42 Sussex Dr., Ottawa, ON (© **613/789-1795**).

Emergencies Dial © **17** for **police** or **medical emergencies,** and © **18** for **fire emergencies.**

Holidays Banks, government offices, post offices, and many stores close for national holidays. *Note:* If a holiday happens on a Thursday, don't expect a business to open until the following Monday. National holidays are as follows: January 1 (New Year's Day), January 3 (All Kings Day), Easter weekend, May 1 (Labor Day), May 8 (Armistice Day), July 14 (Bastille Day), August 24 (St. Barthélemy Saint's Day), November 1 (All Saints Day), November 11 (Armistice Day), and December 25 (Christmas).

Hospitals St. Barts is not the greatest place to find yourself in a medical emergency. Except for vacationing doctors escaping their own practices in other parts of the world, it has only seven resident doctors and about a dozen on-call specialists. The island's only hospital, with the only emergency facilities, is the **Hôpital de Bruyn,** rue Jean-Bart (© **590/27-60-35**), about .4km (¼ mile) north of Gustavia. Serious medical cases are often flown to St. Maarten, Martinique, Miami, or wherever the person or his/her family specifies.

Internet Access Most hotels and resorts offer Wi-Fi. **Centre @ lizés,** rue de la République, Gustavia (© **590/29-89-89**), is a full-service Internet cafe that also offers cellphone and laptop rentals.

Language French is the official language, but English is widely spoken.

Mail The main post office is in Gustavia, on rue du Centenaire (© **590/27-62-00;** closed Sun).

Passports U.S. and Canadian citizens need a passport to enter St. Barts. If you're flying in, you'll need to present your return or ongoing ticket. Citizens of the European Union need only an official photo ID, but passports are always recommended. See "Entry Requirements" earlier in this chapter, for information on how to obtain a passport.

Pharmacies The **Pharmacie de Saint-Barth** is on rue de la République, Gustavia (© **590/27-61-82**). Its only competitor is the **Pharmacie de l'Aéroport,** adjacent to the airport (© **590/27-66-61**). Both are open Monday through Saturday from 8am to 7:30pm; on Sunday one or the other remains open for at least part of the day.

Police See "Emergencies," above.

Smoking While a number of properties offer nonsmoking rooms, there are currently no regulations against smoking.

Taxes   You're assessed a 4€ departure tax if you're heading for another French island; otherwise, you'll pay 8€. (These taxes are included in your airline ticket.) There is no sales tax and no tax on restaurant meals. Hotels now tack on a 5% tourist tax.

Telephones   See "Staying Connected," p. 184.

Time   When standard time is in effect in the United States and Canada (in winter), St. Barts is 1 hour ahead of the U.S. East Coast and 4 hours behind Greenwich Mean Time. When daylight saving time is in effect in the United States, clocks in New York and St. Barts show the same time—5 hours behind Greenwich Mean Time.

Tipping   Hotels usually add a service charge of 10% to 15%; always ask if this is included in the price you're quoted. Restaurants add a 15% service charge. Taxi drivers expect a tip of 10% of the fare.

Toilets   There are public bathrooms on the Quay in Gustavia (next to the Comité du Tourisme de Saint-Barthélemy office). Hotel lobbies and restaurants are your best options, though technically you should be a guest or customer to use one.

Water   The water on St. Barts is generally safe to drink.

Weather   The climate of St. Barts is ideal: dry with an average temperature of 72° to 86°F (22°–30°C).

Index

See also Accommodations and
Restaurant indexes, below.

General Index

A

Accommodations. *See also*
  Accommodations Index
  Anguilla, 111–121
  best, 8–9
  St. Barts, 147–158
  St. Maarten, 69–77
  St. Martin, 77–84
  tips on, 187–188
Act III (St. Martin), 53–54
Air Caraïbes, 128, 171
Air travel
  Anguilla, 87, 90
  St. Barts, 127–128
  St. Maarten/St. Martin, 170–172
Alak Gallery (Anguilla), 102
Albert's Supermarket (Anguilla), 104
American Airlines, 171
American Eagle, 171
Andy's Car and Beach Rentals
  (Anguilla), 92
Anguilla, 85–121, 164–165
  accommodations, 111–121
  art scene, 102
  baby-equipment rentals, 113
  beaches, 4, 94–98
  brief description of, 161–162
  calendar of events, 93–94
  entertainment and nightlife, 101
  exploring, 98
  getting around, 91–93
  getting there, 87, 90, 174–175
  history of, 87
  offshore cays, 5
  outdoor activities, 99–100
  responsible tourism, 183
  restaurants, 7, 101–111
  shopping, 100–101
  telephone, 185
  visitor information, 86–87
  weather, 194
Anguilla Arts and Crafts Shop, 102
Anguilla Day, 94
Anguilla National Trust, 98
Anguilla Regatta, 94, 99
Anguilla Sailing Association, 6, 99
Anguilla Summer Festival, 94
The Anguilla Tourist Board, 86
Anse des Pères (Friar's Bay Beach;
  St. Martin), 24, 61

Anse Heureuse (Happy Bay;
  St. Martin), 25
Anse Marcel (St. Martin), restaurant, 48
Antoine Chapon (St. Martin), 52
Aqua Mania Adventures, 27
Area codes, 188, 192
Art Café (Anguilla), 102
Art galleries, 51–53, 102–103
Artistic Jewelers (St. Maarten), 58
Art of Time (St. Maarten/St. Martin), 58
Atlantis World Casino (St. Maarten), 67
ATMs (automated-teller machines), 177,
  179, 189, 192

B

Baie aux Prunes (Plum Bay;
  St. Martin), 23
Baie de l'Embouchure (St. Martin), 26,
  31, 62
Baie Longue (St. Martin), 23
Baie Nettlé (Nettle Bay; St. Martin),
  12, 24
  restaurants, 47–48
Baie Orientale (Orient Bay; St. Martin),
  25, 61–62
Baie Rouge (Red Beach; St. Martin),
  23–24, 61
Bali Bar (St. Martin), 64
Bamboo Bernies (St. Maarten), 62
Banks, 188–189, 192
Barbecue stands (lolos), 7, 45
Barnes Bay (Anguilla), 95
Bartlett's Collections (Anguilla), 102
Bastille Day (St. Martin), 168
Beach bars and shacks
  Anguilla, 4, 7, 101, 108
  St. Maarten/St. Martin, 61
Beaches, 22–26. *See also specific*
  beaches
  Anguilla, 4, 94–98
  best experiences, 4–6
  St. Barts, 4, 132–134
  St. Maarten/St. Martin, 22–26
Beau Beaus's at Oyster Bay
  (St. Maarten), 60, 61
The Belgian Chocolate Box
  (St. Maarten), 55
Beranger Rental (St. Barts), 131
The Big Event Golf Tournament
  (Anguilla), 93
Bijoux de la Mer (St. Barts), 136
Biking, 99, 128, 131
Bikini Beach (St. Martin), 62
Billfish Tournament (St. Martin), 168
Bird-watching, 28
Bliss (St. Maarten), 60
Blooming Baskets by Lisa
  (St. Maarten), 56
Blue Martini (St. Martin), 65

197

Restaurants